Wisdom With Understanding is Better Than Rubies
Lurine Karon Greenberg Fine Arts Collection

The Double Eagle Guide to

WESTERN STATE PARKS

VOLUME 3
FAR WEST

CALIFORNIA
NEVADA

A DOUBLE EAGLE GUIDE™

DISCOVERY PUBLISHING
BILLINGS, MONTANA USA

The Double Eagle Guide to Western State Parks
Volume 3 Far West

Third Edition

Published by:

Discovery Publishing
Post Office Box 50545
Billings, Montana 59105 USA

Discovery Publishing is an independent, private enterprise. The information contained herein should not be construed as reflecting the publisher's approval of the policies or practices of the public agencies listed.

Information in this book is subject to change without notice.

Frontispiece: Bale Grist Mill State Historic Park, California

10 9 8 7 6 5 4 3 2 1

February 27, 2004 10:13 AM Mountain Time

Produced, printed, and bound in the United States of America.

ISBN 0-929760-37-9

TABLE OF CONTENTS

Double Eagle™ Guides

 INTRODUCTION TO THE *Double Eagle*™ SERIES 

State parks are relative newcomers to the overall public lands picture. While the establishment of Earth's national parks dates back to 1872 with the creation of Yellowstone National Park, state parks have come to the fore of scenic, recreational and historic importance mainly in the latter half of the Twentieth Century. Although history is uncertain as to just when and where the first state park was established, what *is* certain is the overwhelming acceptance and support given to the state park concept by the citizens and visitors of the United States.

Whether you're a veteran of many Western trips or are planning your first visit, this series is for you.

In the *Double Eagle*™ series, our goal is to provide you with reliable, comprehensive, and yet concise, *first-hand* information about these parks—special places which tend to offer more simple (perhaps even more 'natural') enjoyment than that which can be experienced among the awesome spectacles of the West's national parks.

The volumes which comprise the *Double Eagle*™ series constitute a significant departure from the sketchy, plain vanilla approach to information provided by other guidebooks. Here, for the first time, is the most *useful* information about the West's most *useable* public parks. We've included a broad assortment of state parks from which you can choose: From simple, free parks, to areas in deluxe, landscaped surroundings.

The name for this critically acclaimed series was suggested by the celebrated United States twenty-dollar gold piece—most often called the "*Double Eagle*"—the largest and finest denomination of coinage ever issued by the U.S. Mint. The *Double Eagle* has long been associated with the history of the West, as a symbol of traditional Western excellence.

So, too, the *Double Eagle*™ series seeks to provide you with information about the hundreds of small treasures owned, operated, and overseen (but, hopefully, never overlooked) by the citizens of the Western United States.

We hope you'll take pleasure in reading these pages, and come to use the information to enhance your own appreciation for the scenic, recreational and historic legacies of the Western United States.

Enjoy the ride!

Thomas and *Elizabeth Preston*
Publishers

Conventions Used in This Series

The following conventions or standards are used throughout the *Double Eagle*™ series as a means of providing a sense of continuity between one park and the next.

Whenever possible, the parks within each state have been arranged in what we have determined to be a reasonable progression, and based on *typical travel patterns* within a region. Generally speaking, a north to south, west to east pattern has been followed. In certain cases, particularly those involving one-way-in, same-way-out roads, we have arranged the parks in the order in which they would be encountered on the way into the area, so the standard plan occasionally may be reversed.

State Identifier: The state name and number combination in the upper left corner of each park description provides an easy means of cross-referencing the written information to the numbered locations on the maps in the Appendix.

Park Name: The officially designated name for the park is listed in boldface, followed by the specific category of park in which it is classified by its state. ("State Park", "State Recreation Area", "State Historic Park", and so forth.) In most instances, the park name was transcribed directly from the signpost planted at the park entrance; it may (and often does), vary slightly from the name as it appears in other printed sources, (especially in 'official' park literature). One example: Throughout the West, it's quite common to find places with a 'possessive' noun in their names to be spelled without the possessive apostrophe ("Clarks Camp" vs "Clark's Camp"). We have retained that convention whenever we determined it to be historically appropriate. Evidently, the apostrophe was considered a grammatical frill by many of our forebears.

Larger parks with distinctively different major units may be divided into two or more separate descriptions. For example, if "Canyon River State Park" consists of two large areas, the "Mountain Valley" unit and the "Great Plains" unit, each with different access, facilities, and natural features, the two sections might be titled:

CANYON RIVER: MOUNTAIN VALLEY	CANYON RIVER: GREAT PLAINS

Location: This section allows you to obtain a quick approximation of a park's location in relation to nearby key communities, as depicted on the maps in the appendix.

Access: Our *Accurate Access* system makes extensive use of highway mileposts in order to pinpoint the location of access roads, intersections, and other major terminal points. (Mileposts are about 98 percent reliable—but occasionally they are mowed by a snowplow or an errant motorist, and may be missing; or, worse yet, the mileposts were replaced in the wrong spot!) In some instances, locations are noted primarily utilizing mileages between two or more nearby locations—usually communities, but occasionally key junctions or prominent landmarks.

Since everyone won't be approaching a park from the same direction, we've provided access information from two, sometimes three, points. In all cases, we've chosen the access points for their likelihood of use. Distances from communities are listed from the approximate **midtown** point (very often the city hall, couthouse, or post office), unless otherwise specified. Mileages from Interstate highways and other freeway exits are usually given from the approximate center of the interchange. Mileages from access points usually have been rounded to the nearest mile, unless the exact mileage is critical. All instructions are given using the *current official highway map* available free from each state.

Directions are given using a combination of compass and hand headings, i.e., "turn north (left)" or "swing west (right)". This isn't a bonehead navigation system, by any means. When the sun is shining or you're in a region where moss grows on tree trunks, it's easy enough to figure out which way is north. But anyone can become temporarily disoriented on an overcast day or a moonless night while looking for an inconspicuous park turnoff, or while being buzzed by heavy traffic at a key intersection, so we built this redundancy into the system.

Day Use Facilities: Picnic area sizes and number of tables are categorized as: (1) small—up to a dozen; (2) medium—up to 50; (3) large—more than 50. The capacities of parking areas are similarly described. (These are *very* approximate figures because we weren't about to try to *count* all the picnic tables and parking spaces!)

Toilet facilities have been listed thusly: (1) Restrooms—'modern', i.e., flush toilets and usually a wash basin; (2) Vault facilities—'simple', i.e., outhouses, pit toilets, call them what you like. (A rose by any other name.....).

Overnight Facilities: Campgrounds are by far the most common type of overnight facilities offered by state parks. The items in this section have been listed in the approximate order in which a visitor might observe them during a typical swing through a park campground. Following the total number of individual camp units, items pertinent to the campsites themselves are listed, then information related to 'community' facilities. It has been assumed that each campsite has a picnic table.

Site types: (1) Standard—no hookup; (2) Partial hookup—water, electricity; (3) Full hookup—water, electricity, sewer.

We have extensively employed the use of *general* and *relative* terms in describing the size, separation, and levelness of the campsites ("medium to large", "fairly well separated", "basically level", etc.). Please note that "separation" is a measure of relative privacy and is a composite of both natural visual 'screens' and spacing between campsites. The information is presented as an *estimate* by highly experienced observers. Please allow for variations in perception between yourself and the reporters.

Parking Pads: (1) Straight-ins, (sometimes called "back ins" or "spurs")—the most common type, are just that—straight strips angled off the driveway; (2) Pull-throughs—usually the most convenient type for large rv's, they provide an in-one-end-and-out-the-other parking space; pull-throughs may be either arc-shaped and separated from the main driveway by some sort of barrier or 'island' (usually vegetation), or arranged in parallel rows; (3) Pull-offs—essentially just wide spots adjacent to the driveway. Pad lengths have been categorized as: (1) Short—a single, large vehicle up to about the size of a standard pickup truck; (2) Medium—a single vehicle or combination up to the length of a pickup towing a single-axle trailer; (3) Long—a single vehicle or combo as long as a crew cab pickup towing a double-axle trailer. Normally, any overhang out the back of the pad has been ignored in the estimate, so it might be possible to slip a crew cab pickup hauling a fifth-wheel trailer in tandem with a ski boat into some pads, but we'll leave that to your discretion.

Fire appliances have been categorized in three basic forms: (1) Fireplaces—angular, steel or concrete, ground-level; (2) Fire rings—circular, steel or concrete, ground-level or below ground-level; (3) Barbecue grills—angular steel box, supported by a steel post about 36 inches high. (The trend is toward installing steel fire rings, since they're durable, relatively inexpensive—60 to 80 dollars apiece—and easy to install and maintain. Barbecue grills are often used in areas where ground fires are a problem, as when charcoal-only fires are permitted.)

Certain parks also offer other types of overnight facilties, such as a park-operated lodge, cabins, or group buildings.

Travelers' supply points have been described at five levels: (1) Camper Supplies—buns, beans and beverages; (2) Gas and Groceries—a 'convenience' stop; (3) Limited—at least one store which approximates a small supermarket, more than one fuel station, a general merchandise store, hardware store, and other basic services; (4) Adequate—more than one supermarket, (including something that resembles an IGA or a Safeway), a choice of fuel brands, and several general and specialty stores and services; (5) Complete—they have a major discount store.

♿ Parks reported by state agencies to have facilities for physically challenged persons that conform to the requirements of the Americans with Disabilities Act of 1990 (ADA) have been highlighted with this familiar symbol. In most parks, a minimum you can expect is equal access to restrooms. In many places, special handicapped-access picnic or camp sites, fishing piers and other recreational facilities are also provided, especially in larger parks. Some parks which are not listed as having handicapped access may indeed have some facilities that offer it on a limited basis, usually at restrooms, but they may not technically conform to the rigid standards of the ADA. If you rely on these facilities, it might be a good idea to double check for their existence and condition prior to visiting the park, using the ☎ information.

Park managers, attendants and camp hosts can be expected to be on-site or readily available during the regular season in more than 85 percent of state parks.

Activities & Attractions: As is mentioned a number of times throughout this series, the local scenery may be the principal attraction of the park (and, indeed, may be the *only* one you'll need). Other nearby attractions/activities have been listed if they are low-cost or free, and are available to the general public. An important item: *Swimming and boating areas very often do not have lifeguards.*

Natural Features: Here we've drawn a word picture of the natural environment in and around each park. Please remember that seasonal, even daily, conditions will affect the appearance of the area. A normally "sparkling stream" can be a muddy torrent for a couple of weeks in late spring; a "deep blue lake" might be a nearly empty hole in a drought year; "lush vegetation" may have lost all its greenery by the time you arrive in late October. In the interest of simplicity and easy readability, we list broadleaf trees (i.e., "deciduous" trees, such as cottonwood, maple, oak) as "hardwoods"; cone-bearing needle trees (pines, Western cedar, spruce, etc.) as "conifers". We typically call the relatively small Eastern redcedar and Western junipers "evergreens". This information might be especially helpful to you in determining the amount of shade you can expect to find to help cool you in midsummer. Elevations above 500′ are rounded to the nearest 100′; lower elevations are rounded to the nearest 50′. (Some elevations are estimated, but no one should develop a nosebleed or a headache because of a 100′ difference in altitude.)

Season & Fees: Seasons listed are approximate, since weather conditions, particularly in mountainous or hilly regions, may require adjustments in opening/closing dates. Day use areas are generally available sunrise to sunset; historic sites are typically open during standard business hours; campground entrance gates are usually unlocked from 6:00 a.m. to 10:00 p.m. Fee information listed here and in the Appendix was obtained directly from the responsible agencies a few hours before press time. Fees should be considered *minimum* fees since they are always *subject to adjustment* by agencies or legislatures. Discounts and special passes are usually available for seniors and disabled persons.

Mail & Phone: The exact mailing address of the park is listed, followed by a telephone number which can be called in order to obtain information about current conditions in that park. In the case of 'satellite' or smaller parks, the 'master' park or district office which is listed in this section can be contacted. We've accented the phone number with a ☎ symbol for quick reference. It could be very helpful while you're in a highwayside phone booth fumbling for a quarter or your 'calling card', poking the buttons on the touch-tone pad, and simultaneously trying to hold the handset up to your ear as you're calling a park for reservations, current weather info, or whatever.

Park Notes: Consider this section to be somewhat more subjective in nature than the others. In order to provide our readers with a well-rounded report, we have listed personal comments related to our field observations. (Our enthusiasm for the West is, at times, unabashedly proclaimed. So if the text sometimes reads a bit like a tourist promotion booklet, please bear with us—there's a lot to be enthusiastic about!)

Throughout the series, certain small, relatively undeveloped 'satellite' park areas are given abbreviated 'thumbnail' descriptions in the *Park Notes* section of a principal park. Since these spots often are little-used outback areas, it might pay to check them out if you're in the neighborhood and looking for a simple, tranquil place to sit for a while.

(Indeed, as you read through an occasional marginal park's description, you too may wonder *why* it deserves designation and funding as a state park. In virtually every state, some parks almost certainly have been purchased and/or maintained as a result of local or state political influence—so-called "pork-barrel politics"—rather than for their scenic, recreational or historic value. With all due respect to the noble swine, we privately refer to these as "pork parks" or simply "porkers". In your travels, you too may find a candidate for this special designation.)

Style...

Throughout the *Double Eagle*™ series, we've utilized a free-form writing style. Complete sentences, phrases, and single words have been incorporated into the park descriptions as appropriate under the circumstances. We've adopted this style in order to provide our readers with detailed information about each item, while maintaining conciseness, clarity, and conversationality.

Print...

Another departure from the norm is our use of print sizes which are 20 percent larger (or more) than ordinary guidebooks. We also use more efficient page layouts for less paper waste. It's one thing to read a guidebook in the convenience and comfort of your well-lit living room. It's another matter to peruse the pages while you're bounding and bouncing along in your car or camper as the sun is setting; or by a flickering flashlight inside a breeze-buffeted dome tent. We hope this works for you, too.

Maps...

After extensive tests of the state maps by seasoned travelers, both at home and in the field, we decided to localize all of the maps in one place in the book. Travelers felt that, since pages must be flipped regardless of where the maps are located, it would be more desirable to have them all in one place. We're confident that you'll also find this to be a convenient feature. Likewise, we determined that states should be shown in their entirety, rather than fragmented into regions. Although this makes for 'cramped quarters' in a few high-density recreation areas, map readers preferred the overall 'big picture' approach. Cities shown on the maps are keyed to the cities listed in the *Location* and *Access* sections of the text.

About 'Regs'...

Although this series is about public parks, you'll find comparatively few mentions of rules, regulations, policies, statutes, decrees or dictates. Our editorial policy is simply this: (1) It's the duty of a citizen or a visitor to know his legal responsibilities (and, of course, his corresponding *rights*); (2) Virtually every park has the appropriate regulations publicly posted for all to study; and (3) If you're reading this *Double Eagle*™ Guide, chances are you're in the upper ten percent of the conscientious citizens of the United States or some other civilized country and you probably don't need to be constantly reminded of these matters.

A Final Word...

We've tried very, very hard to provide you with accurate information about the West's great recreation opportunities. But occasionally, all is not as it's supposed to be.....

If a park's access, facilities or fees have been recently changed, please let us know. We'll try to pass along the news to other travelers.

If the persons in the next picnic or camp site flip a frisbee that periodically plops into your potato salad, or keep their generator poppety-popping past midnight so they can cook a turkey in the microwave, blame the bozos, not the book.

If the beasties are a bit bothersome in that beautiful spot down by the bog, note the day's delights and not the difficulties.

Thank you for reading—and using—our book. We hope you'll have many terrific trips!

California State Parks

Northern California

Tomales Bay State Park

California

Northwest Corner

JEDEDIAH SMITH REDWOODS
State Park

Location: Northwest corner of California northeast of Crescent City.

Access: From U.S. Highway 199 at milepost 5 (0.7 mile east of the junction of U.S. 199 and California State Highway 197, 9 miles northeast of Crescent City, 77 miles southwest of Grants Pass, Oregon), turn south/west (i.e., right if approaching from Crescent City), into the main park entrance station; just inside the entrance, turn north (right) and proceed 0.2 mile to the day use area; or just after the entrance, jog left for a few yards, then right into the campground.

Day Use Facilities: Medium-sized picnic area; drinking water; restrooms; 2 medium-sized parking lots.

Overnight Facilities: *Jed Smith Campground*: 108 campsites; (hike-bike sites are also available); sites are small to small+, level, with fair to good visual separation; parking pads are packed gravel, primarily short to medium-length straight-ins; adequate space for a medium to large tent in most sites; storage cabinets; large, barbecue-height fireplaces; firewood is available for gathering on nearby national forest land, or b-y-o; water at several faucets; restrooms with showers; holding tank disposal station; paved driveways; complete supplies and services are available in Crescent City.

Activities & Attractions: Visitor center and museum featuring exhibits related to local flora and fauna; self-guided nature trail; guided nature walks in summer; swimming area; campfire center for scheduled evening programs; fishing.

Natural Features: Located along the banks of the Smith River in a dense forest of lofty redwoods, and an almost uncountable number of other varieties of trees, shrubs, ferns and small plants; picnic and camp sites are well-shaded/sheltered; picnic sites border a sandy river beach, some campsites are along the riverbank; summers are typically sunny and hot, winters are very rainy; park area is 9560 acres; elevation 150´.

Season & Fees: Open all year; please see Appendix for reservation information, park entry and campground fees.

Mail & Phone: Jedediah Smith Redwoods State Park, c/o 4241 Kings Valley Road, Crescent City, CA 95531; ☎(707) 458-3310 or ☎(707) 464-9533.

Park Notes: From all the stories you hear about Jed Smith, and from all of the historical markers relating his exploits that are placed around the West, you might think the man was the ancient Paul Bunyan of this part of the continent. Smith was indeed a giant among men—not in his slender stature, but in his skilled woodsmanship, his enthusiasm for the Western Wilderness, and his unquenchable thirst for always wanting to see what was on the other side of the mountain.

Jedediah Strong Smith was born in upstate New York in 1799, but he had moved west to join the ranks of the Mountain Men by the time he was 20. Smith's many remarkable journeys included one during which he passed through this region and discovered an overland route from Northern California to the Columbia River. In his brief lifetime he blazed a hundred trails for the rest of us to follow. He died in a Comanche ambush while leading a wagon train to Santa Fe, at the age of 32. Smith once commented that redwoods were the most noble trees he had ever seen. He probably would be honored knowing a place like this uncommonly beautiful spot, the northernmost of the California state parks, was named after him.

▲ **California 2**

PELICAN
State Beach

Location: Northern California Coast north of Crescent City.

Access: From U.S. Highway 101 at a point 100 yards south of the agricultural check station at the California-Oregon border, 20 miles north of Crescent City, turn west onto a paved local road and go 50 yards, then turn north (right) for another 100 yards to the parking area; from there it's a 100-yard walk to the beach. (Note: if you're southbound from Oregon, the turnoff will be the very first right turn south of the bug station, so stay along the right edge of the highway.)

Day Use Facilities: Small parking area.

Overnight Facilities: None; nearest public campground is in Jedediah Smith Redwoods State Park.

Activities & Attractions: Surf fishing for perch; dip netting for smelt.

Natural Features: Located on a beach and on a short bluff on a coastal plain; vegetation consists of grass, shrubs and small evergreens; park area is 5 acres; sea level.

Season & Fees: Open all year; (no fee).

Mail & Phone: c/o Del Norte Coast Redwoods State Park.

Park Notes: It may be small, but it's a nice little beach that doesn't see a lot of use. Another recreation area in this locale which doesn't see much use either is the Lakes Earl and Talawa Project. The entire area contains about 10,000 acres, half of which is managed by the state parks department and the other half by the fish & game people. The area is made up of grassland, wetland, and vegetated dunes on the Smith River flood plain along Pelican Bay north of Crescent City. There are some hiking trails and limited boating opportunities. Several environmental (primitive) campsites, which reportedly are seldom used, are also available. Best time for camping is March and April. If you'd like to take advantage of the secluded location, your best bet would be to contact the park offices at Jed Smith or Del Norte Coast Redwoods. They can fix you up with a permit, directions, and the numbers for the combination lock on the gate at the parking lot.

▲ **California 3** ♿

DEL NORTE COAST REDWOODS
State Park

Location: Northern California Coast south of Crescent City.

Access: From U.S. Highway 101 at milepost 20 +.3 (6 miles south of Crescent City, 15 miles north of Klamath), turn east onto a paved park access road; proceed 1.3 miles to the park entrance station; continue down for 0.9 mile to a 'T' intersection; turn left or right to the Mill Creek camp areas.

Day Use Facilities: Trailhead parking.

Overnight Facilities: *Mill Creek Campground*: 142 campsites in 2 loops; (several walk-in sites are also available); sites are small+ to medium+, reasonably level, with fairly good to excellent separation; parking pads are hard-surfaced, medium to medium+ straight-ins; tent spots are large and generally private; storage cabinets; fireplaces; b-y-o firewood is recommended; water at several faucets; restrooms with showers; holding tank disposal station; paved driveways; complete supplies and services are available in Crescent City.

Activities & Attractions: Hiking trails include several interconnecting routes around the campground, also Last Chance Trail along an ocean bluff, and Damnation Creek Trail to an ocean beach; (trailheads for the latter 2 trails are near milepost 16, 4 miles south of the campground turnoff); nature trail; guided nature walks and campfire programs in summer; limited trout fishing in Mill Creek.

Natural Features: Located along the banks of Mill Creek in a redwood forest, bordered by steep, forested hills (campground); dense undergrowth provides excellent privacy for many campsites; some sites are creekside; a profusion of wildflowers is seen in spring; regional climate is typically temperate and foggy, but the campground's microclimate is fairly sunny and warm in summer; densely forested hills lie throughout much of the park; park area is 6375 acres; sea level to 1000´.

Season & Fees: April to October, with limited availability other times; please see Appendix for reservation information, park entry and campground fees.

Mail & Phone: Del Norte Coast Redwoods State Park, 4241 Kings Valley Road, Crescent City, CA 95531; ☎(707) 464-9533.

Park Notes: The park's lands are along a seven-mile corridor on both sides of the main highway, roughly between mileposts 15 and 22, and border portions of Redwood National Park. Mill Creek is one of the finest camps in the state park system. If the Enchanted Forest had a campground, it might look like this.

▲ California 4 ♿

PRAIRIE CREEK REDWOODS
State Park

Location: Northern California Coast south of Crescent City.

Access: (Northbound) From U.S. Highway 101 at a point 4 miles north of Orick, turn northerly onto Drury Scenic Parkway and proceed 2 miles; turn west onto a park access road and proceed 0.15 mile west then south to the visitor center; continue for 0.4 mile south to the picnic area, or another 0.1 mile to the main campground; or continue northerly on the Scenic Parkway for an additional 9 miles of redwood scenery. **Alternate Access:** (Southbound) From U.S. Highway 101 at a point 4 miles south of Klamath, turn southerly onto Drury Scenic Parkway and proceed 9 miles to the main park entrance.

Additional Access (for Gold Bluffs Beach): From U.S. 101 near milepost 123 +.8 (1.5 miles north of Orick), turn west onto Davison Road and proceed 4 miles on a narrow, steep, winding, rough, gravel/dirt road to the Gold Bluffs Beach area; (no long vehicles or vehicles with trailers are allowed on Davison Road).

Day Use Facilities: Medium-sized picnic area; drinking water; restrooms; several small parking areas.

Overnight Facilities: *Elk Prairie Campground*: 75 campsites in 3 loops; (hike-bike sites are also available); a dozen sites along the edge of the prairie are medium-sized, level, with nominal separation; remaining sites are level, and vary from small to spacious, with fairly good to very good separation; parking pads are paved, short to medium-length straight-ins; large tent spots; fireplaces or fire rings; firewood is usually for sale, or b-y-o; water at several faucets; restrooms with showers; holding tank disposal station; paved driveways; (primitive campsites are also available at Gold Bluffs Beach); gas and groceries in Orick and Klamath.

Activities & Attractions: 70 miles of hiking trails within the park, including the 4.2 mile James Irvine Trail which leads from the main park area to the beach; self-guided nature trail; visitor center with extensive exhibits; campfire circle; guided nature walks and evening programs in summer; stream fishing.

Natural Features: Located in a forested area along the edge of a small prairie/meadow; most sites are shaded/sheltered by tall trees and considerable undergrowth providing good separation; some sites are creekside; sites along the edge of the prairie are essentially unsheltered; Gold Bluffs Beach area includes secluded, pleasant Fern Canyon, north of the camping area; park area is 12,500 acres; sea level to 300′.

Season & Fees: Open all year; please see Appendix for reservation information, park entry and campground fees.

Mail & Phone: Prairie Creek Redwoods State Park, Orick, CA 95555; ☎(707) 488-2171.

Park Notes: Prairie Creek is probably best known for its several resident herds totaling about 200 Roosevelt elk. The elk are commonly seen browsing in the meadow on the east edge of the main park area just off the highway. Although the park's elk are often thought of as 'tame' elk because they feed in the open, the critters are simply reverting back to their original way of life. Like the grizzly, the elk was principally an animal of the plains and open hillsides until it was driven into the forests by the coming of civilization.

California 5

HUMBOLDT LAGOONS: STONE LAGOON

State Park

Location: Northern California Coast north of Eureka.

Access: From U.S. Highway 101 at milepost 117 +.3 (17 miles north of Trinidad, 4 miles south of Orick), turn west onto a paved access road and go 0.2 mile down a very steep, narrow road to the beach.

Day Use Facilities: Small picnic area; vault facilities; medium-sized parking lot.

Overnight Facilities: Primitive camping opportunities ('open camping') are available on this beach; boat-in camps are available on the southwest shore of the Stone Lagoon, with access from the visitor center parking lot; (use the sight tubes positioned in the parking lot to locate your landing point).

Activities & Attractions: Beachcombing; seasonally operated visitor center with exhibits and audio-visual programs, 2 miles south on the highway; motorless boating.

Natural Features: Located on an ocean beach at the north tip of Stone Lagoon; a conifer and brush clad bluff rises behind the beach; total park area is 1500 acres; sea level.

Season & Fees: Open all year; (no fee).

Mail & Phone: c/o Prairie Creek Redwoods State Park; park phone ☎(707) 488-5435 (seasonally).

Park Notes: When we hear the word "lagoon", we might think of palms, sunshine, sand, and placid (or even stagnant) waters. Well, with Humboldt Lagoons we've got the sand part right anyway. These lagoons are anything but placid and stagnant. Open to the sea, they're at the mercy of wind and waves, which first build 'barrier beaches' that impound the waters and create the lagoons. Lambasted by really heavy weather and freshwater runoff, the barriers are often breached and their contents spill into the ocean. Then the cycle starts all over again.

California 6

HUMBOLDT LAGOONS DRY LAGOON

State Park

Location: Northern California Coast north of Eureka.

Access: From U.S. Highway 101 at milepost 114 +.4 (14 miles north of Trinidad, 7 miles south of Orick), turn west onto a paved access road and proceed westerly for 0.5 mile; from this point, the environmental campsites can be reached via a marked trail which goes up a bluff for 200 to 400 yards to the campsites; or continue past the camp turnoff for another 0.5 mile to the day use area and the beach.

Day Use Facilities: Small picnic area; vault facilities; medium-sized parking lot.

Overnight Facilities: Environmental (primitive) campsites with tables, fire rings, storage cabinets, small tent areas, vaults.

Activities & Attractions: Beachcombing; seasonally operated park visitor center with exhibits and audio-visual programs, 1 mile north on the highway.

Natural Features: Located on a driftwood-strewn beach (day use) and on a short bluff above the beach (campsites); the bluff is topped by conifers and shrubs; sea level.

Season & Fees: Open all year; (no fee).

Mail & Phone: c/o Prairie Creek Redwoods State Park; park phone ☎(707) 488-5435 (seasonally).

Park Notes: Dry Lagoon, rather than being a duplicate of its sister ponds in the park, Big and Stone Lagoons, gradually has been turned into a freshwater marsh, bringing with its transformation the standard group of plants and animals. The Dry Lagoon beach is loaded with enormous driftwood logs, witnesses to the ferocity of North Coast weather. But plan to b-y-o firewood for your outing anyway. It would take three years to burn one of those beached behemoths whole—and it would take about the same amount of time to cut one into pieces small enough to dry and burn. An adjacent state park unit, Harry A. Merlo State Recreation Area, is an 800-acre strip along the highway on Big Lagoon, south of Dry Lagoon, that has no facilities but provides fishing and limited boating access.

▲ California 7 ♿

PATRICK'S POINT
State Park

Location: Northern California Coast north of Eureka.

Access: From U.S. Highway 101 at milepost 106 (15 miles south of Orick, 6 miles north of Trinidad), turn southwest onto Patrick's Point Drive and proceed 0.2 mile; turn west (right) onto the park access road and proceed 0.1 mile to the entrance station; continue a few yards to a fork; turn northwest (right) to Patrick's Point and the Agate Beach camp and picnic areas or south (left) to Palmer's Point and the camp areas near Abalone Point.

Day Use Facilities: Medium-sized picnic area; 2 group picnic areas (reservable); drinking water; restrooms; medium-sized parking lot.

Overnight Facilities: 128 campsites in 2 main areas; (hike-bike sites are also available); sites are small to medium-sized, basically level, with nominal to good separation; parking pads are hard-surfaced, mostly short to medium-length straight-ins; ample space for large tents in most sites; storage cabinets; fireplaces or fire rings; firewood is usually for sale, or b-y-o; water at several faucets; restrooms with showers; paved driveways; groceries in Trinidad; gas and groceries in Orick.

Activities & Attractions: Hiking trails, principally the Rim Trail which follows the coastline for 2 miles from Agate Beach on the north to Palmer's Point at the south end of the park; beachcombing, especially for agates; rock climbing on 'Ceremonial Rock', an ancient sea stack which rises 107 feet above a meadow; guided nature walks and campfire programs in summer; small museum.

Natural Features: Located above the ocean in a mixed environment of meadows and forests; most sites are situated on light to moderately forested flats sheltered by tall hardwoods and conifers, plus ferns and other undergrowth; a few sites are on more open, grassy sections; coastal fog and clouds keep the climate cool year 'round; buckets of rain in winter; park area is 632 acres; sea level to 200′.

Season & Fees: Open all year; please see Appendix for reservation information, park entry and campground fees.

Mail & Phone: Patrick's Point State Park, 4150 Patrick's Point Drive, Trinidad, CA 95570; ☎(707) 677-3570.

Park Notes: Patrick's Point is in an ideal location. It has many pleasantly secluded campsites in a forest atmosphere, within an easy walk of stretches of ocean beach and some superb vistas. Woodsmen traditionally refer to the peace and beauty of the outdoors as the "Cathedral in the Pines". Well,

Patrick's Point's variation on that theme is "Wedding Rock". The rock is a sea stack which rises nobly above the surf. It was named in 1930 when the park's first ranger and his bride exchanged their vows on its crest. Reportedly, Wedding Rock continues to be an outdoor altar for couples who choose to make unpretentious nuptial arrangements.

California 8

TRINIDAD
State Beach

Location: Northern California Coast north of Eureka.

Access: From U.S. Highway 101 at milepost 100 +.7, take the Trinidad Exit and proceed west on Main Street for 0.2 mile, then hang a right onto Stagecoach Road, drop down the hill for a few yards, then turn left into the park.

Day Use Facilities: Medium-sized picnic area; drinking water; restrooms; medium-sized parking lot.

Overnight Facilities: None; nearest public campground is in Patrick's Point State Park.

Activities & Attractions: Trail down to the beach.

Natural Features: Located on a sandy beach and on a high bluff; the blufftop area has a large lawn flanked by stands of conifers; park area is 159 acres; sea level to 100´.

Season & Fees: Open all year; (no fee).

Mail & Phone: c/o Patrick's Point State Park.

Park Notes: Good ocean views from the blufftop at Trinidad. Nice picnic spot too. Little River State Beach, south of here, is also relatively easy to reach. Take the Little River State Beach/Crannell Road Exit at milepost 97 between Eureka and Trinidad. Beach access is across a brushy flat from parking spots along the shoulder of a west frontage road. Little River itself flows behind and parallel to the shore, then exits Humboldt County at the north end of the beach.

California 9 ♿

FORT HUMBOLDT
State Historic Park

Location: Northwest California in Eureka.

Access: From U.S. Highway 101 at milepost 76 at the south end of Eureka, turn east for 1 block to Fort Avenue, then go north (left) on Fort Avenue into the park.

Day Use Facilities: Small picnic area; drinking water; restrooms; small parking lot

Overnight Facilities: None; nearest public campground is in Patrick's Point State Park.

Activities & Attractions: Restoration and preservation of Fort Humboldt; fort museum; logging museum.

Natural Features: Located on a bluff/hill above Humboldt Bay; a large parade ground of mown grass dotted with conifers occupies the center of the park; picnic sites are on the parade ground; park area is 12 acres; elevation 50´.

Season & Fees: Open all year; please see Appendix for park entry fees.

Mail & Phone: Fort Humboldt State Historic Park, 3431 Fort Avenue, Eureka, CA 95501; ☎(707) 445-6567.

Park Notes: By the early 1850's, white settlers had begun moving into the Humboldt Bay area, causing friction with the Indians. To protect both parties, Fort Humboldt was established in 1853 and was operated until 1866. The fort's bright white wooden buildings present a fresh contrast against the North Coast's often gray skies. Machinery from the early days of the logging industry is featured in an outdoor display that covers a couple of acres. Interpretive signboards explain the uses of assorted pieces of heavy equipment. The unobstructed, typically breezy parade ground covers most of the park's 12 acres. It makes a first-rate place for kite-flying.

California 10 ♿

GRIZZLY CREEK REDWOODS
State Park

Location: Northwest California southeast of Eureka.

Access: From California State Highway 36 at milepost 17 +.7 (11 miles east of Carlotta, 30 miles west of Mad River), turn south into the park.

Day Use Facilities: Medium-sized picnic area; drinking water; restrooms; medium-sized parking area.

Overnight Facilities: 30 campsites; (environmental/primitive sites are available 3 miles west at Cheatham Grove); sites are small to medium+, level, with fair to very good separation; parking pads are paved short to long straight-ins, some are extra wide; plenty of space for tents in most sites; storage cabinets; fireplaces and fire rings; firewood is usually for sale, or b-y-o; water at several faucets; restrooms with showers; paved driveways; gas and groceries in Carlotta; limited+ supplies and services are available in Fortuna, 20 miles west.

Activities & Attractions: Hiking, including a 1.25-mile Memorial Trail which is accessible by crossing a 'summer only' bridge to the south bank of the river; self-guided nature trail (0.5 mile) into a grove of virgin redwoods; small visitor center with exhibits; guided nature walks and campfire programs in summer; fishing for trout in summer, upstream from the park (said to be good); fishing for salmon and steelhead in fall (good to very good); designated swimming beach.

Natural Features: Located on a flat along the north bank of the Van Duzen River in the Van Duzen River Valley; dense vegetation is comprised of huge redwoods mixed with small hardwoods; bordered by timbered hills; Grizzly Creek meets the river along the west edge of the picnic area; most campsites are in dense shade/shelter, some campsites are near fairly open, grassy riverside areas; park area is 393 acres; elevation 400´.

Season & Fees: Open all year; please see Appendix for reservation information, park entry and campground fees.

Mail & Phone: Grizzly Creek Redwoods State Park, 16949 Highway 36, Carlotta, CA 95528; ☎(707) 777-3683.

Park Notes: Grizzly Creek Redwoods was established to set aside virgin groves of redwoods in the Van Duzen River Valley. Ironically, picnic and camp sites are within a few yards of the highway and its heavy logging truck traffic. The loggers begin to roll before daybreak and provide a graphically audible example of the expression "a rude awakening" for campers. Sites are still very much in demand during the summer season, though. If Grizzly Creek Redwoods' small campground is full, you might find a rustic campsite available at a Van Duzen County park, locally known as 'Swimmers Delight', located a few miles west on Highway 36.

California 11

HUMBOLDT REDWOODS: NORTH
State Park

Location: Northwest California southeast of Eureka.

Access: From U.S. Highway 101 (northbound) near milepost 35 near Dyerville (2.5 miles north of Weott), take the exit signed for "Rockefeller Forest" & "Founders Tree" to a 4-way intersection; continue east (ahead) to Founders Grove; *or* go south (right) on Avenue of the Giants for 0.3 mile, then turn west (right) for 0.3 mile to Federation Grove; *or* turn north (left) and go 0.2 mile across the river bridge, then west through the freeway underpass; from the west side of the freeway, travel south then west on Bull Creek Flats Road for 1.5 miles to the Rockefeller Nature Trail; or continue for another 3.6 miles, then turn north (right) onto a paved access road for 0.2 mile to Albee Creek Campground. **Alternate Access:** From Highway 101 (southbound), take the South Fork-Honeydew Exit (also signed for "Rockefeller Forest", "Founders Tree") to the west side of the freeway and onto Bull

Creek Flats Road and continue as above to the campground; or go east under the freeway to the Founders Tree and Federation Grove areas.

Day Use Facilities: Small picnic area, drinking water, restrooms, medium-sized parking lot in Federation Grove.

Overnight Facilities: *Albee Creek Campground*: 39 campsites; (environmental-primitive campsites are located 0.6 mile southwest); sites are small to small+, with nominal to fairly good separation; parking pads are gravel, short to medium-length straight-ins; most pads will require a little additional leveling; medium to large, sloped areas for tents; storage cabinets; fireplaces; b-y-o firewood is recommended; water at several faucets; restrooms with showers; paved driveways; gas and groceries in Weott.

Activities & Attractions: Largest grove of old growth redwoods in the world at Rockefeller Forest; nature trails at Rockefeller Forest and Founders Grove; tallest tree in the park at Founders Grove; Hearthstone Fireplace (a stone, foursquare fireplace with a common chimney) at Federation of Women's Clubs Grove.

Natural Features: Located near the confluence of the Eel River, the South Fork of the Eel River and Bull Creek (Founders and Federation Groves, Rockefeller Forest); located on a slope along the edge of a large clearing/meadow at the confluence of Bull and Albee Creeks (campground); campsites are very lightly to densely shaded/sheltered by redwoods interspersed with slender hardwoods; creekside elevation 300′.

Season & Fees: Day use areas open all year; campground open May to October; please see Appendix for reservation information, park entry and campground fees.

Mail & Phone: See Central area, below.

Park Notes: Unlike the other principal campgrounds in the park, Albee Creek has a distant view. Most of the campsites are actually within the forest, but a 30-second walk would put you into the clearing and give you a visual shot up the valley to the nearby mountains. Albee Creek is the most remote of the park's trio of highway-accessible campgrounds, but if its more solitude you seek, there are also six trail camps for backpackers in the interior of the park. Each small camp has piped water and vaults. Complete directions and the necessary permits can be obtained from the park office.

▲ California 12 ♿

Humboldt Redwoods: Central

State Park

Location: Northwest California southeast of Eureka.

Access: From U.S. Highway 101 at milepost 33 +.2 at the Weott Exit, (22 miles north of Garberville, 3 miles south of Dyerville, 25 miles south of Fortuna), turn west onto Newton Road; proceed west 0.2 mile to a 'T' intersection; turn south (left) onto Avenue of the Giants (Road 254) and proceed south for 1.5 miles; turn east into Burlington Campground; or continue south for a few yards to the visitor center; or from the 'T' intersection above, turn north (right) onto Avenue of the Giants and travel 0.2 mile to the Marin Garden Club Grove. (Note: continuing south on Avenue of the Giants past the visitor center for 1.8 miles provides an alternate access to the South areas, below.)

Day Use Facilities: Small picnic area, drinking water, restrooms, medium sized parking lot at the visitor center.

Overnight Facilities: *Burlington Campground*: 58 campsites; (hike-bike sites are available 1.7 miles north at the Marin Garden Club Grove, check in at Burlington first); sites are small, level, with minimal separation; parking pads are paved, short straight-ins; tent spots are moderately large; storage cabinets; fire rings; firewood is usually for sale, or b-y-o; water at several faucets; restrooms with showers; holding tank disposal station nearby at Williams Grove; paved driveways; gas and groceries in Weott.

Activities & Attractions: Large visitor center with flora, fauna, and historical exhibits, an audio-visual program, and an interpretive garden; nature walks and other interpretive programs, marathons and campfire programs are scheduled throughout the summer (a current calendar is available from the park office); over 100 miles of hiking and horse trails, including the strenuous Grasshopper Trail which leads to Grasshopper Peak at 3379´; (a detailed brochure/map with contour lines is available).

Natural Features: Located on a forested flat in a narrow valley across the Avenue from the South Fork of the Eel River (campground); the entire valley has huge redwoods towering over a forest floor of hardwoods and ferns; very little light filters down through the 'giants', and the campground generally remains heavily shaded, with a unique atmosphere; the entire park encompasses some 51,000 acres; park elevation ranges from 100´ along the river to 3400´ in the highlands.

Season & Fees: Open all year; please see Appendix for reservation information, park entry and campground fees.

Mail & Phone: Humboldt Redwoods State Park, P.O. Box 100, Weott, CA 95571; ☎(707) 946-2311.

Park Notes: As California's premier sanctuary for *Sequoia sempervirens*, the regal coast redwood, Humboldt Redwoods has an atmosphere—a mystique if you will—that gives it a unique status among the Northern California redwood parks. Spearheaded by the Save-the-Redwoods League, an ongoing movement to purchase and set aside the redwood forests has reinstated over 500 memorial redwood groves to the public domain, including more than a hundred parcels just in Humboldt Redwoods alone.

▲ California 13 ♿

Humboldt Redwoods: South

State Park

Location: Northwest California southeast of Eureka.

Access: From U.S. Highway 101 at milepost 28 at the Myers Flat Exit, (5 miles south of Weott, 17 miles north of Garberville), from the east side of the freeway, go northeast on Avenue of the Giants for 0.7 mile, then turn north (left) onto the campground access road and proceed 0.1 mile to Hidden Springs Campground; or from the west side of the freeway, travel north on Avenue of the Giants (through the town of Myers Flat) for 1.2 miles to Williams Grove, or another 1.1 miles to Garden Club of America Grove, both on the west (left) side of the Avenue.

Day Use Facilities: Medium-sized picnic area, drinking water, restrooms, group picnic and camp areas, 2 medium-sized parking lots at Williams Grove; small picnic area, drinking water, restrooms, medium-sized parking lot at Garden Club of America Grove.

Overnight Facilities: *Hidden Springs Campground*: 155 campsites in a complex of strings and loops; sites are small to medium-sized, with good to very good separation; parking pads are paved, short to medium-length straight-ins; most pads will require additional leveling; small to medium-sized areas for tents, mostly sloped; fire rings; b-y-o firewood is recommended; restrooms with showers; holding tank disposal station at Williams Grove; paved driveways; camper supplies in Myers Flat.

Activities & Attractions: River trail between Williams Grove and Garden Club of America Grove (makes connections with other trails all the way to Albee Campground in the northwest corner of the park); trail between Hidden Springs and Williams Grove; Children's Forest Trail at Williams Grove; fishing; campfire programs; visitor center, near park headquarters, several miles northwest on Avenue of the Giants.

Natural Features: Located on a densely forested hillside above the South Fork of the Eel River (Hidden Springs Campground); virtually all campsites are surrounded by dense vegetation, primarily tall redwoods, plus some hardwoods and ferns; Williams Grove and Garden Club America Grove day use areas are along the east riverbank in a similarly forested setting; picnic sites vary from shady to sunny; elevation 250´ in the Groves, 450´ at Hidden Springs.

Season & Fees: Day use areas open all year; campground open April to October; please see Appendix for reservation information, park entry and campground fees.

Mail & Phone: See Central area, above.

Park Notes: The impressive 5000-acre Garden Club of America Grove is located on the west side of the river, across from the day use area. (However, the stately redwoods in the Garden Club picnic area are no less impressive.) Campsites at Hidden Springs are attractively finished, many with rail fences around the terraced sites and stairs leading to their tables. Another nearby park area, Franklin K. Lane Grove, is located on the Avenue near the southeast tip of the park, 0.4 mile north of Phillipsburg and 8.5 miles south of Hidden Springs. It has small picnic and parking areas, and restrooms. The grove is separated from the main park by about 2 miles.

California 14

Benbow Lake

State Recreation Area

Location: Northwest California north of Leggett.

Access: From U.S. Highway 101 at milepost 8 +.6 (2 miles south of Garberville, 23 miles north of Leggett), for the day use area, from the off-ramp proceed to the west side of the freeway, go north on a frontage road, then curve around to the west and south for a total of 0.35 mile to the day use entrance station; for the campground, proceed to the east side of the highway, and go east on Lake Benbow Drive for 0.1 mile to a 'T' intersection; turn south (right) onto Benbow Drive and proceed 1 mile south and west; turn north (right) onto the campground access road, cross the bridge and continue for 0.25 mile north to the campground entrance.

Day Use Facilities: Large picnic area; group picnic area (reservable); drinking water; restrooms; large parking lot.

Overnight Facilities: 75 campsites in 2 loops (one on each side of the highway connected by an underpass); sites are medium to large, with fair to good separation; parking pads are hard-surfaced, medium to long, mostly straight-ins, plus a few pull-throughs; tent spots are large, level, many are grassy; storage cabinets; fire rings; b-y-o firewood is recommended; water at several faucets; restrooms with cold showers; paved driveways; limited supplies and services are available in Garberville.

Activities & Attractions: Limited boating (motorless); designated swimming area; hiking; fitness course in the day use area; guided activities, including nature walks and canoe hikes; campfire programs; performance platform/bandstand for special programs and festivals in summer; winter fishing (steelhead and salmon).

Natural Features: Located on a flat along the South Fork of the Eel River; picnic sites are very lightly to lightly shaded by hardwoods and conifers on a long, wide strip of mown lawn along the riverbank; campground vegetation, consists of very light to medium-dense Doug firs, redwoods, madrones, oaks and grass; the lake and river valley are flanked by forested hills to the west and tree-dotted slopes to the east; park area is 1200 acres, including a 25-acre summer lake; elevation 400´ to 1000´.

Season & Fees: Day use area open all year, campground open April to November (depending on weather); please see Appendix for reservation information, park entry and campground fees.

Mail & Phone: c/o CDPR Eel River District Office, Humboldt Redwoods State Park, P.O. Box 100, Weott, CA 95571; ☎(707) 946-2311.

Park Notes: Here's a novel wrinkle: Benbow Dam is installed across the river each spring to create a summer lake. The impoundment is created just downstream of the day use area. The lake's 25-acres may make it look like a sidewalk puddle compared to some of the whopper ponds in the state; but there are actually about 6 miles of waterfront property within the park, so there's still plenty of room along the meandering river to wade, splash, stroll or sit.

▲ California 15 ♿

RICHARDSON GROVE
State Park

Location: Northwest California north of Leggett.

Access: From U.S. Highway 101 at milepost 1 +.7 (7 miles south of Garberville, 18 miles north of Leggett), turn west into the park, then south to the entrance station; from just inside the entrance, the Huckleberry camp area is to the west (right), the Madrone camp loop is 0.2 mile straight ahead; or turn east (left) from inside the entrance and go under the highway for 0.2 mile to the day use area and visitor center, or continue past the day use area and across the river bridge for another 0.4 mile to the Oak Flat camp area.

Day Use Facilities: Medium-large picnic area; drinking water; restrooms; large parking lot; concessioned store.

Overnight Facilities: 169 campsites in 3 loops; (hike-bike sites and a small group camp are also available); sites vary from small to medium-sized, with nominal to good separation; parking pads are paved, short to medium-length, mostly straight-ins; many pads will require additional leveling; medium to large tent spots, may be a bit sloped; storage cabinets; fire rings; b-y-o firewood is recommended; water at several faucets; restrooms with showers; holding tank disposal station; paved driveways; camper supplies at the park store; limited supplies and services are available in Garberville.

Activities & Attractions: Hiking trails; nature trail; visitor center with displays relating to Northwest California Indians and natural history; campfire circle for scheduled interpretive programs in summer; guided walks and other activities in summer; limited fishing (winter steelhead and salmon); designated, gravel swimming beach.

Natural Features: Located in the forested valley along the South Fork of the Eel River; most camp and picnic sites are densely forested in a mixture of conifers, including many tall redwoods, and hardwoods; sites in Oak Flat are on a semi-open area just above the riverbank; South Fork flows through a wide riverbed at this point; its size fluctuates considerably from a low level late in summer to great volumes (even flooding) in winter and spring; (the bridge to Oak Flat is removed each autumn); park area is 1000 acres; elevation 450´.

Season & Fees: Open all year; please see Appendix for reservation information, park entry and campground fees.

Mail & Phone: Richardson Grove State Park, 1600 U.S. Highway 101, Garberville, CA 95440; ☎(707) 247-3318.

Park Notes: The camp sites here vary considerably in size and shelter. If circumstances allow, you may want to take a look at all three loops before settling on a site that suits your needs and preferences. The picnic ground doesn't leave much in the way of choice—the entire riverside spot, in the deep shadows of tall redwoods, is terrific. Ditto the group camp. The park is named for F.W. Richardson, twenty-fifth governor of California.

▲ California 16

SMITHE REDWOODS
State Reserve

Location: Northwest California south of Garberville.

Access: From U.S. Highway 101 at milepost 96 +.5 (3.5 miles north of Leggett, 21 miles south of Garberville), turn west into the parking lot.

Day Use Facilities: Restrooms; small parking lot.

Overnight Facilities: None; nearest public campground is in Standish-Hickey State Recreation Area.

Activities & Attractions: Trail through a redwood grove.

Natural Features: Located in a grove of redwoods along the east bank of the South

Fork of the Eel River; park area is 622 acres; elevation 700´.

Season & Fees: Open all year; (no fee).

Mail & Phone: c/o CDPR Eel River District Office, Humboldt Redwoods State Park, P.O. Box 100, Weott, CA 95571; ☎(707) 946-2311.

Park Notes: The principal feature of the reserve is the Frank and Bess Smithe Redwood Grove, through which you can walk at a leisurely pace right from the roadside parking area. There are good river views within a few yards of the highway. Much of the park lies in steep, forested, largely inaccessible terrain. If you're on a camping trip and you find that the area's large state parks with standard campgrounds have the "Campground Full" shingle hung out, you might find a spot at a nearby primitive, wayside camp. Reynolds Wayside Campground is on the west side of U.S. 101, three miles north of the Smithe Grove. Take the off-ramp for State Highway 271 to reach Reynolds.

▲ California 17 ♿

STANDISH-HICKEY
State Recreation Area

Location: Northwest California south of Garberville.

Access: From U.S. Highway 101 at milepost 93 +.9 (1 mile north of Leggett, 24 miles south of Garberville), turn south to the park entrance station (Highway 101 runs in an east-west direction along this segment); turn left into the Rock Creek area, right into the Hickey area, or proceed 0.5 mile down a steep access road and across the river to the Redwood area.

Day Use Facilities: Small picnic area; restrooms nearby.

Overnight Facilities: 162 campsites in 3 sections; (a hike-bike site is also available); sites are smallish, with nominal separation; most parking pads are packed gravel, short to short+ straight-ins, some are extra wide; most tent spots are medium-sized; parking pads and tent spots in the Redwood Area are quite small and rather sloped; sites in the Rock Creek and Hickey areas are reasonably level; storage cabinets; fireplaces or fire rings; b-y-o firewood is recommended; water at several faucets; restrooms with showers; paved driveways; limited supplies and services are available in Garberville.

Activities & Attractions: Many miles of hiking trails, including Big Tree Loop Trail which leads to the 225-foot-tall Miles Standish Tree; campfire center; ranger-assisted activities; swimmin' holes on the river; kayaking in season; fishing (mostly during the winter steelhead and salmon runs).

Natural Features: Located along both banks of the South Fork of the Eel River; South Fork flows through a very narrow, steep-walled, rocky gorge in this section; picnic sites and most campsites are situated on a forested bluff above the north bank of the river; some sites are along the river's south bank; sites receive medium shade/shelter from tall redwoods and other conifers, tall hardwoods and moderate undergrowth; park area is 1012 acres; elevation 800´.

Season & Fees: Open all year; please see Appendix for reservation information, park entry and campground fees.

Mail & Phone: Standish-Hickey State Recreation Area, P.O. Box 208, Leggett, CA 95455; ☎(707) 925-6482.

Park Notes: Interestingly, campsites in the Redwood area are accessible only in summer because a temporary bridge across the river must be removed each fall. The natural, 15-foot-deep swimmin' holes scooped into the gravelly riverbed are some of the park's main attractions.

▲ California 18

ADMIRAL WILLIAM STANDLEY
State Recreation Area

Location: Northwest California north of Willits.

Access: From U.S. Highway 101 at milepost 69 +.5 in midtown Laytonville, head generally westerly on Branscomb Road (paved) for 13 miles to the park. (Branscomb Road actually dips far to the southwest for 6 miles, then picks up the South Fork of the Eel River and follows the stream as it gradually curves back northwesterly to the park.)

Day Use Facilities: Small parking area.

Overnight Facilities: None; nearest public campground is in Standish-Hickey State Recreation Area.

Activities & Attractions: Fishing.

Natural Features: Located in a dense, conifer forest along the South Fork of the Eel River in the Coast Range; park area is 45 acres; elevation 1700´.

Season & Fees: Open all year, subject to weather conditions.

Mail & Phone: c/o CDPR Eel River District Office, Humboldt Redwoods State Park, P.O. Box 100, Weott, CA 95571; ☎(707) 946-2311.

Park Notes: While most state parks get more than their share of visitors, it's virtually guaranteed that you'll not encounter the teeming masses yearning to be free in this far-removed spot (except maybe on Independence Day weekend).

North Coast

California 19

SINKYONE WILDERNESS
State Park

Location: Northwest California north of Fort Bragg.

Access: From California State Highway 1 at milepost 90 +.9 (13.5 miles north of Westport, 14.5 miles southwest of Leggett), head north on Usal Road (Mendocino County Road 431, dirt, rough) for 6 miles to the Usal Beach Campground and the Lost Creek Trailhead. **Additional Access:** From U.S. Highway 101 in Garberville, from the west side of the freeway, go northwest on Redwood Drive for 2.2 miles into the community of Redway; pick up Redway Drive-Thorne Road and follow Thorne westerly out of town for 6 miles to the community of Briceland; the road then becomes Briceland-Thorne Road (also called Briceland-Whitehorn Road); continue southwest and south for another 10.5 miles to the settlement of Whitehorn; finally, go 9 more miles to the north trailhead at Bear Harbor. (Note: roads between Whitehorn and Bear Harbor are dirt, narrow, twisty, steep, and are really not for rv's; a solid piece of road iron with good springs and shocks, beefy tires and an extra measure of ground clearance would be good to have.)

Day Use Facilities: Shared with camping facilities.

Overnight Facilities: *Usal Beach Campground*: 15 primitive campsites; (9 hike-in trail camps are also available); fire rings; b-y-o firewood; b-y-o drinking water; vault facilities; nearest supplies (gas and groceries) are in Westport.

Activities & Attractions: 17-mile Lost Coast Trail follows the coastline from Usal Beach to Bear Harbor; visitor center/office at Needle Rock at the north end of the park near Bear Harbor.

Natural Features: Located along a rugged section of the Coast Range; dense forests interspersed with meadows and grassy slopes make up the principal vegetation; park area is 7000 acres; sea level to 1700´.

Season & Fees: Open all year, subject to weather conditions.

Mail & Phone: c/o CDPR Eel River District Office, Humboldt Redwoods State Park, P.O. Box 100, Weott, CA 95571; ☎(707) 946-2311.

Park Notes: Even magnificently engineered Highway 1 couldn't penetrate this terrain. This is the last sizable section of coastal wilderness north of San Francisco and it also goes by the name of the "Lost Coast". *Sinkyone* is the name of the Indian tribe which first occupied this territory.

California 20 ♿

WESTPORT UNION LANDING
State Beach

Location: Northern California Coast north of Fort Bragg.

Access: From California State Highway 1 at milepost 80 +.5 (3 miles north of Westport, 19 miles north of Fort Bragg, 24 miles southwest of Leggett), turn west into the park entrance; camp and picnic sites are located in 7 sections within 1 mile north or south of the entrance.

Day Use Facilities: 2 small picnic areas; drinking water; vault facilities; small parking lots.

Overnight Facilities: 130 campsites; sites are very small, with zilch to zero separation; parking surfaces are gravel, short straight-ins, or short to medium-length pull-offs; a little additional leveling will be required in many sites; adequate space for a small tent in most sites; fire rings; b-y-o firewood; water at several faucets; vault facilities; paved main driveway; gas and groceries in Westport.

Activities & Attractions: Beach access; surf fishing.

Natural Features: Located on a short, grassy, treeless bluff at the ocean's edge; hills and headlands closely border the beach; park area is 40 acres; sea level.

Season & Fees: Open all year; please see Appendix for campground fees.

Mail & Phone: c/o CDPR Mendocino Coast District Office, P.O. Box 440, Mendocino, CA 95460; ☎(707) 937-5804.

Park Notes: Picnic and camp sites in this beach park are situated along the remains of Old Highway 1. The park closely parallels the new highway for nearly two miles. If you're camping, for several bucks you get a parking spot, a table and a fire ring. But the views are very good.

California 21 ♿

MacKERRICHER
State Park

Location: Northern California Coast north of Fort Bragg.

Access: From California State Highway 1 at milepost 64 +.9 (3 miles north of Fort Bragg, 12 miles south of Westport), turn west onto a paved access road and proceed 0.15 mile to the park entrance station; Cleone camping area is just ahead and to the left of the entrance; or jog north (right) for a few yards then turn left and continue west for 0.2 mile to the Pinewood camp area, or 0.5 mile west to the picnic area and the Surfwood camping area.

Day Use Facilities: Medium-sized picnic area; drinking water; restrooms; medium-sized parking lot.

Overnight Facilities: 143 campsites, including 12 walk-in sites, in 3 loops; sites are small to medium-sized, mostly level, with nominal to very good separation; parking pads are short to medium-length, gravel/sand or paved, straight-ins or pull-offs; tent spots are generally large; fireplaces; firewood is usually for sale, or b-y-o; water at several faucets; restrooms with showers; holding tank disposal station; paved driveways; adequate supplies and services are available in Fort Bragg.

Activities & Attractions: Surf fishing and abalone hunting; designated scuba areas; fishing for stocked trout on Lake Cleone; hand-propelled boating and small boat launch on the lake; beach hiking trail from Ten Mile River at the north tip of the park to Pudding Creek Beach south of the main park area; trail around Lake Cleone; seal and whale watching at Laguna Point (accessible via a local road underpass from near the picnic area); equestrian trails; guided nature walks and campfire programs in summer.

Natural Features: Located along the Pacific Ocean just south of Laguna Point; Mill Creek flows westward into small, freshwater Lake Cleone and then continues on to the sea; picnic sites are on the shore of Lake Cleone; many of the campsites are in dense vegetation of tall conifers and underbrush, other sites are more in the open; park area is 1600 acres; sea level.

Season & Fees: Open all year; please see Appendix for reservation information, park entry and campground fees.

Mail & Phone: c/o CDPR Mendocino District Office, P.O. Box 440, Mendocino, CA 95460; ☎(707) 937-5804.

Park Notes: Most people probably see only the developed area of the park. (Nothing wrong with that—it's certainly a good one). But there are seven miles of beach and dunes to be explored as well, most of it north of the main park zone. The relatively mild climate (usually cool, sometimes foggy in summer, chilly but not cold, though occasionally rainy in winter), contributes to the excellent picnicking, camping and beach walking opportunities during most of the year.

California 22

JUG HANDLE

State Reserve

Location: Northern California Coast north of Mendocino.

Access: From California State Highway 1 at milepost 56 (5 miles north of Mendocino, 5 miles south of Fort Bragg), turn west into the parking lot.

Day Use Facilities: Small picnic area; drinking water; vault facilities; medium-sized parking lot.

Overnight Facilities: None; nearest public campground is in Russian Gulch State Park.

Activities & Attractions: Ecological Staircase Nature Trail includes 2 sections: Headlands Loop Trail (0.5 mile), and Pygmy Forest Trail (2.5 miles); (a well-prepared, detailed guide booklet is available).

Natural Features: Located on an oceanside bluff above Jug Handle Bay and along Jug Handle Creek; (the park and creek are often spelled as a single word "Jughandle"); park area is 769 acres; elevation 100´.

Season & Fees: Open all year; (no fee).

Mail & Phone: c/o CDPR Mendocino District Office, P.O. Box 440, Mendocino, CA 95460; ☎(707) 937-5804.

Park Notes: The trail is a time traveling tool that takes you back about a half-million years past an ascending succession of five wave-cut terraces (hence the "staircase" metaphor). In the Pygmy Forest are miniature pines and cypress growing in a mineral-rich, infertile soil called "hardpan". The stunted trees, only two to five feet tall, are 50 to 100 years old. If you're on a leisurely trip along the coast, this would be a worthwhile way to spend 30 minutes to three hours, depending upon how far along the trails you wanted to go.

California 23

CASPAR HEADLANDS

State Beach/State Reserve

Location: Northern California Coast north of Mendocino.

Access: From California State Highway 1 at milepost 54 +.6 (0.7 mile south of Caspar, 3.5 miles north of Mendocino) turn west onto Point Cabrillo Drive and proceed 0.8 mile to the state beach (across from the private campground); or continue for another 0.3 mile to the state reserve. (Point Cabrillo Drive is a loop road; access is also possible from Russian Gulch SP, at the south end of Point Cabrillo Drive; from the park entrance, go northwest on Point Cabrillo Drive for 1.8 miles to Caspar Headlands; this back road approach would be good for walkers or bicyclists stopping or staying at Russian Gulch.)

Day Use Facilities: Small parking lot in the state reserve.

Overnight Facilities: None; nearest public campground is in Russian Gulch State Park.

Activities & Attractions: Beachcombing; scenic and scientific observation.

Natural Features: Located on a cove (beach), and on an oceanside bluff (reserve); blufftop is carpeted with grass and small, brightly hued plants and a few bushy evergreens; park area is 3 acres for each unit; sea level to 50´.

Season & Fees: State beach open all year. Official signs posted at the state reserve gate read: "Portions of lands adjoining to Caspar Headlands Estates have been established as a California state reserve area for the purpose of scenic or scientific observation.....Permission to enter must be obtained from the California Department of Parks and Recreation". (See Mail & Phone, below.)

Mail & Phone: c/o CDPR Mendocino District Office, P.O. Box 440, Mendocino, CA 95460; ☎(707) 937-5804.

Park Notes: The reserve overlooks an interesting group of large, surf-splashed rocks. Since it isn't right on the main road, and because a special permit is needed in order to conduct scenic or scientific observation, you may find a measure of seaside solitude here.

▲ California 24 ♿

RUSSIAN GULCH
State Park

Location: Northern California Coast north of Mendocino.

Access: From California State Highway 1 at milepost 53 (2 miles north of Mendocino, 8 miles south of Fort Bragg), turn west and immediately south for 0.1 mile to the park entrance station; go 0.1 mile beyond the entrance to a 4-way intersection; turn west (right) and proceed 0.2 mile to the picnic area; or from the 4-way, continue south and then east (left, under the highway) for 0.2 mile, then turn south (right) to the beach and group camp or continue east for another 0.3 mile to the campground.

Day Use Facilities: Small picnic area, vault facilities, small parking lot on the bluff; restrooms with freshwater rinse showers at the beach.

Overnight Facilities: 30 campsites; (a group camp is also available, by reservation); sites are small to small+, basically level, with fair to fairly good separation; parking pads are packed gravel, mostly short straight-ins; most sites are best-suited for small or medium-sized tents; storage cabinets; fire rings; b-y-o firewood; water at several faucets; restrooms with showers; paved driveways; gas and groceries in Mendocino; adequate supplies and services are available in Fort Bragg.

Activities & Attractions: Hiking on about 10 miles of scenic trails in the vicinity, including Falls Loop Trail to a small (35′) waterfall, and a beach trail; 3-mile bike trail on an old road; diving for abalone; stream fishing for small rainbow trout; recreation hall; access to a backcountry horse camp.

Natural Features: Located just east of where Russian Gulch meets the Pacific Ocean; picnic sites are on a small, lightly wooded bluff; campsites are all in a canyon with a dense carpet of ferns topped by fairly dense hardwoods, and conifers including second-growth redwoods; a small, all-season stream flows past many campsites; park area is 1300 acres; sea level to 100′.

Season & Fees: Open all year; please see Appendix for reservation information, park entry and campground fees.

Mail & Phone: c/o CDPR Mendocino District Office, P.O. Box 440, Mendocino, CA 95460; ☎(707) 937-5804.

Park Notes: Any park with "Gulch" in its name is sure to bring in a crowd, and this one is no exception. The depth of the gulch itself is emphasized by the arched bridge which crosses the chasm high above the beach. From under the shadow of the span, you can hear the surf booming and echoing against the rocky canyon walls and bouncing off the bottom of the bridge. Some yards inland from the edge of the bluff near the picnic area you can also hear the whoosh of the waves reverberating inside a wide, ocean blowhole ringed by grass and bushes (and a fence). Most of these coastal oddities (such as the well-publicized "Devil's Punchbowl" in Oregon) are smaller and much closer to the outer edge of their oceanside shelf or bluff than this one.

California 25 ♿

Mendocino Headlands
State Park

Location: Northern California Coast in Mendocino.

Access: From California State Highway 1 at milepost 50 +.8 in Mendocino, turn west onto Little Lake Road/Mendocino County Road 408 and proceed 0.2 mile into midtown Mendocino and a 'T' intersection; jog south (left) for a few yards, then right and continue west on Little Lake Road for 0.8 mile to the view areas at the tip of the headland; or continue around northerly and easterly to viewpoints (and restrooms) along the north side of the headland. (If you're southbound from Fort Bragg, at the north city limit of Mendocino you could angle off the highway onto Lansing Street and then head westerly on local roads for 1.2 miles to the end of the point.) **Additional Access** (beach area): From Highway 1 at the south end of Mendocino, at the north end of the Big River Bridge, turn east onto a paved access road and proceed 0.15 mile down to a parking area along the river; from there you can walk a couple-hundred yards along the riverbank to the beach, if water and weather conditions are favorable.

Day Use Facilities: Restrooms; several small parking areas.

Overnight Facilities: None; nearest public campground is in Van Damme State Park.

Activities & Attractions: Viewpoints.

Natural Features: Located along a small beach and on a blufftop plain, covered mostly with grass, plus a grove of trees; forested hills rise just east of the highway; park area is 340 acres; sea level to 50´.

Season & Fees: Open all year; (no fee).

Mail & Phone: c/o CDPR Mendocino District Office, P.O. Box 440, Mendocino, CA 95460; ☎(707) 937-5804.

Park Notes: Tighten the ribbon on your bonnet before you step out of the car here. The short grass and small plants on the bluff don't do much to slow down the wind, which has been picking up speed all the way from Japan. The typically stiff breeze heightens the wild atmosphere of Mendocino. So do the winter whales, which often make their appearance a short distance offshore of the hundreds of rocks which dot the surf in this area.

California 26 ♿

Van Damme
State Park

Location: Northern California Coast south of Mendocino.

Access: From California State Highway 1 at milepost 48 (2.5 miles south of Mendocino, 0.5 mile north of the town of Little River), turn east into the campground or west into the day use area. **Alternate Access** (for the Pygmy Forest Trail and other trail access): From Highway 1 near milepost 47 +.5 at the south edge of the town of Little River, travel east on Little River-Comptche Road (Airport Road) for 3.5 miles, then turn north (right) into the small parking area.

Day Use Facilities: Vault facilities; large parking lot.

Overnight Facilities: 74 campsites in 2 sections; (10 walk-in sites, a group camp and enroute sites are also available); sites are small to medium-sized, with fair to very good separation; parking pads are packed/oiled gravel, most are short to medium-length straight-ins, plus a few pull-offs; creekside sites are generally level, highland sites tend to be a little sloped; many large tent spots; fire rings; firewood is usually for sale, or b-y-o; water at several faucets; restrooms and showers; holding tank disposal station; paved driveways; gas and groceries in Little River and Mendocino; adequate supplies and services are available in Fort Bragg.

Activities & Attractions: Hiking, including Bog Trail and Fern Canyon Trail; Pygmy Forest Discovery Trail (self-guided nature trail); Van Damme Beach, on a fairly well-sheltered cove, is a designated underwater area; diving for abalone; campfire circle; small interpretive center with sea-related exhibits and audio-visual programs.

Natural Features: Located on the beach (day use), and in and above Fern Canyon; campsites are located along Little River in the canyon, or in forested areas around a fairly open highland meadow; walk-in sites are tucked away along a forest trail at the east end of the canyon; enroute sites are in the beach parking lot; medium to dense vegetation consists of hardwoods, conifers and large ferns; park area is 2163 acres; sea level to 50′.

Season & Fees: Open all year; please see Appendix for reservation information, park entry and campground fees.

Mail & Phone: c/o CDPR Mendocino District Office, P.O. Box 440, Mendocino, CA 95460; ☎(707) 937-5804.

Park Notes: If you're not into abalone hunting or the beach is too populated, you might consider taking a relatively easy, one-way walk through the deep forest. The plan will work if someone can drop you off at the Pygmy Forest parking lot. From there, you can take the main Fern Canyon Trail back to the campground and the beach; or take a shortcut along the old logging road. The trip is 4 to 5 miles, depending upon which route you follow. (A trail map is available at the visitor center.)

▲ California 27

Greenwood Creek
State Beach

Location: Northern California Coast south of Mendocino.

Access: From California State Highway 1 near milepost 34 in the small community of Elk (100 yards south of the Elk Post Office, 6 miles south of the junction of Highway 1 & State Highway 128), turn west into the park.

Day Use Facilities: Small picnic area; vault facilities; small parking lot.

Overnight Facilities: None; nearest public campground is in Van Damme State Park.

Activities & Attractions: Trail leads several 10ths of a mile down to the beach.

Natural Features: Located on a long, sandy beach and on a bluff above the beach; blufftop vegetation consists mostly of large, bushy evergreens, plus some grass and shrubs, trimmed by a rail fence; sea level to 150′.

Season & Fees: Open all year; (no fee).

Mail & Phone: c/o CDPR Mendocino District Office, P.O. Box 440, Mendocino, CA 95460; ☎(707) 937-5804.

Park Notes: At lower tides, tunnels in the large rocks offshore are exposed, imparting a touch of added interest to an already interesting spot. This is a fine stop.

▲ California 28

Manchester
State Beach

Location: Northern California Coast south of Mendocino.

Access: From California State Highway 1 at milepost 21 +.4 (1 mile north of Manchester), turn west onto Kinney Road; proceed 0.7 mile, then turn north (right) into the campground; or continue past the campground turnoff for another 0.3 mile, then turn north (right) to the day use area.

Day Use Facilities: Small picnic area; vault facilities; medium-sized parking area.

Overnight Facilities: 46 campsites; (hike-bike sites and a reservable group camp are also available); most sites are small to medium-sized, level, with fair separation; parking pads are gravel, short to medium-length, wide straight-ins; adequate space for large tents in most sites; fire rings; b-y-o firewood; water at several faucets; vault facilities; holding tank disposal station; paved driveways; gas and groceries+ in Manchester.

Activities & Attractions: Short trails to the beach; fishing; small campfire circle.

Natural Features: Located on a beachside plain covered with tall grass, dense bushes and some tall evergreens; a dune separates the plain from the beach; Alder Creek and Brush Creek flow through the park, some distance north and south respectfully, of the camp/picnic area; park area is 1400 acres; sea level.

Season & Fees: Open all year; please see Appendix for reservation information and campground fees.

Mail & Phone: c/o CDPR Mendocino District Office, P.O. Box 440, Mendocino, CA 95460; ☎(707) 937-5804.

Park Notes: Manchester has a reputation for being one of the best surf fishing beaches on the Mendocino Coast. During the winter rains the park's two creeks are said to tbe good for steelhead and salmon. The picnic/camp area is situated roughly midway along the park's four+ miles of beach. This is one of those simple, windswept North Coast beach camps. Likeable.

California 29

NAVARRO RIVER REDWOODS: PAUL M. DIMMICK

State Park/Wayside Campground

Location: Northwest California southeast of Mendocino.

Access: From California State Highway 128 at milepost 8 (8 miles southeast of the junction of Highway 128 & State Highway 1 near Albion, 21 miles northwest of Boonville) turn south into the campground.

Day Use Facilities: Small picnic area.

Overnight Facilities: 28 campsites; sites are small to medium sized, respectably level, with fair to fairly good separation; parking pads are dirt/gravel, short to medium-length straight-ins or pull-offs; ample space for large tents; fireplaces or fire rings; b-y-o firewood; water at several faucets; restrooms; paved driveways; gas and groceries in Navarro, 6 miles east.

Activities & Attractions: Fishing.

Natural Features: Located in a redwood forest on a flat along the banks of the Navarro River; total park area is 674 acres; area for this park unit is 12 acres; elevation 50´.

Season & Fees: Open all year, subject to weather conditions; (the campground is often flooded in late winter and spring); please see Appendix for campground fees.

Mail & Phone: c/o CDPR Mendocino District Office, P.O. Box 440, Mendocino, CA 95460; ☎(707) 937-5804.

Park Notes: The towering trees and dense foliage create a neat atmosphere for Dimmick's riverside campsites. The only real drawback to staying here in summer might be the heavy daytime traffic; but then again, this *is* a "wayside" campground. It's still a nice spot to spend a night. (We know.) Navarro River Redwoods' other park unit is Navarro Beach, located 8 miles west of Dimmick Campground at the junction of Highways 1 & 128. Navarro Beach has a few primitive campsites on a grassy flat near the mouth of the river at the ocean.

California 30 ♿

HENDY WOODS

State Park

Location: Northwest California southeast of Mendocino.

Access: From California State Highway 128 at milepost 20 +.15 (20 miles southeast of the junction of State Highways 1 & 128 near Albion, 6 miles east of Navarro, 3 miles west of Philo), turn south onto Philo-Greenwood Road (Mendocino County Road 132) and proceed 0.5 mile; turn east (left) onto a paved park access road and go 0.3 mile to the park entrance station; continue for 0.8 mile, then turn left into the campground; or continue past the campground turnoff for an additional 0.4 mile to the picnic area.

Day Use Facilities: Medium-sized picnic area; drinking water; restrooms; medium-sized parking lot.

Overnight Facilities: 92 campsites in 2 loops; sites are small+ to generously medium-sized, level, with very good separation; parking pads are paved, medium-length straight-ins; really nice, large tent spots, many on a thick carpet of forest material; fire rings and fireplaces; firewood is usually for sale, or b-y-o; water at several faucets; restrooms with showers;

holding tank disposal station; paved driveways; gas and groceries in Philo and Navarro.

Activities & Attractions: Hendy Woods Grove (a stand of old-growth redwoods); hiking trails, including a handicapped-access trail; equestrian trail; canoeing and kayaking (late winter and spring); stream fishing; guided nature walks and campfire programs are scheduled in summer.

Natural Features: Located on a large, densely forested flat along the Navarro River in Anderson Valley; park vegetation consists of huge redwoods, ferns, and a good assortment of other small forest plants; park area is 693 acres; elevation 200′.

Season & Fees: Open all year, subject to weather conditions; (portions of the park tend to flood in late winter and spring); please see Appendix for reservation information, park entry and campground fees.

Mail & Phone: c/o CDPR Mendocino District Office, P.O. Box 440, Mendocino, CA 95460; ☎(707) 937-5804.

Park Notes: Hendy Woods is particularly noted for it virgin redwoods groves—the last sizable stands in Anderson Valley. Two other nearby state park units, Mailliard Redwoods and Montgomery Woods State Reserves, have features similar to Hendy Woods. A creek flows through the 242-acre Mailliard Redwoods State Reserve and there's a tiny picnic area and matching parking space. To reach this secluded little spot, from Highway 28 at a point 9 miles southeast of Boonville and 6 miles northwest of Yorkville, travel southwest on Fish Rock Road (narrow, winding) for 3.5 miles to the reserve. Even more secluded is Montgomery Woods State Reserve. The easiest route to Montgomery Woods is from U.S. 101 in Ukiah. Take the northernmost Ukiah exit, then from the east side of the freeway, go north on North State Street for 0.4 mile. Turn northwest onto Orr Springs Road (Comptche Road) and follow it for 13 miles (paved for the first 11 miles, then gravel) to the 1142-acre reserve. Montgomery Woods has small picnic and parking areas, a creek, and a three-mile loop trail that passes through five groves of virgin redwoods. A guide pamphlet is available at the trailhead.

California

North Bay

California 31

SALT POINT: WOODSIDE
State Park

Location: Northern California Coast northwest of Bodega Bay.

Access: From California State Highway 1 at milepost 39 +.8 (7 miles north of the community of Fort Ross, 9 miles south of Stewarts Point), turn east onto the park access road; proceed east for 0.2 mile to the hike-bike camps; or turn south (just past the disposal station, before the hike-bike area) and proceed 0.8 mile to the main camp loops and the walk-in camp.

Day Use Facilities: Drinking water; restrooms; medium-sized parking lot.

Overnight Facilities: 79 campsites in 2 loops; (10 hike-bike sites and 20 walk-in campsites are also available); sites are medium to large with fair to very good separation; parking pads are paved, medium to long straight-ins; many pads may require additional leveling; most tent spots are large, but may be a bit sloped; storage cabinets; fire rings; firewood is usually for sale, or b-y-o; water at faucets throughout; restrooms; holding tank disposal station; paved driveways; camper supplies in Stewarts Point; gas and groceries+ in Gualala, 20 miles north.

Activities & Attractions: Underwater Reserve; designated scuba and skin diving areas; hiking and equestrian trails including 0.6 mile Gerstle Trail which leads from Woodside down to the ocean beach; (a detailed brochure/map with contour lines is available); whale-watching in winter.

Natural Features: Located on heavily timbered hills above the coastline; tall conifers and hardwoods are the predominant form of vegetation; a considerable quantity of underbrush and some ferns help to provide privacy for the campsites; the walk-in sites are tucked away in the forest; park area is 6000 acres; sea level to 1000´, Woodside elevation 100´.

Season & Fees: Open all year; please see Appendix for reservation information, park entry and campground fees.

Mail & Phone: Salt Point State Park, 25050 Coast Highway 1, Jenner, CA 95450; ☎(707) 847-3221.

Park Notes: It's not uncommon to find Pacific Blacktail deer wandering through Woodside's campsites. Three miles upcoast from Woodside and on the same side of the highway is Kruse Rhododendron State Reserve. The 317-acre reserve contains a mixture of second-growth redwoods, Doug firs, oaks, ferns, and thousands of rhododendrons which are at their finest when the pink flowers bloom in spring. The reserve also has 5 miles of hiking trails which pass through the dense forest and across wooden bridges that span small canyons. The turnoff to Kruse Rhododendron is at milepost 42 +.7, then go a half mile east on a paved road to the parking lot.

California 32

SALT POINT:
GERSTLE COVE
State Park

Location: Northern California Coast northwest of Bodega Bay.

Access: From California State Highway 1 at milepost 39 +.9 (7 miles north of the community of Fort Ross, 9 miles south of Stewarts Point), turn west onto a park access road and proceed 0.15 mile to the campground; or continue west on the access road past the camp turnoff for an additional 0.5 mile to the parking areas at the Underwater Reserve on Gerstle Cove; or swing left at the bottom of the hill and go a final 0.5 mile to the South Gerstle Cove picnic area. **Additional Access:** At Highway 1 milepost 41 +.2, (a mile north of Gerstle Cove) turn west into the Stump Beach day use area; or at milepost 42 +.6, turn left into the Fisk Mill Cove day use area.

Day Use Facilities: Small picnic area, vault facilities and small parking areas at South Gerstle Cove and Stump Beach; medium-sized picnic area, vault facilities and 2 medium-sized lots at Fisk Mill Cove.

Overnight Facilities: 30 campsites; (a group camp is also available, by reservation); sites are small, with nominal to fairly good separation; parking pads are paved, mostly short to short+ straight-ins; some will probably require a little additional leveling; medium to large areas for tents; fire rings; firewood is usually for sale, or b-y-o; water at several faucets; restrooms; holding tank disposal station; paved driveways; camper supplies in Stewarts Point.

Activities & Attractions: Gerstle Cove Marine Reserve; designated scuba and skin diving areas; trails to the beach from most day use areas; hiking/horse trails east of the highway.

Natural Features: Located on a hillside above the Pacific Ocean; conifers provide very light shade/shelter for most picnic sites; campsites are generally well sheltered by tall conifers; elevation at Gerstle Cove and other areas west of the highway, sea level to 100´.

Season & Fees: Open all year; please see Appendix for reservation information, park entry and campground fees.

Mail & Phone: Salt Point State Park, 25050 Coast Highway 1, Jenner, CA 95450; ☎(707) 847-3221.

Park Notes: This stretch of the coast is a bit rockier and more heavily forested than many of the other Northern California coastal access points. The campground here is sometimes called "Moonrock". (But what or who is 'Gerstle'; is it anything like *gestalt*?) Gerstle Cove Marine Reserve in the well-sheltered waters at the north end of the Cove was one of the first underwater parks to be designated in California.

▲ California 33 ♿

Fort Ross

State Historic Park

Location: Northern California north of Bodega Bay.

Access: From California State Highway 1 at milepost 33 (12 miles northwest of Jenner, 2 miles south of the hamlet of Fort Ross), turn west onto the park access road and proceed 0.25 mile to the park.

Day Use Facilities: Small picnic area; drinking water; restrooms; large parking lot.

Overnight Facilities: None; nearest standard public campground is in Salt Point State Park; (a 25-site primitive campground with limited availability is located 1.7 miles south of Fort Ross SP, at the bottom of a ravine off the west side of the highway.)

Activities & Attractions: Paved trail (0.3 mile) from the parking lot to a restoration of Fort Ross; (ask at the visitor center for handicapped access arrangements); visitor center with exhibits and audio-visual programs.

Natural Features: Located on a bluff above the ocean; park vegetation consists of large, open grassy tracts and stands of conifers; park area is 1165 acres; elevation 100´.

Season & Fees: Open all year; please see Appendix for park entry fees.

Mail & Phone: Fort Ross State Historic Park, 19005 Coast Highway 1. Jenner, CA 95450; ☎(707) 847-3286.

Park Notes: The village and fortress of Ross, several houses and a stout wooden fort, was founded in 1812 by Russian and Alaskan Indian seal fur hunters. The extensive reconstruction allows you to see Fort Ross somewhat as it was when the Russians set up housekeeping here. One original building, the commandant's residence, still stands inside the stockade and was restored to its original appearance. The stockade and the twin-domed chapel crowned by a Saint Cyril's Cross also have been authentically rebuilt.

▲ California 34

Sonoma Coast: Goat Rock

State Beach

Location: Northern California Coast north of Bodega Bay.

Access: From California State Highway 1 at milepost 19 +.2 (8 miles north of Bodega Bay, 0.6 mile south of the Russian River Bridge south of Jenner), turn west onto a park access road and proceed 1.9 miles to the beach.

Day Use Facilities: Several picnic tables; vault facilities; medium-sized parking lot, plus scattered parking.

Overnight Facilities: None; nearest public campground is in the Wright's Beach unit of the park; also, several primitive campsites are located 2 miles east of Goat Rock on the edge of a large flat bordering the south bank of the Russian River and Willow Creek, off the east side of Highway 1.

Activities & Attractions: Beachcombing.

Natural Features: Located on a beach and on a high bluff above the beach; vegetation consists mainly of short grass; the wide Russian River enters the ocean at the north end of the beach; total park area is 5000 acres; sea level to 100´.

Season & Fees: Open all year; (no fee).

Mail & Phone: Sonoma Coast State Beach, Bodega Bay, CA 94923; ☎(707) 875-3483 or☎(707) 875-3382.

Park Notes: Goat Rock might be the most interesting of the string of individually named beaches that make up Sonoma Coast State Beach. It's the first (southbound) or last beach you'll encounter on this stretch of the coast. South of here every few tenths of a mile to Bodega Bay there are highwayside pull-offs for nearly a dozen small beaches, points, and coves. Portuguese Beach and Schoolhouse Beach, both in the vicinity of milepost 15, are two of the largest and perhaps most scenic. Easy trails lead to some beaches; borderline, bluff-to-beach scrambles are the accesses to others.

▲ California 35 ♿

SONOMA COAST:
WRIGHT'S BEACH
State Beach

Location: Northern California Coast north of Bodega Bay.

Access: From California State Highway 1 at milepost 16 +.8 (6 miles north of Bodega Bay), turn west onto a park access road and proceed 0.2 mile to the park.

Day Use Facilities: Small picnic area; drinking water; restrooms; small and medium-sized parking areas.

Overnight Facilities: 30 campsites; sites are very small to small, level, with nil to nominal separation; parking pads are sand/gravel, short straight-ins; enough space for small tents in most sites; fire rings; firewood is usually for sale, or b-y-o; water at central faucets; restrooms; paved driveways; gas and groceries in Bodega Bay, or Jenner, 5 miles north.

Activities & Attractions: Beach access.

Natural Features: Located at breaker-level on a sandy beach; bushy trees and shrubs provide some shelter/shade; closely bordered by a bluff; sea level.

Season & Fees: Open all year; please see Appendix for reservation information, park entry and campground fees.

Mail & Phone: Sonoma Coast State Beach, Bodega Bay, CA 94923; ☎(707) 875-3483 or☎(707) 875-3382.

Park Notes: The tiny campground at Wright's Beach is close enough to the ocean to be awash at high tide (almost). (It would be an OK place to stay, provided you're willing to sell off a block of your IBM stock in order to pay the rent.)

▲ California 36 ♿

SONOMA COAST:
BODEGA DUNES/BODEGA HEAD
State Beach

Location: Northern California Coast near Bodega Bay.

Access: From California State Highway 1 at milepost 11 +.7 (1 mile north of the town of Bodega Bay), turn west onto a park access road and proceed 0.4 mile to the entrance station; just past the entrance, turn west (left) and proceed 0.8 mile out to South Salmon Creek Beach; or continue ahead past the entrance for 0.3 mile to the Bodega Dunes main camp loops. **Additional Access** (for Bodega Head): From Highway 1 at milepost 11 +.1 on the north edge of Bodega Bay, (0.6 mile south of the Bodega Dunes turnoff above), turn west onto Bay Shore Road and go 0.3 mile west and south to a 3-way intersection at the bottom of the hill; turn west (right) onto Bay Flat Road and proceed 3.5 miles to the headland.

Day Use Facilities: Small picnic area, vaults, medium-sized parking lot at South Salmon Creek Beach; vault facilities and 3 small parking lots at and near Bodega Head.

Overnight Facilities: *Bodega Dunes Campground*: 98 campsites; (hike-bike sites are also available); sites are small, level, with nominal to fairly good separation; parking pads are hard-surfaced, mostly short straight-ins; adequate space for medium to large tents in most sites; fire rings; firewood is usually for sale, or b-y-o; water at several faucets; restrooms with showers; holding tank disposal station; paved driveways; gas and groceries in Bodega Bay.

Activities & Attractions: Trails to the beach and out to Bodega Head from Bodega Dunes; campfire center.

Natural Features: Located in a dunes area on Bodega Bay (campground), on a 2-mile-long beach along the northwest side of the peninsula (South Salmon Creek Beach) and on a rocky point (Bodega Head); campsites are very lightly to lightly shaded but well-sheltered from wind by large, full evergreens and dense, ceiling-height bushes; most other areas are covered with tall grass plus a few small evergreens; sea level to 50´.

Season & Fees: Open all year; please see Appendix for reservation information, park entry and campground fees.

Mail & Phone: Sonoma Coast State Beach, Bodega Bay, CA 94923; ☎(707) 875-3483 or☎(707) 875-3382.

Park Notes: Only a few Bodega Dunes campsites overlook the bay, but the sea's edge is only a short walk from any campsite. There is much more dense, low-level vegetation in this campground than in most other state beach campgrounds on the North Coast. The views from Bodega Head are worth the cost of a couple of miles off the highway.

▲ California 37 ♿

Tomales Bay
State Park

Location: Northern California Coast north of San Francisco.

Access: From California State Highway 1 near milepost 28 +.5 at the south edge of the town of Point Reyes Station, turn west onto Sir Francis Drake Boulevard and travel west and northwest (through the hamlet of Inverness) for 6.5 miles to a fork; take the right fork onto Pierce Point Road and proceed 1.2 miles; turn north (right) onto the park access road for 0.8 mile to the park entrance; continue ahead for 0.45 mile to Hearts Desire Beach, or a final 0.2 mile to the bluff (upper) area.

Day Use Facilities: Medium-sized picnic area, drinking water, dressing rooms/restrooms and large parking lot at Hearts Desire Beach; medium-sized picnic area, drinking water, restrooms and large parking lot in the upper area.

Overnight Facilities: Hike/bike campsites in the upper area; groceries in Inverness, 4 miles southeast.

Activities & Attractions: Designated swimming/wading areas; 4 sandy beaches (3 beaches are accessible via hiking trails (0.4 mile to 4 miles).

Natural Features: Located along the shore and on Inverness Ridge above Tomales Bay; park vegetation consists of stands of medium-tall pines, hardwoods and some dense undergrowth; the park preserves what is said to be one of the finest groves of virgin Bishop pine, a relatively small tree which commonly develops a well-weathered appearance; park area is 1857 acres; sea level to 100´.

Season & Fees: Open all year; please see Appendix for park entry fees.

Mail & Phone: Tomales Bay State Park, Star Route, Inverness, CA 94937; ☎(415) 669-1140.

Park Notes: There are some really dandy picnic sites on a small shelf in the ridge section above Hearts Desire Beach. The views of fjord-like Tomales Bay from within the park are good, but particularly from up on top. The waters and beaches of the 14-mile-long, mile-wide bay are quite well-sheltered from most heavy weather by the ridge.

▲ California 38 ♿

Armstrong Redwoods
State Reserve

Location: Northern California northwest of Santa Rosa.

Access: From California State Highway 116 in Guerneville (15 miles northwest of Sebastopol, 14 miles northeast of Jenner), travel north on Armstrong Woods Road for 2.5 miles to the park entrance; continue ahead for 0.6 mile to the picnic area.

Day Use Facilities: Large picnic area; group picnic area (reservable); drinking water; restrooms; 2 medium-sized parking lots.

Overnight Facilities: None; nearest public campground is in Austin Creek State Recreation Area.

Activities & Attractions: Grove of virgin redwoods, including the 310´ Parson Jones tree and the 1400-year-old Colonel Armstrong Tree; Redwood Forest Theater, 1200-seat amphitheater, which can be used for plays, concerts, weddings and other appropriate special events (available by reservation); trails along the stream and along bordering ridges.

Natural Features: Located in a grove of redwoods and some hardwoods along Fife

Creek; picnic sites are situated in a nice spot between 2 forks of the stream; park area is 752 acres; elevation 150´.

Season & Fees: Open all year; please see Appendix for park entry fees.

Mail & Phone: Armstrong Redwoods State Reserve, 17000 Armstrong Woods Road, Guerneville, CA 95446; ☎(707) 869-2015.

Park Notes: The redwoods here are genuine, first-run articles—not the second growth poles you might find in some previously logged locations in this neck o' the woods. The park was set aside as a natural area in 1870 by a lumberman, Colonel James Armstrong. If you want to take pictures on your outing, bring a camera with a flash. Even at noon on a cloudless day, very little sunlight filters down through the towering trees to the forest floor.

California 39

AUSTIN CREEK
State Recreation Area

Location: Northern California northwest of Santa Rosa.

Access: From California State Highway 116 in Guerneville (15 miles northwest of Sebastopol, 14 miles northeast of Jenner), travel north on Armstrong Woods Road for 2.3 miles to the entrance to Armstrong Redwoods State Reserve; continue through the reserve for 0.6 mile; (abandon all hope of turning around past this point—and your trailer, if you have one—anything longer than 20 feet, or with a trailer, is officially barred from making the run to the top); head up a steep, sinuous, single-lane (but paved) track for 2.3 miles to the day use and trailhead parking lot or a final 0.2 mile to the campground.

Day Use Facilities: Medium-sized parking lot.

Overnight Facilities: *Bullfrog Pond Campground*: 24 campsites; (3 trail camps for hikers and equestrians are also available); sites are small to small+, sloped, with minimal to fair separation; parking pads are gravel, short straight-ins; small to large tent areas; storage cabinets; fire rings; b-y-o firewood; water at several faucets; restrooms; paved driveways; adequate supplies and services are available in Guerneville.

Activities & Attractions: Hiking and horse trails (a detailed brochure/map with contour lines is available).

Natural Features: Located on hilly, densely forested terrain; campsites are generally well sheltered and shaded by hardwoods and conifers, and some sites overlook 2-acre Bullfrog Pond; park area is 4200 acres; park elevation 200´ to 1800´, Bullfrog Pond campground elevation 1400´.

Season & Fees: Open all year; please see Appendix for reservation information and campground fees.

Mail & Phone: Austin Creek State Recreation Area, 17000 Armstrong Woods Road, Guerneville, CA 95446; ☎(707) 869-2015.

Park Notes: It's amazing how totally different this spot is from Armstrong Redwoods, in the valley just below. In the redwood grove, it's mild and shadowy and moist; up on top, it's sunshine and blue sky and dry air (May to October, anyway). And the great views are something else! (So is the drive up; we keep some loose change in the ash tray, and about three dollars in dimes and quarters slid out on one of the steeper sections.) To be sure, all of Austin Creek isn't like this. The majority of the park's wild acres lie on the mountainsides and in the valleys flanking Austin Creek and its tributaries. Most of the 20 miles of trails also closely follow the streams.

California 40 ♿

CLEAR LAKE
State Park

Location: Northwest California north of Santa Rosa.

Access: From California State Highway 29 at milepost 34.2 at the east edge of Kelseyville, (9 miles southeast of Lakeport), turn north onto Main Street; follow a well-signed, zig-zag route (or just follow the traffic) along Main Street, Gaddy Lane and

Soda Bay Road for 4.1 miles to the park; turn north (left) onto the park access road and proceed 0.2 mile to the entrance station; go 0.2 mile, then turn left into Cole Creek Campground, or 0.4 mile past Cole Creek to the main day use areas and Kelsey Creek Campground; continue past Kelsey Creek for an additional 0.6 mile or 1 mile to Lower and Upper Bayview Campgrounds. (Note: this is the simplest routing of at least 5 accesses from State Highways 29, 175 and 281; they all eventually lead to Soda Bay Road.)

Day Use Facilities: Large picnic area; large group picnic area (reservable); drinking water; restrooms; medium-sized and large parking lots.

Overnight Facilities: *Cole Creek Campground*: 26 campsites; (hike-bike sites are also available); *Kelsey Creek Campground*: 65 sites; sites in both campgrounds are medium to large, level, with nominal to fair separation; parking pads are paved, medium to medium+ straight-ins; excellent, grassy tent spots; *Upper and Lower Bayview Campgrounds*: 31 campsites in Lower Bayview and 35 sites in Upper Bayview; sites are mostly medium-sized, with nominal to fair separation; parking pads are paved, short to medium-length straight-ins; many pads may require additional leveling; medium to large tent spots, some may be sloped; *all campgrounds*: storage cabinets; fireplaces; b-y-o firewood is recommended; water at faucets throughout; restrooms with showers; holding tank disposal station near the visitor center; paved driveways; adequate supplies and services are available in the Kelseyville-Lakeport area.

Activities & Attractions: Boating; boat launch; fishing for largemouth bass, crappie, bluegill and catfish; swimming beach; visitor center; campfire circle; Indian Nature Trail; hiking trails; interpretive programs in summer.

Natural Features: *Kelsey Creek*: located on the south shore of Clear Lake, between the lake and the Kelsey Creek bayou; most sites have lake views; *Cole Creek*: located along Cole Creek a few hundred yards from the lake shore; large hardwoods provide light to medium shade in both areas, with some open grassy sections in Kelsey Creek; *Upper and Lower Bayview*: located on a hill above Soda Bay; large oak trees and sparse grass are the predominant forms of vegetation; some sites have lake views through the trees; the lake is ringed by wooded hills and mountains; summer temperatures commonly exceed 90° F; park area is 565 acres; elevation 1300´.

Season & Fees: Open all year; please see Appendix for reservation information, park entry and campground fees.

Mail & Phone: Clear Lake State Park, 5300 Soda Bay Road, Kelseyville, CA 95451; ☎(707) 279-2267 or ☎(707) 279-8650.

Park Notes: For such a relatively small park (it covers less than a square mile), this place is loaded with a variety of natural settings and facilities, hence the rather involved descriptions above. Choosing a campsite at Clear Lake is difficult: to camp on top, with more commanding views; or to stay at lake level, closer to the park's activities. The lake is popular with picnickers, boaters, campers and mosquitoes. Clear Lake is the largest natural lake totally within California. Yes, Tahoe is larger; but the key words here are *totally within* California.

▲ **California 41**

ANDERSON MARSH
State Historic Park

Location: Northwest California north of Santa Rosa.

Access: From California State Highway 53 near milepost 1 +.5 (near the southeast tip of Clear Lake, 1.5 miles south of the town of Clear Lake, 1.5 miles north of the junction of State Highways 53 & 29 in the community of Lower Lake), turn west into the park.

Day Use Facilities: Small picnic area; drinking water; restrooms; parking area.

Overnight Facilities: None; nearest public campground is in Clear Lake State Park.

Activities & Attractions: 4 hiking trails, varying from 0.8 mile to 1.6 miles, through varying topography; guided tours of the former Anderson Ranch buildings and a reconstructed Pomo Indian village; visitor center.

Natural Features: Located at the southeast tip of Clear Lake, principally on wetlands or tule marsh, plus grassland and some oak woodlands; Cache Creek flows through the center of the park; bordered by wooded hills; park area is 870 acres; elevation 1300´.

Season & Fees: Open all year; please see Appendix for park entry fees.

Mail & Phone: mail c/o CDPR Clear Lake District Office, 5300 Soda Bay Road, Kelseyville, CA 95451; park phone ☎(707 994-0688.

Park Notes: Anderson Marsh holds half of what's left of the original tule marsh associated with Clear Lake, so it's ecological importance is quite clear (no pun intended). The marsh areas provide food and breeding areas for the lake's many forms of aquatic, land, and bird life. The ranch buildings, plus more than two dozen Indian archaeological sites, constitute the historic side of the park.

▲ California 42

ROBERT LOUIS STEVENSON

State Park

Location: Northern California northwest of Napa.

Access: From California State Highway 29 at milepost 45 +.5 (8 miles north of Calistoga, 8 miles south of Middletown), turn east into the parking lot. (Note: this spot is between a pair of blind turns on the highway, so visibility is limited; unless you park in the very small pull-off on the west side of the highway, you'll have to do a mad dash from the parking lot across the often-busy road to the picnic area and trailhead.)

Day Use Facilities: Small picnic area; small parking lot.

Overnight Facilities: None; nearest public campground is in Bothe-Napa Valley State Park.

Activities & Attractions: Trail to the Stevenson monument (1.0 mile) and to the summit of Mount Saint Helena (5.0 miles); (be sure to fill up with drinking water in town).

Natural Features: Located on Mount Saint Helena; the mountain is forested with tall hardwoods and conifers; park area is 3670 acres; elevation 2200´ to 4343´.

Season & Fees: Open all year; (no fee).

Mail & Phone: c/o CDPR Napa District Office, 3801 Saint Helena Highway North, Calistoga, CA 94515; ☎(707) 942-4575.

Park Notes: Robert Louis Stevenson spent several years in California in the 1880's. Reputedly, some of the scenic descriptions in his classic *Treasure Island* were modeled after the natural surroundings in the area. Stevenson's *Silverado Squatters* was about life in this region, and in it Stevenson sketched Mount Saint Helena: "It looks down on much green, intricate country ... From its summit you must have an excellent lesson of geography ... Its sides are fringed with forest; and the soil, where it is bare, glows warm with cinnabar. Life in its shadow goes rustically forward."

▲ California 43 ♿

BOTHE-NAPA VALLEY

State Park

Location: Northern California northwest of Napa.

Access: From California State Highways 29/128 at milepost 33 +.5 (3 miles southeast of Calistoga, 4 miles northwest of St. Helena), swing south/west onto the park access road and proceed 0.2 mile to the entrance station and then the visitor center; just past the visitor center, turn west (right) and proceed 0.2 mile to the campground; or continue on the main park road past the campground turnoff for 0.1 mile to the picnic area and the swimming pool.

Day Use Facilities: Large picnic area; group picnic area with ramada; drinking water; restrooms; parking along the park road; horse trailer parking lot.

Overnight Facilities: 50 campsites, including 9 walk-in units; (a group camp is also available); sites are small, with nominal to fairly good separation; parking pads are packed/oiled gravel, short to short+ straight-ins; some pads may require a little additional leveling; small to medium-sized areas for tents; storage cabinets; fire rings or fireplaces; firewood is usually for sale, or b-y-o; water at several faucets; restrooms with showers; adequate supplies and services are available in Calistoga.

Activities & Attractions: 7 miles of hiking trails; history trail to Bale Grist Mill (see separate info); small (motel-size), creek-fed swimming pool (in the day use area, a few feet from the highway); visitor center with interpretive displays and a 3D map of the region; (a park brochure/map showing contour lines and the locations of many Napa Valley wineries is available).

Natural Features: Located on the northwest edge of Napa Valley; picnic area is on a grassy flat, with light to medium shade provided by tall conifers; campsites are moderately shaded/sheltered by hardwoods and some conifers; bordered by forested hills; park area is 1917 acres; elevation 350´.

Season & Fees: Open all year; please see Appendix for reservation information, park entry and campground fees; (camping limited to one night only, subject to change).

Mail & Phone: Bothe-Napa Valley State Park, 3801 Saint Helena Highway North, Calistoga, CA 94515; ☎(707) 942-4575.

Park Notes: What does this park have in common with San Francisco's famous landmark, Coit Tower? Bothe-Napa Valley SP formerly was the vacation home of "Firebelle Lillie" Coit, who was known for her lifelong admiration for firefighters. As an eight-year-old child in 1851, she was rescued from a burning hotel by a San Francisco volunteer fireman. For the rest of her long life, Lillie chased clanking fire engines and cheered the firefighters at every opportunity. Her exploits made her the darling of the media. When sent to the family retreat here (called "Lonely" in those days) her cigar smoking, poker playing, and wild buggy driving (sort of a real-life Mr. Toad in *Wind in the Willows*), scandalized her very proper Calistoga neighbors. At her death in 1929, she willed $100,000 to "beautify the city" of San Francisco. The upshot of the bequest was Coit Tower, shaped like a fire hose nozzle. "Lonely" eventually became this state park.

▲ California 44 ♿

Bale Grist Mill

State Historic Park

Location: Northern California northwest of Napa.

Access: From California State Highways 29/128 at milepost 31 +.9 (4 miles southeast of Calistoga, 3 miles northwest of St. Helena), turn west onto a park access road and proceed 0.3 mile to the parking lot; a paved trail leads 0.2 mile to the mill.

Day Use Facilities: Small main parking lot, plus designated lot for buses and rv's.

Overnight Facilities: None; nearest public campground is in Bothe-Napa Valley State Park.

Activities & Attractions: Grain mill with functioning water wheel, dating back to the 1840's; exhibits explaining the use of water power; short history trail; mill pond.

Natural Features: Located along Mill Creek (of course!); vegetation consists of a mixture of hardwoods and conifers; park area is 1 acre; elevation 350´.

Season & Fees: Open all year; please see Appendix for park entry fees.

Mail & Phone: c/o CDPR Napa District Office, 3801 Saint Helena Highway North, Calistoga, CA 94515; ☎(707) 942-4575; or park phone ☎(707) 963-2236.

Park Notes: This tiny park provides a neat opportunity to see one of the few, fully functioning water wheels available to the public. (Champion Lake State Park near Imperial, Nebraska has one too, if you're ever in that neighborhood.) The mill is complete with a 36´ wooden, flume-fed wheel, gearworks, and massive millstones. Especially if you have kids, grandchildren, friends who are kids, or students, this place is worth a visit.

California 45

ANNADEL
State Park

Location: Northern California east of Santa Rosa.

Access: From California State Highway 12 near milepost 21 (5 miles east of Santa Rosa, 17 miles north of Sonoma), turn southwest onto Los Alamos Road for 0.1 mile to a 'T' intersection; jog right onto Melita Road for 100 yards, then bear left onto Montgomery Drive and go 0.3 mile to a point just before the bridge; turn left onto Channel Drive and continue south, east, then southeast on Channel Drive for 1.1 miles to the park entrance station; go past the entrance on a narrow, paved roadway for 0.8 mile to the Quarry picnic area or for a final 0.4 mile to the main parking lot. **Additional Access** (for the Lawndale Trailhead)**:** From Highway 12 near milepost 26 (10 miles southeast of Santa Rosa), turn south onto Lawndale Road and proceed 2 miles to the trailhead.

Day Use Facilities: Small picnic area and small parking lot at Quarry; picnic tables and vault facilities adjacent to the large, main parking lot; medium-sized parking lot at Lawndale; drinking water at the park office, near the entrance station.

Overnight Facilities: None; nearest public campground is in Spring Lake county park, 2 miles west.

Activities & Attractions: 35 miles of trails for hikers, bicyclists and equestrians (a detailed trail guide/map with contour lines is available); fishing (said to be good) for bass and bluegill at Lake Ilsanjo (trail access only).

Natural Features: Located on the east slopes of 1887´ Bennett Mountain and adjacent hills and valleys; vegetation consists of large, dense stands of hardwoods and conifers interspersed with open meadows; park area is 4900 acres; elevation 350´ to 1880´.

Season & Fees: Open all year; please see Appendix for park entry fees.

Mail & Phone: Annadel State Park, 6201 Channel Drive, Santa Rosa, CA 95405; ☎(707) 539-3911.

Park Notes: Most of the park's trails climb and descend gradually, even though the elevation change within this relatively small area is quite dramatic. The climate from late spring to early winter is good to excellent for trail pursuits. Summer afternoon temps can reach into the high 80's and the 90's, but the thing to do is get out early because there's only occasional morning fog here to veil the view.

California 46

SUGARLOAF RIDGE
State Park

Location: Northwest California east of Santa Rosa.

Access: From California State Highway 12 at milepost 26 +.1 (11 miles east of Santa Rosa, 11 miles north of Sonoma), turn northeast onto Adobe Canyon Road; proceed 3.35 miles on a fairly narrow, winding, steep, paved road to the park entrance station; just beyond the entrance, bear left at the fork to the picnic area or right to the campground.

Day Use Facilities: Medium-sized picnic area; drinking water; restrooms; medium-sized parking lot.

Overnight Facilities: 50 campsites in a loop and a string; (a large group camp is also available, by reservation); sites are small, with nominal to fair separation; parking pads are gravel, medium to long straight-ins; some pads may require additional leveling; good tent spots in most sites; fire rings; b-y-o firewood; water at several faucets; restrooms; paved driveways; complete supplies and services are available in Santa Rosa.

Activities & Attractions: 25 miles of hiking and equestrian trails within the park connect to miles of trails in nearby Hood Mountain Regional Park; nature trail; (a detailed brochure/trail map with contour lines is available); small visitor center; campfire center.

Natural Features: Located on the west slope of the Coast Range; an interior large, grassy, open area is ringed by camp and picnic sites, large hardwoods and some underbrush; Sugarloaf Ridge itself runs northwest-southeast along the park's southern boundary and tops-out at 1939´; Bald Mountain and Red Mountain rise to 2729´ and 2547´ at the north end of the park, and Little Bald Mountain rises to 2275´ near the southeast corner; park area is 2500 acres; elevation ranges from 600´ to 2729´, elevation at the picnic area and campground is 1100´.

Season & Fees: Open all year; please see Appendix for reservation information, park entry and campground fees.

Mail & Phone: Sugarloaf Ridge State Park, 2605 Adobe Canyon Road, Kenwood, CA 95452; ☎(707) 833-5712.

Park Notes: Sugarloaf Ridge seems to be geared especially toward ecology-conscious visitors. Many of the programs and much of the park literature are directed toward appreciating and preserving the natural environment. Sugarloaf Ridge supposedly takes its name from large, solid, conical mounds of sugar which were found in old-time grocery stores. (In summer, it's color and texture also make it resemble a big hunk of pound cake.) The elevation at the center of the park is 1000´ higher than nearby Santa Rosa. If you don't have the time to go up into the hills, you can still see the cone-topped ridge from the valley by looking up and northeast from the main highway near its junction with Adobe Road.

▲ **California 47** ♿

JACK LONDON
State Historic Park

Location: Northern California southeast of Santa Rosa.

Access: From California State Highway 12 at milepost 30 +.7 near the town of Glen Ellen (9 miles north of Sonoma, 13 miles south of Santa Rosa) turn southwest onto Arnold Drive and proceed 1 mile into midtown Glen Ellen; turn west onto London Ranch Road and go 0.9 mile to the park entrance station; just beyond the entrance, turn left to the main parking lot and museum, or right to the ranch area.

Day Use Facilities: 2 small picnic areas; drinking water; restrooms; 2 large parking lots.

Overnight Facilities: None; nearest public campground is in Sugarloaf Ridge State Park.

Activities & Attractions: Beauty Ranch, home of the early twentieth century fiction writer Jack London; working ranch exhibits; trails to London's grave (0.5 mile) and Wolf House (0.6 mile), 0.5 self-guiding loop trail through Beauty Ranch; museum in the 'House of Happy Walls', built in 1919 by London's widow, Charmian, includes many of his works and the collection of objects gathered in their travels around the world.

Natural Features: Located in the foothills of Sonoma Mountain above Sonoma Valley; (one of London's best-known books, *Valley of the Moon*, is descriptive of this valley); much of the park is moderately to densely wooded with oaks, eucalyptus, madrones, other hardwoods and some conifers; park area is 795 acres; elevation 700´.

Season & Fees: Open all year; please see Appendix for park entry fees.

Mail & Phone: Jack London State Historic Park, 2400 London Ranch Road, Glen Ellen, CA 95442; ☎(707) 938-5216.

Park Notes: Although Jack London was born in San Francisco in 1876, Oakland is generally considered to be his home town. As a young man, London worked his way around the Oakland waterfront, around California and around the world. His adventures eventually led to his becoming one of the most popular and prolific novelists and short story writers of the twentieth century. Known best for *Call of the Wild*, *White Fang* and *The Sea Wolf*, London drew on first-hand experience in the Far North and at sea.

The park highlights the life London led here at Beauty Ranch between 1905 until his death in 1916. Not satisfied with being just a world-famous literary figure, London established Beauty Ranch in order to experiment with and perfect new agricultural techniques, in his words "to make two blades of grass grow where one blade grew before". He raised fine horses, livestock, fruit and vegetable crops. The eucalyptus trees here are part of some 150,000 units he planted at a 1910 cost of $50,000. If you take the trail to Wolf House, you'll see the remnants of a magnificent, shattered dream. Designed by London to be his principal residence and built of stone, lava rock, redwood and other native materials, the house was destroyed one night in 1913 just before its completion by a fire of mysterious origins. London continued his adventurous, hard-working, hard-spending, hard-drinking lifestyle until his death here in 1916 at the age of 40. London once wrote: "Everything I build is for the years to come".

▲ **California 48** ♿

SONOMA: MISSION & TOWN

State Historic Park

Location: Northern California north of San Francisco.

Access: From California State Highway 12 in midtown Sonoma at the town plaza, go east then north around the plaza to Spain Street; most park buildings are situated on the north side of Spain Street, east and west of 1st Street East.

Day Use Facilities: Small picnic area in the mission courtyard; picnic tables and drinking water in the plaza; restrooms at the mission and near the barracks; large, city parking lot between 1st East & 1st West, north of the historic area; streetside parking is also available.

Overnight Facilities: None; nearest public campground is in Sugarloaf Ridge State Park.

Activities & Attractions: Restored and renovated Mission San Francisco Solano, Toscano Hotel, Blue Wing Inn and Army barracks, complete with period furniture.

Natural Features: Located in-town in the Sonoma Valley; park contains several gardens/courtyards; total park area is 64 acres; elevation 100´.

Season & Fees: Open all year; please see Appendix for park entry fees.

Mail & Phone: Sonoma State Historic Park, 20 East Spain Street, Sonoma, CA 95476; ☎(707) 938-1519 (district office) or☎(707) 938-0151 (mission) or☎(707) 938-2588 (barracks).

Park Notes: Sonoma's history dates back to 1823 when the Mission San Francisco Solano, the most northerly of the Franciscan missions was founded. The present chapel was constructed in the 1840's by General Vallejo. Sonoma was the headquarters for the Bear Flag Revolt in 1846, which was the impetus for California's independence, and California's famous grizzly bear flag was designed here. The barracks served the Mexican and American military, then it was turned into a winery by the good general. The Blue Wing Inn was a gambling hall and saloon, and now holds concessioners' shops. And the Toscano Hotel, with its authentic furnishings right down to the bottle of Red Eye on the bar, goes back to the late 1800's. (Reportedly, it was an "unpretentious, inexpensive hotel", but by the looks of the present interior, it certainly wasn't a two-bit flophouse.) All of the buildings in this section of the park are within a block of the plaza, so the sidewalk tour method works very well here.

▲ **California 49**

SONOMA: VALLEJO HOME

State Historic Park

Location: Northern California north of San Francisco.

Access: From California State Highway 12 at a point 0.3 mile west of the town plaza in midtown Sonoma, turn north onto 3rd Street West and proceed 0.4 mile to the park. (If you have the time, it would be a pleasant, 15 minute walk from the main park downtown on Spain Street to the Vallejo Home, or vice versa.)

Day Use Facilities: Small (very nice) picnic area; drinking water; restrooms; medium-sized parking lot.

Overnight Facilities: None; nearest public campground is in Sugarloaf Ridge State Park.

Activities & Attractions: Restored, Gothic-Victorian style home of General M.G. Vallejo.

Natural Features: Located at the base of a hill in the Sonoma Valley; landscaping consists of a variety of large hardwoods, shrubs, flowers, lawns and gardens; (to some extent, the vegetation reflects Vallejo's long-time interest and accomplishments in horticulture); bordered by open fields; elevation 100´.

Season & Fees: Open all year; please see Appendix for park entry fees.

Mail & Phone: Sonoma State Historic Park, 20 East Spain Street, Sonoma, CA 95476; ☎(707) 938-1215.

Park Notes: Born in Monterey in 1807, Mariano Guadalupe Vallejo distinguished himself early in life as an outstanding student, military cadet and army officer. As a reward for his leadership, he obtained huge land grants from the Mexican government and was named *Commandante General* of all Mexican forces in California. By 1846, his portfolio totaled 175,000 acres of California real estate. It was probably more than just luck that brought him—one of the principal Mexican government officials—securely through the days of the Bear Flag Revolt and the Republic of California and into the mainstream of California state politics. But Vallejo's holdings had already begun to dwindle during the revolt and a continuous string of economic and political setbacks gradually wore away at his fortune. The General spent his last 30 years reading and writing and receiving guests at this home, which he named *Lacrima Montis*, (sometimes spelled *Lachryma Montis*) "Tear of the Mountain", a Latinization of "Crying Mountain", the Indian phrase for an all-season spring on this land. Vallejo died in 1890 and is buried in a small cemetery on a hill overlooking Sonoma.

▲ California 50

PETALUMA ADOBE
State Historic Park

Location: Northern California north of San Francisco.

Access: From California State Highway 116 in Petaluma at a point 0.8 mile east of the junction of Highway 116 & U.S. 101, turn northeast onto Casa Grande Road and proceed 1.8 miles; turn southeast (right) onto Adobe Road and go 0.2 mile, then turn north (left) onto the park access road for 0.1 mile to the parking lot. **Alternate Access:** From Highway 116 (if approaching from Sonoma) at milepost 41 +.7, travel northwest on Adobe Road for 2 miles to the park.

Day Use Facilities: Medium-sized picnic area; drinking water; restrooms; medium-sized parking lot.

Overnight Facilities: None; nearest public campground is in China Camp State Park.

Activities & Attractions: Self-guided tours of the partially restored structure and authentic furnishings of the ranch home of General M. G. Vallejo; some of the displays include 'beehive' charcoal kilns, blacksmith apparatus, a classic wooden cart and other simple farm equipment; guided tours for groups, by reservation.

Natural Features: Located on a knoll amid open fields dotted with oak; a stream flows down through the grounds; picnic sites are lightly shaded; park area is 41 acres; elevation 150´.

Season & Fees: Open all year; please see Appendix for park entry fees.

Mail & Phone: Petaluma Adobe State Historic Park, 3325 Adobe Road, Petaluma, CA 94952; ☎(707) 762-4871.

Park Notes: General Mariano Vallejo founded *Rancho Petaluma* in 1834 following a land grant from the Mexican governor of California. When you come here and see the large home with its first and second floor verandas all around, and its sizeable courtyard, take into account that what you're seeing is only *half* of the original house and a tiny fraction of the general's domain. Rancho Petaluma covered 66,000 acres—100 square miles—between Petaluma and Sonoma, and San Francisco Bay to what is now the town of Glen Ellen. But this spread was only a little more than a third of Vallejo's total holdings in California. To a greater extent, Vallejo was an absentee *hacendado* and spent only short periods here each year. A bronze bust of the general near the courtyard depicts him as a distinguished gentleman with a respectably receding hairline and fashionable, big ol' pork chop sideburns—the very image of the potentate he was.

California 51

OLOMPALI
State Historic Park

Location: Northern California north of San Francisco

Access: From U.S. Highway 101 (southbound) at a point 3 miles north of Novato, 3 miles south of Petaluma, take the Olompali Exit and proceed 0.5 mile to the park entrance; from U.S. 101 (northbound) continue north past the park and take the San Antonio Road Exit; do a '180', then head southbound on U.S. 101 to the Olompali Exit and continue as above.

Day Use Facilities: Small parking area.

Overnight Facilities: None; nearest public campground is in China Camp State Park.

Activities & Attractions: Site of a major Miwok Indian village; hiking trails; guided nature walks; interpretive programs.

Natural Features: Located in the Petaluma River Valley in the shadow of 1557′ Burdell Mountain; vegetation consists of stands of hardwoods and open grassy sections; elevation 100′ to 1500′.

Season & Fees: Open all year, with limited days and hours of availability; (please check with the park for a current schedule); please see Appendix for park entry fees.

Mail & Phone: mail c/o CDPR Marin District, 1455A East Francisco Boulevard, San Rafael, CA 94901; park phone ☎(415) 892-3383.

Park Notes: This park is undergoing development and the village site is being excavated by archaeologists.

California 52 ♿

SAMUEL P. TAYLOR
State Park

Location: Northern California northwest of San Francisco.

Access: From U.S. Highway 101 near San Rafael, take the Sir Francis Drake Boulevard Exit; travel northwest on Sir Francis Drake Boulevard (through the towns of San Anselmo, Fairfax and Lagunitas) for 16 miles; turn south (left) to the park entrance station and proceed 0.1 mile to the picnic area, another 0.1 mile to the lower camp area or a final 0.2 mile to the upper camp loop. **Alternate Access:** From California State Highway 1 in the town of Olema, turn east onto Sir Francis Drake Boulevard and proceed 5.1 miles to the Redwood Grove turnoff and continue as above.

Day Use Facilities: Medium-sized picnic area; group picnic area (reservable); drinking water; restrooms; medium-sized parking area.

Overnight Facilities: 60 campsites, plus enroute sites for self-contained vehicles in the picnic area; (2 group camps and an equestrian camp are also available); lower loop sites are small, level, with nominal separation; parking pads are packed gravel, short straight-ins; small to medium+ tent areas; upper loop sites are small+, with nominal to fairly good separation; parking pads are paved, medium to long straight-ins which might require a little additional leveling; medium to large tent areas; fireplaces or fire rings in the lower loop, barbecue grills and fire rings in the upper loop; b-y-o firewood; water at faucets throughout; restrooms with showers; holding tank disposal station; paved driveways; groceries+, 2 to 3 miles east; adequate supplies and services are available in Fairfax.

Activities & Attractions: Paved bike/horse/hike trail from Redwood Grove to the settlement of Tocoloma, 3 miles west; several additional miles of hike/horse trails.

Natural Features: Located in a densely forested canyon along and above the banks of Lagunitas Creek (also called Papermill Creek); redwoods tower above hardwoods, bushes and ferns; park area is 2708 acres; elevation 150´.

Season & Fees: Open all year; please see Appendix for reservation information, park entry and campground fees.

Mail & Phone: Samuel P. Taylor State Park, P.O. Box 251, Lagunitas, CA 94938; ☎(415) 488-9897.

Park Notes: There's a really pretty picnic area on a little shelf above the stream with just enough daylight showing through the redwoods to make a near-perfect spot. The picnic and camp areas are trimmed with what must be three miles of rail fence. You couldn't go wrong in any of the campsites, as long as your camping ensemble fits in the available space. The paved path is a real bonus. It's on the opposite side of the stream from the highway. You may still hear the traffic, but it won't be whooshing past your left ear.

California 53 ♿

China Camp
State Park

Location: Northern California north of San Francisco.

Access: From U.S. Highway 101 near milepost 12 +.5 on the north end of San Rafael, take the North San Pedro Road Exit and proceed 3 miles to the park boundary; 0.05 mile inside the boundary, turn south (right) onto a paved access road and proceed 0.4 mile to the Back Ranch Meadows Campground; or continue southeast on the main park road for 0.6 mile to the Miwok Meadows group day use area on the right, another 0.8 mile to the Buckeye Point, Weber Point and China Camp Point picnic areas, all on the left, or for an additional 0.3 mile to the historic area, also on the left; continue beyond the historic area for a final 0.5 mile to the east park boundary. **Alternate Access:** From U.S. 101 near milepost 10 +.5 in San Rafael, take the Third Street/Point San Pedro Road Exit and proceed 4.5 miles to the east park boundary and reverse the above directions. (Note: the Alternate Access is a 'back door' approach, but it may be a slightly more convenient route if you're coming up '101 from The City.)

Day Use Facilities: Small picnic areas, drinking water, vault facilities, small parking areas at Buckeye Point, Weber Point. China Camp Point and at the village; large group day use area at Miwok Meadows (available by reservation only).

Overnight Facilities: 30 primitive walk-in campsites (scattered around a wooded hillside, 25 to 100 yards from the parking lot), plus about 20 enroute sites for self-contained vehicles in the paved, level parking lot; water at central faucets; vault facilities; complete supplies and services are available in San Rafael.

Activities & Attractions: Remains of a historic Chinese fishing village; museum; trails into the hills (a large brochure/map with contour lines is available); fishing; small boat launch area.

Natural Features: Located on a bayside plain and in the hills above the bay; vegetation consists of open grassy/brushy areas, plus large sections of hardwoods; picnic and camp sites are very lightly to lightly shaded; good views of San Francisco Bay from throughout the park; park area is 1640 acres; sea level to 700´.

Season & Fees: Open all year; please see Appendix for reservation information, park entry and campground fees.

Mail & Phone: China Camp State Park, RR 1 Box 244, San Rafael, CA 94901; ☎(415) 456-0766.

Park Notes: *Wa Jen Ha Lio*. This was one of the earliest, largest and most productive Chinese fishing villages in California. China Camp was in operation by 1870 and it was home to several thousand Chinese immigrants and their descendants who introduced the use of commercial netting to catch bay shrimp off Point San Pedro. The shrimp were then dried and shipped to Chinese people all over the world. China

Camp represents the last surviving Chinese shrimping village in the state. A few buildings and foundations remain on the shoreside site.

California 54 ♿

Mount Tamalpais

State Park

Location: Northern California northwest of San Francisco.

Access: From California State Highway 1 (northbound) at milepost 3 +.4 (3 miles west of the junction of Highway 1 & U.S. 101 near Mill Valley), head northwest on Panoramic Highway for 5.1 miles to the Bootjack picnic area, or another 0.3 mile to a 3-way junction and the Pantoll campground; continue southwest on Panoramic Highway for another 3.6 miles to Stinson Beach; from Highway 1 (southbound) in Stinson Beach, proceed northeast on Panoramic Highway and reverse the above directions. **Additional Access:** From the junction at Pantoll, travel north on Pantoll Road for 1 mile, then northeast on Ridgecrest Boulevard for 3 miles to the summit of Mount Tamalpais at East Peak; from Stinson Beach, travel southeast on Highway 1 for 0.8 mile to the Steep Ravine camp. (Note: the above routing via the park's main road, Panoramic Highway, will serve the majority of travelers; short, paved roads are available for local exploration.)

Day Use Facilities: Small picnic area, small group picnic area, drinking water, restrooms and large parking lot at Bootjack; small picnic area, drinking water, restrooms and parking lot at the visitor center; Mountain Theater.

Overnight Facilities: *Pantoll Campground*: 16 park 'n walk campsites, plus approximately 25 enroute sites for self-contained vehicles, and a hike-bike site; park 'n walk sites are small, sloped, with fair separation; parking is in a fairly level, paved lot; tent areas are medium to large and somewhat level; storage cabinets; fireplaces; firewood is usually for sale, or b-y-o; water at several faucets; restrooms. *Steep Ravine Environmental Campground*: 6 primitive campsites and 10 small cabins; campsites have small to medium-sized tent areas, table, fireplace, storage cabinet; cabins have a 'sleeping platform', table, inside wood stove and outdoor fireplace; firewood is available; water at faucets; vault facilities; (2 group camps, and a small backpack camp for individuals and groups are also available, in other areas in the park); complete supplies and services are available in Mill Valley.

Activities & Attractions: More than 50 miles of trails within the park, connecting to a 200-mile system of trails on adjacent public land; (a brochure/map with contour lines is available); horses are allowed on fire roads and designated trails; bicycles are allowed on designated fire roads and paved roads; 3 designated hang glider launch points; visitor center at East Peak; "Mountain Theater", with room for about 3,000 individuals, (via a 0.7 mile trail from the Bootjack parking lot, or 0.2 mile trail from the Ridgecrest Boulevard parking lot).

Natural Features: Located on and around Mount Tamalpais; the park's vegetation consists of dense sections of hardwoods and conifers, open meadows, and brushy hillsides; most picnic and camp sites (except enroute sites) are well-shaded/sheltered by tall conifers and/or hardwoods; park area is 6200 acres; sea level to 2586′.

Season & Fees: Open all year; please see Appendix for reservation information and campground fees.

Mail & Phone: Mount Tamalpais State Park, 801 Panoramic Highway, Mill Valley, CA 94941; ☎(415) 388-2070.

Park Notes: "Mount Tam" itself is a triple-peaked ridge with a difference of a few feet between its highest points. *Tamalpais* is said to mean "Land of the Tamal (Indians)". The Cushing Memorial Theater ("Mountain Theater") is a large, outdoor amphitheater of native stone which was built by the CCC during the 1930's. Its serves as the stage for the long-run, annual "Mountain Play" and is sometimes used for weddings and other special occasions.

California 55 ♿

ANGEL ISLAND
State Park

Location: Northern California north of San Francisco.

Access: From the mainland: ferry service is available from Tiburon, San Francisco or Vallejo (ferry phone numbers, below); the only other access is by private craft to the harbor at Ayala Cove.)

Day Use Facilities: Large picnic area, drinking water and restrooms at Ayala Cove (Hospital Cove) on the northwest side of the island; group picnic area with drinking water and restrooms at East Garrison-Quarry Point on the middle-east side of the island (reservations required).

Overnight Facilities: Primitive campsites in 4 locations, 2 each on the southwest and southeast quadrants of the island (available by reservation only).

Activities & Attractions: Remains of military installations dating from the Civil War Era to the defunct Nike Missile days of the Cold War; hiking and bicycling on the park's trails and fire roads; a paved road follows the west, north and east shores of the island; (a large, color map with contour lines and marked historic sites is available); fishing for rockfish and stripers; fishing pier at Ayala Cove; athletic field at East Garrison; limited courtesy dock space and mooring buoys at Ayala Cove.

Natural Features: Located on Angel Island in San Francisco Bay; vegetation consists of a potpourri of hardwoods, evergreens, shrubs, brush and wildflowers—both native and that which was introduced by transients from around the world over the years; picnic sites are lightly to moderately shaded; sheltered, sandy beaches at Ayala Cove and Quarry Point; the island is topped by 781´ Mount Livermore; park area is 758 acres; sea level to 781´.

Season & Fees: Open all year; no dogs; please see Appendix for reservation information, park entry and campground fees.

Mail & Phone: Angel Island State Park, P.O. Box 318, Tiburon, CA 94920; park office ☎(415) 435-1915; ferry from Tiburon ☎(415) 435-2131; ferry from San Francisco or Vallejo ☎(415) 546-2815 or 546-2896.

Park Notes: Angel Island is the only state park on the California Coast which formerly served in a major, modern U.S. military capacity. Its military activity antedates that of many of the other West Coast forts-turned-state parks by some years. (See Fort Stevens State Park in Oregon, Forts Columbia, Flagler, Worden State Parks et. al. in Washington, in *Volume I Pacific Northwest* of this series.) Like its Northwest counterparts, shore batteries for harbor defense were installed during the Spanish American War era. Known as Fort McDowell during most of its twentieth century service, it was one of the country's largest military induction centers. It was also an immigration station and a World War II transient camp for Japanese pow's. Angel Island was given its Honorable Discharge from the Army in 1962 when the Nike missile battery was decommissioned and nearly the entire isle became a state park. (Nike was the Greek goddess of victory, and park boosters might say that she switched sides somewhere along the way.)

California 56 ♿

CANDLESTICK POINT
State Recreation Area

Location: Western California in San Francisco.

Access: From U.S. Highway 101 in the southeast corner of San Francisco (2 miles south of the junction of U.S. 101 & Interstate 80), take the Third Street/Bayshore Boulevard Exit and go northeast on Third Street to Jamestown Avenue; turn southeast (right) onto Jamestown Avenue and proceed 0.8 mile; turn southwest (sharp right, just past the stadium) onto Harney Way for 0.1 mile, then left into the Last Port picnic area; or continue east on Jamestown Avenue past Harney Way and around to the east side of the stadium for another 0.55 mile (be in the far right lane); turn east (right) into the main park area.

Day Use Facilities: Several small picnic areas; small group picnic areas; some sites have small windbreaks; drinking water; restrooms; very large parking lot in the main area, small lot in the Last Port area.

Overnight Facilities: None; nearest public campground is in China Camp State Park.

Activities & Attractions: Paved and packed-sand paths/trails; walking, jogging and fitness courses; fishing for perch and shark; 2 fishing piers.

Natural Features: Located on Candlestick Point on the west shore of San Francisco Bay; landscaping consists of acres of lawns, planted shrubs and flowers, conifers and hardwoods; park area is 45 acres; sea level.

Season & Fees: Open all year; please see Appendix for park entry fees.

Mail & Phone: c/o CDPR San Francisco District Office, 1150 Carroll Avenue, San Francisco, CA 94124; ☎(415) 557-4069.

Park Notes: Candlestick Park's presence is unmistakably evident from near the sra's parking lot. But once you wander out onto the point among all the trees and grass, you probably won't even remember that the world-famous sports complex is in the neighborhood (until a player in the stadium hits a touchdown, or whatever they do there).

California 57

BENICIA

State Recreation Area

Location: Western California northeast of Oakland.

Access: From Interstate 780 at the northwest tip of Benicia (2.5 miles southeast of the junction if I-780 & I-80 in Vallejo), take the Columbus Parkway/Benicia SRA Exit; from the west side of the freeway, go west on State Park Road for 0.1 mile to the park entrance station; continue west for 0.2 mile, then the park road curves south for another 0.9 mile to the picnic area or a final 0.4 mile to the last parking lot and turnaround. (Note: if northbound on I-780, continue north off the ramp for 0.3 mile to Rose Drive, then go across the freeway to the park road; if southbound, the off-ramp swings around onto a right-hand cloverleaf; about half-way around the circle, exit left off the cloverleaf onto the park road.)

Day Use Facilities: Medium-sized picnic area, plus scattered additional tables; drinking water; restrooms; several medium-sized parking lots.

Overnight Facilities: None; nearest public campground is in Bothe-Napa Valley State Park.

Activities & Attractions: Shore fishing for salmon (fall), shad, stripers, sturgeon.

Natural Features: Located on a plain on Southampton Bay near the confluence of the Sacramento River and the upper end of San Francisco Bay; park vegetation consists of very large tracts of natural grass, plus lawns dotted with hardwoods and some conifers; picnic sites have very light to light-medium shade; park area is 467 acres; sea level.

Season & Fees: Open all year; please see Appendix for park entry fees; automatic gate ("iron ranger") requires fee in dollar bills.

Mail & Phone: Mail c/o Benicia Capitol State Historic Park; park phone ☎(707) 648-1911.

Park Notes: The level park road is a very popular spot with walkers, joggers, cyclists and strollers (both the two-legged and the small four-wheeled types). Pleasant scenery.

California 58

BENICIA CAPITOL

State Historic Park

Location: Western California northeast of Oakland.

Access: From Interstate 780 in Benicia, take the Central Benicia/East Second Street Exit and proceed southwest on East Second for 0.3 mile; turn northwest (right) onto Military East for 0.1 mile, then turn southwest (left) onto First Street and go

0.35 mile (5 blocks); the park is on the northwest corner of First and G Streets (on your right).

Day Use Facilities: Small picnic area; drinking water; restrooms; streetside parking.

Overnight Facilities: None; nearest public campground is in Bothe-Napa Valley State Park.

Activities & Attractions: Restored site of the Third Capitol of California; museum with period furnishings.

Natural Features: Located in-town; park grounds are landscaped with manicured lawns, hardwoods and small gardens; park area is 1 acre; elevation 20´.

Season & Fees: Open all year; (days and hours may vary, contact the park for a current schedule); please see Appendix for park entry fees.

Mail & Phone: Benicia Capitol State Historic Park, 115 West G Street, P.O. Box 5, Benicia, CA 94510; ☎(707) 745-3385.

Park Notes: Erected in 1852, this building was ostensibly meant to be the Benicia city hall. It was offered for use as the state capitol and was accepted posthaste by the legislature. Benicia was the capital of California from February 4, 1853 to February 25, 1854. This was one of four locations of what became known as the "Capitol on Wheels", before a permanent home for California government was found. Benicia was named for Francisca Benicia Vallejo, wife of powerful General Mariano Vallejo (also see the Sonoma County state parks). As the story goes, in 1847 local officials first proposed that the newly founded town be named "Francisca". Politics being what they are, the city fathers of another local burg, Yerba Buena, objected to what they saw as patronization of the general, and in a quick game of one-upmanship, changed the name of their city to San Francisco. To avert confusion over two similar names, Benicia subsequently took its present pleasant name.

▲ **California 59** ♿

Mount Diablo
State Park

Location: Western California northeast of Oakland.

Access: From Interstate 680 in Walnut Creek (*northbound*) take the Ygnacio Valley Road Exit, travel northeast on Ygnacio Valley Road for 2.2 miles; turn southeast (right) onto Walnut Avenue and go 1.6 miles, then jog right onto Oak Grove for 100 yards, then left onto North Gate Road for 1.7 miles to the northwest park entrance; proceed 4.5 miles to the camp and picnic area and the park office at Junction; continue on the main road for another 2 miles to the Horseshoe/Rock City/Artist Point day use areas; (from the Artist Point area, go west for 0.5 mile on a side road to Live Oak Campground) or go southerly for 1 final mile to the south entrance station. From I-680 in Walnut Creek (*southbound*) take the North Main Exit and go south on North Main for 0.6 mile, then turn left onto Ygnacio Valley Road and continue as above. **Alternate Access:** From Interstate 680 in Danville at the Diablo Road Exit, head easterly on Diablo Road for 2.9 miles; turn north (left) onto Mount Diablo Scenic Road and proceed 3.7 miles to the south entrance station and continue in reverse of the above. **Additional Access:** From Junction, travel northeasterly on the summit road (paved) for 2 miles to a half-dozen small picnic areas scattered along the road, or an additional 0.5 mile to Juniper Campground, or a final 2 miles to the summit of Mount Diablo. (Note: The north road climbs/descends more gradually and has fewer switchbacks than the south road.)

Day Use Facilities: Rock City/Artist Point/Horseshoe picnic areas combined have a medium number of tables scattered over a wide area, also drinking water, central restrooms, vaults, scattered parking; Summit Road picnic areas are small, scattered, with vault facilities nearby.

Overnight Facilities: 58 campsites in 3 major areas (*Junction*, *Live Oak*, *Juniper*); (4 standard group camps and 2 group horse camps are also available, by reservation);

sites are small to small+, with minimal to nominal separation; parking pads are gravel, mostly short straight-ins, plus some medium+ pull-throughs in Juniper; many pads will require additional leveling; small to medium-sized tent areas; assorted fire appliances; b-y-o firewood; water at faucets; vault facilities; (restrooms nearby at Junction); complete supplies and services are available in Walnut Creek.

Activities & Attractions: Observation deck at the summit; miles of hiking trails (a detailed brochure/map is available); small interpretive center.

Natural Features: Located on the summit and sides of Mount Diablo; the mountain is cloaked with large, open grassy areas and stands of oaks, plus a few tall conifers; most picnic and camp sites receive very light to light-medium shade; park area is 18,000 acres; elevation 300′ to 3849′.

Season & Fees: Open all year; please see Appendix for reservation information, park entry and campground fees.

Mail & Phone: Mount Diablo State Park, P.O. Box 250, Diablo, CA 94528; ☎(415) 837-2525.

Park Notes: From Mount Diablo's summit you can see about half of California (or so it might seem). Actually, on a clear day you can see portions of nearly two-thirds of the state's 58 counties, or roughly one-fourth of its land area (about 40,000 square miles). Skilled observers say that, under perfect conditions and aided by binocs, they can see Half Dome in Yosemite, 135 miles southeast, or Lassen Peak, 165 miles north. It is claimed that the view is excelled only by the panorama from Africa's 19,000′ Mount Kilimanjaro. To get a good visual effect from this solitary peak, you don't *have* to drive all the way to the top—but just about everyone does.

California

South Bay

California 60

MONTARA
State Beach

Location: Central California Coast south of San Francisco.

Access: From California State Highway 1 at milepost 36 +.5 just inside the north city limits of Montara, opposite Second Street (8 miles north of Half Moon Bay) turn west into the main parking lot.

Day Use Facilities: Vault facilities; small parking lot.

Overnight Facilities: None; nearest public campground is in Half Moon Bay State Beach.

Activities & Attractions: Beach trail; beachcombing; fishing.

Natural Features: Located on a sandy beach and on a short bluff above the beach; a small headland rises at the north end of the beach and a low hill forms the south boundary; beach property extends back into the hills about a half-mile from the ocean; park area is 680 acres; sea level to 100′.

Season & Fees: Open all year; (no fee).

Mail & Phone: c/o CDPR San Mateo Coast District Office, 95 Kelly Avenue, Half Moon Bay, CA 94019; ☎(415) 726-6238.

Park Notes: Montara is a mile-long, fairly wide beach—possibly the nicest beach on this section of the coast. Two other state beach properties are located north of here. Grey Whale Cove State Beach is concession-operated, and is near milepost 37 +.9 at the north tip of Montara SB. It has a tiny parking lot on a small shelf below the highway and high above the beach. A steep driveway leads to the lot, a steep trail leads to the sand. Grey Whale Cove covers a couple of acres—1 horizontal, the other vertical. Pacifica State Beach, on the other hand, is completely on the level, in topographic respects, anyway. It covers a half-mile strip of sand abeam of the Linda

Mar district in the southwest corner of Pacifica. A large parking lot is located on the west side of Highway 1, between Crespi Drive and Linda Mar Boulevard. Pacifica State Beach is operated by the city of the same name.

California 61 ♿

Half Moon Bay

State Beach

Location: Central California Coast south of San Francisco.

Access: From California State Highway 1 at milepost 28 +.7 near the south end of the city of Half Moon Bay, turn west onto Kelly Avenue; go 0.65 mile down to the end of Kelly, then hang a short right and you're in the Francis Beach picnic and camp areas; or from Highway 1 near mileposts 30, 30 +.5 and 31 (within 2 miles north of Kelly Avenue), go west onto Venice Boulevard, Young Avenue or Roosevelt Boulevard for 0.4 mile to the park's Venice Beach, Dunes Beach or Roosevelt Beach areas, respectively.

Day Use Facilities: Medium-sized picnic area, drinking water, restrooms, large parking lot at Francis Beach.

Overnight Facilities: 50 campsites in a semi-parking lot arrangement; (hike-bike sites, enroute sites, and a primitive group camp in a separate area, are also available); sites are tiny but level; separation—zero; parking slots are paved, mostly short to medium-length straight-ins; small to medium-sized tent spots in some sites, none in others; storage cabinets; barbecue grills or fireplaces; b-y-o firewood; water at central faucets; restrooms; cold outside showers; holding tank disposal station; paved driveways; adequate+ supplies and services are available in Half Moon Bay.

Activities & Attractions: Beach access.

Natural Features: Located on a wide, sandy beach and on a short bluff at the edge of the beach; park vegetation consists of grass and a few trees; bordered by residential and light agricultural zones; coastal hills rise a couple of miles behind the beach; park area is 170 acres; sea level.

Season & Fees: Open all year; please see Appendix for reservation information, park entry and campground fees.

Mail & Phone: Half Moon Bay State Beach, 95 Kelly Avenue, Half Moon Bay, CA 94019; ☎(415) 726-6238.

Park Notes: The Central Valley is famous for winter fog, and the San Francisco Peninsula is the Valley's summer coastal counterpart. A big reason for the fog here *is* the Central Valley. Rising hot air in the Valley draws cold, moist air inland from the ocean and bingo! A blanket of fog is pulled over the head and shoulders of Half Moon Bay. You don't sun yourself on a beach blanket in this park—you bundle yourself in it. (Mark Twain once remarked that the coldest winter he ever experienced was the summer he spent around here.) Half Moon Bay is a burgeoning getaway community. The town, its location and climate might remind you of Lincoln City or Seaside, Oregon, if you're numbered among the millions who've ever been to those two weekenders' havens.

California 62

San Gregorio

State Beach

Location: Central California Coast south of Half Moon Bay.

Access: From California State Highway 1 at milepost 18 +.1 (0.1 mile south of the junction of Highway 1 & State Highway 84, 10 miles south of Half Moon Bay) turn west and proceed 0.1 mile to the park.

Day Use Facilities: Small picnic area; vault facilities; large parking lot.

Overnight Facilities: None; nearest public campground is in Butano State Park.

Activities & Attractions: Beachcombing; fishing.

Natural Features: Located on a beach and on a short rise above the beach; vegetation consists of large, grassy sections, some small plants and a solitary cypress; San Gregorio Creek meets the sea at the south edge of the park; bordered by hills and headlands; park area is 172 acres; sea level.

Season & Fees: Open all year; please see Appendix for park entry fees.

Mail & Phone: c/o CDPR San Mateo Coast District Office, 95 Kelly Avenue, Half Moon Bay, CA 94019; ☎(415) 726-6238.

Park Notes: Captain Gaspar De Portola and his party of Spanish explorers camped in this pretty spot by San Gregorio Creek for three days of R & R, October 24-27, 1769. The group had come searching for an overland route from San Diego to Monterey Bay, but missed their destination. They discovered San Francisco Bay instead.

▲ California 63

POMPONIO
State Beach

Location: Central California Coast south of Half Moon Bay.

Access: From California State Highway 1 at milepost 16 +.6 (11 miles south of Half Moon Bay) turn west into the park.

Day Use Facilities: Small picnic area; vault facilities; medium-sized parking lot.

Overnight Facilities: None; nearest public campground is in Butano State Park.

Activities & Attractions: Beachcombing; fishing.

Natural Features: Located on a medium-sized beach and on a very short shelf above the beach; vegetation consists of bushes, small plants and grass; small hills and headlands complete the scene; park area is 410 acres; sea level.

Season & Fees: Open all year; please see Appendix for park entry fees.

Mail & Phone: c/o CDPR San Mateo Coast District Office, 95 Kelly Avenue, Half Moon Bay, CA 94019; ☎(415) 726-6238.

Park Notes: There are good upcoast views from here. If you stop at this or any of the other beaches along this section of coast, try to determine which vegetation is responsible for the quite noticeable (at times, anyway) turpentine aroma.

▲ California 64

PESCADERO
State Beach

Location: Central California Coast south of Half Moon Bay.

Access: From California State Highway 1 at 3 points between mileposts 13 +.5 and 14 +.5 (13-14 miles south of Half Moon Bay: turn west into the parking areas; (the southernmost entrance is at the junction of Highway 1 & Pescadero Road).

Day Use Facilities: Several picnic tables; vault facilities; medium and large parking lots.

Overnight Facilities: None; nearest public campground is in Butano State Park.

Activities & Attractions: Paths and steps down to the beach; guided nature walks of Pescadero Marsh, scheduled regularly (contact the park office for a calendar).

Natural Features: Located on a sandy and rocky beach and on medium-high bluffs/dunes above the beach; vegetation consists of shrubs, some larger bushes and grass; park area is 638 acres; sea level to 50′.

Season & Fees: Open all year; please see Appendix for park entry fees (charged seasonally at the developed facility at the north end of the park).

Mail & Phone: Mail c/o CDPR San Mateo Coast District Office, 95 Kelly Avenue, Half Moon Bay, CA 94019; park phone ☎(415) 879-0832.

Park Notes: The largest beach is at the northernmost of the 3 park access points. At the south end, large rock formations just offshore and the shoreline rock shelves are the main features. In the middle, fairly good-sized dunes predominate.

▲ California 65

BUTANO
State Park

Location: Central California coastal area north of Santa Cruz.

Access: From California State Highway 1 at milepost 13 +.7 (14 miles south of Half Moon Bay, 33 miles north of Santa Cruz), turn east onto Pescadero Road and travel 2.5 miles; turn south (right) onto Cloverdale Road and proceed 4.3 miles to Butano Park Road; turn east, (left) and proceed 0.2 mile to the park entrance station and the picnic area; or continue for another mile to the campground. **Alternate Access:** From Highway 1 at milepost 5 +.75, turn east onto Gazos Creek Road and proceed 2.1 miles to Cloverdale Road; turn north (left) onto Cloverdale Road and go 1.3 miles to Butano Park Road, and continue as above. (Note: the alternate access is handier if you're coming from Santa Cruz, but it's also more winding.)

Day Use Facilities: Small picnic area.

Overnight Facilities: *Ben Reis Campground*: 35 campsites, including 14 walk-in units located several yards from a parking area; (hike-bike sites are also available; a trail camp can be used, by reservation); sites are medium-sized, with fairly good separation; parking pads are gravel, short to medium-length straight-ins; some pads will require additional leveling; large, basically level, tent areas; fireplaces or fire rings; b-y-o firewood; water at several faucets; restrooms; paved, narrow driveways; limited supplies and services are available in Pescadero, 9 miles northwest.

Activities & Attractions: Several foot trails and fire roads lead 4-5 miles from the entrance or from the campground to the northeast corner of the park; guided nature walks and campfire programs in summer.

Natural Features: Located on the west slopes of the Santa Cruz Mountains, in a very dense forest of redwoods, some oaks, shrubs and ferns; most of the long, narrow park flanks Little Butano Creek, a small, typically seasonal, stream; park area is 3200 acres; elevation 250´ to 1700´.

Season & Fees: Open all year; please see Appendix for reservation information, park entry and campground fees.

Mail & Phone: Butano State Park, P.O. Box 9, Pescadero, CA 94060; ☎(408) 338-6132.

Park Notes: Most of the park is deep in the dense woods, but from one trail-accessible high point near the park entrance you can look out to the ocean and Ano Nuevo Island. In keeping with the natural theme of the park, the campground provides a very subdued, unembellished, forest environment.

▲ California 66

BEAN HOLLOW
State Beach

Location: Central California Coast south of Half Moon Bay.

Access: From California State Highway 1 at milepost 11 +.1 turn west into the park.

Day Use Facilities: Small picnic area; restrooms; medium-sized parking area.

Overnight Facilities: None; nearest public campground is in Butano State Park.

Activities & Attractions: Hiking/nature trail (2 miles, 1.5 hours, a guide pamphlet is available); fishing.

Natural Features: Located on 2 sections of beach on a cove and on a bluff above the beach; low headlands border the cove; park area is 44 acres; sea level.

Season & Fees: Open all year; (no fee).

Mail & Phone: c/o CDPR San Mateo Coast District Office, 95 Kelly Avenue, Half Moon Bay, CA 94019; ☎(415) 726-6238.

Park Notes: With a down-home name like this, how could anybody pass up a chance to stop.

▲ California 67 ♿

Año Nuevo
State Reserve

Location: Central California Coast northwest of Santa Cruz.

Access: From California State Highway 1 at milepost 1 +.6 (10 miles north of Davenport, 15 miles south of Pescadero), turn west into the park access road and proceed 0.3 mile to the visitor center. (An additional day use access point is located near milepost 6.)

Day Use Facilities: Drinking water; restrooms and vault facilities; medium-sized parking lot.

Overnight Facilities: None; nearest public campground is in Butano State Park.

Activities & Attractions: Guided tours during the elephant seal breeding season, December to April, reservations required; several hiking trails; visitor center.

Natural Features: Located on a beach and a bushy coastal plain; the forested Santa Cruz Mountains rise to the east; park area is 1200 acres; sea level.

Season & Fees: Open all year; no dogs allowed; please see Appendix for reservation information and park entry fees.

Mail & Phone: Mail c/o CDPR San Mateo Coast District Office, 95 Kelly Avenue, Half Moon Bay, CA 94019; park phone ☎(415) 879-0595 or ☎(415) 879-0852 or ☎(415) 979-0227.

Park Notes: "Northern Elephant Seal breeding season is always an exciting event", say the park's promotional posters. To visit Año Nuevo State Reserve during this season you must be on a guided walk led by a trained volunteer naturalist. There's a narrow observation 'window' for this occasion. The bulls (which commonly are the length and weight of a compact car, but can be as long and hefty as a loaded mini-pickup) make their grand appearances beginning in early December and continue arriving through February. By mid-March, though, mom and pop have left on the honeymoon, leaving behind the weaned pups who hang around through April. The three-mile round-trip on the guided walk takes about 2.5 hours.

▲ California 68 ♿

Wilder Ranch
State Historic Park

Location: Central California Coast west of Santa Cruz.

Access: From California State Highway 1 at milepost 21 +.8 (5 miles west of Santa Cruz, 7 miles southeast of Davenport), turn south/west onto a park access road and go 0.2 mile to the main parking lot.

Day Use Facilities: Picnic area; drinking water; restrooms; large parking lot.

Overnight Facilities: None; nearest public campground is in New Brighton State Beach.

Activities & Attractions: Many of the original buildings of a 19th and 20th century dairy farm; 22-acre "cultural preserve"; hiking/nature trail; orientation information is available in the ranch house/interpretive center.

Natural Features: Located on a coastal plain/terrace, with a backdrop of rolling, tree-dotted hills; the central ranch area is landscaped with lawns, hardwoods and gardens; park area is 2800 acres; sea level to 100´.

Season & Fees: Open all year; no dogs permitted.

Mail & Phone: c/o CDPR Pajaro Coast District Office, 101 Madeline Drive, Aptos, CA 95003; ☎(408) 688-3241.

Park Notes: First established in 1791 by Mission Santa Cruz as *Rancho del Matadero*, this spread became a dairy operation run by the Wilder family for more than 100 years into the mid-twentieth century. Many of the original buildings, including the Victorian ranch house, still stand. Plans call for incorporating a working model of a dairy ranch within the framework of the park. And how 'bout this, veggie lovers: 12 percent of the nation's crop of *brussels sprouts* are grown on cropland within the park. The 1.2-mile scenic trail from the parking lot goes across a level terrace, past the Sea of Sprouts and out to the edge of the bluff. The trail follows the coastline to Old Landing Cove, where harbor seals use a large flat rock to *siesta* during low tides. A hanging garden of ferns grows from the ceiling of a log-jammed sea cave in the cove. Sheltered from the salt spray, the delicate ferns flourish in soil moistened by underground springs.

▲ California 69 ♿

NATURAL BRIDGES
State Beach

Location: Central California Coast in Santa Cruz.

Access: From California State Highway 1 near milepost 20 in the far southwest corner of Santa Cruz, turn south onto Western Drive and proceed 0.1 mile to a 'T', then jog west (right) on Mission Street for 50 yards, then turn south (left) onto Natural Bridges Drive; go south on Natural Bridges Drive for 0.4 mile, then east (left) on Delaware Avenue for 0.1 mile and then south (right) on Swanton Boulevard for 0.3 mile to a 'T' at West Cliff Drive; swing west (a sharp right) to the park entrance and go down 0.1 mile to the main parking lot. (Note: the route zigzags through a light industrial and residential district; alternatively, you could come all the way out to the far west end of West Cliff Drive from Lighthouse Field State Beach.)

Day Use Facilities: Medium-sized picnic area; drinking water; restrooms with freshwater rinse showers; large parking lot in the picnic area, medium-sized lot at the park entrance.

Overnight Facilities: None; nearest public campground is in New Brighton State Beach.

Activities & Attractions: Small visitor center; nature trail through monarch butterfly habitat; paved trail to the beach; beach overlook point.

Natural Features: Located on the beach and on a densely wooded, hilly section a few yards north of the beach; park area is 65 acres; sea level.

Season & Fees: Open all year; please see Appendix for park entry fees.

Mail & Phone: Natural Bridges State Beach, 2531 West Cliff Drive, Santa Cruz, CA 95060; ☎(408) 423-4609.

Park Notes: There are well-weathered rock formations and shelves along this section of coast, and some of the more interesting shapes are on this beach. Thousands of monarch butterflies annually spend the winter in the small wooded area here. Monarchs are very picky (or shall we say "discriminating") when it comes to selecting their winter surroundings, and the microclimate has to be perfect. Natural Bridges is one of about 100 dispersed wintering sites along the Central and Southern California Coast, and it's one of the best. As many as 200,000 monarchs have spent the winter in the park's eucalytus grove.

▲ California 70

LIGHTHOUSE FIELD
State Beach

Location: Central California Coast in Santa Cruz.

Access: From California State Highway 1 in the southwest corner of Santa Cruz (1.7 miles southwest of the San Lorenzo River bridge), turn southeast onto Bay Street and proceed 1 mile to a 'T' intersection; turn west (right) onto West Cliff Drive and go 0.5 mile to the park.

Day Use Facilities: Small picnic area and sitting benches; drinking water; restrooms; half-dozen small and medium-sized parking lots; (streetside parking is also available).

Overnight Facilities: None; nearest public campground is in New Brighton State Beach.

Activities & Attractions: Steps down to the beach; paths crisscross the field; seal-watching at Seal Rock, just offshore; Mark Abbott Memorial Lighthouse (small surfing museum inside), overlooks the beach.

Natural Features: Located on the beach and on a bluff above Monterey Bay; the 'field' is a several-acre meadow with small plants, bushes, wildflowers, grass, well-dotted with large evergreens, on the north side of West Cliff Drive; planted vegetation consists of sections of lawns along the edge of the bluff; sea level to 50´.

Season & Fees: Open all year; (no fee).

Mail & Phone: c/o CDPR Pajaro Coast District Office, 101 Madeline Drive, Aptos, CA 95003; ☎(408) 688-3241.

Park Notes: The park extends for about 0.6 mile along West Cliff Drive, and Lighthouse Field covers a little less than a square mile behind the beach. This is Surf City North. On a good day, there'll be almost as many spectators as there are surfers and seals. In reasonably clear weather, you can see all the way across the bay to Monterey.

▲ California 71 ♿

TWIN LAKES

State Beach

Location: Central California Coast in Santa Cruz.

Access: From California State Highway 1 near milepost 15 on the east side of Santa Cruz, take the Soquel Avenue Exit, then go southwest on Soquel Avenue for 0.2 mile; turn south (left) onto 7th Avenue and travel 1.4 miles to the intersection of 7th Avenue and Eaton Street; continue south on 7th for a final 0.3 mile to the Schwan Lagoon area; or turn west (right) onto Eaton Street and go 0.55 mile across the harbor bridge and onto Murray Street, then turn south (left) onto Seabright Avenue for 0.2 mile to the Seabright Beach area.

Day Use Facilities: Benches, restrooms, freshwater rinse showers, limited streetside parking near both areas.

Overnight Facilities: None; nearest public campground is in New Brighton State Beach.

Activities & Attractions: Beach access; Santa Cruz City Museum, adjacent to Seabright Beach; small craft harbor.

Natural Features: Located along the beach and around a lagoon, in a residential district; park area is 110 acres; sea level.

Season & Fees: Open all year; (no fee).

Mail & Phone: c/o CDPR Pajaro Coast District Office, 101 Madeline Drive, Aptos, CA 95003; ☎(408) 688-3241.

Park Notes: Seabright Beach is, subjectively, the preferred spot, mostly because the beach area is much greater than the one at Schwan lagoon, but Seabright is also a little farther from the traffic mainstreams. This is a sailboat-watcher's paradise. There must be a thousand sailboats parked (berthed, docked, moored, whatever) in the harbor. The long, rectangular harbor and Schwan Lagoon comprise the "Twin Lakes". (Some maps and a few local beachcombers still refer to Schwan Lagoon as "Schwan Lake", but maybe that's just an unintended pun.)

▲ California 72 ♿

HENRY COWELL REDWOODS

State Park

Location: Central California coastal area north of Santa Cruz.

Access: From California State Highway 1 at milepost 17 +.5 in midtown Santa Cruz, take the State Highway 9/River Street Exit and travel north on Highway 9 for 4.8 miles; turn east (right) onto a park access road and proceed 0.4 mile to the day use area. **Additional Access** (campground): From Highway 1 at the Ocean Street-Felton Exit in Santa Cruz at milepost 17 +.3, turn north onto Ocean Street and proceed 0.2 mile; bear right onto Graham Hill Road, go northerly for 3 miles, then turn west (left) onto a park access road for 0.2 to the campground entrance station. **Alternate Access:** From the intersection of California State Highway 9 and Graham Hill Road in midtown Felton, travel south on Highway 9 for 0.6 mile to the day use area turnoff; or from that same intersection in Felton, travel southeast on Graham Hill Road for 2 miles to the campground access road.

Day Use Facilities: Large picnic area; drinking water; restrooms; several parking lots; concession stand.

Overnight Facilities: *Graham Hill Campground*: 113 campsites; (bike sites are also available); sites are medium to medium+ in size, with good separation; parking pads are gravel/dirt, medium-length straight-ins; good to excellent tent-pitching opportunities; at least half of the parking pads and tent areas are essentially level, others are a touch sloped; storage cabinets; fireplaces or fire rings; b-y-o firewood; water at faucets throughout; restrooms with showers; paved driveways; groceries on Graham Hill Road within 2 miles north and south; complete supplies and services are available in Santa Cruz.

Activities & Attractions: 15 miles of hiking and horse trails; redwood groves; trail from the campground to an observation deck; steelhead and salmon fishing in winter.

Natural Features: Located in the western foothills of the Santa Cruz Mountains; the picnic area overlooks the banks of the San Lorenzo River, which winds southerly through the center of the park; most picnic and camp sites are well sheltered/shaded; park area is 4300 acres; elevation 100´ to 500´.

Season & Fees: Open all year; please see Appendix for reservation information, park entry and campground fees.

Mail & Phone: Henry Cowell Redwoods State Park, 101 North Big Trees Park Road, Felton, CA 95018; ☎(408) 335-4598 (office) or☎(408) 438-2396 (campground).

Park Notes: Think of the park as being shaped like a drinking gourd. The day use area is in the 'handle'; the campground is on the rim of the 'bowl'. Except for service roads and trails, the remaining 90 percent of the dipper is semi-wilderness. The most-frequented place in the park is the Redwoods Grove, within a couple-hundred yards by trail from the day use parking area. A second, smaller stand of redwoods, the Cathedral Redwoods, is deep within the park's interior. Interestingly, in a park known for its redwoods, the campground's trees are primarily large, full oaks and ponderosa pines. No matter—it's a really nice place.

▲ California 73

SANTA CRUZ MISSION
State Historic Park

Location: Central California coastal area in Santa Cruz.

Access: From California State Highway 1 on the west side of Santa Cruz, at the intersection of Highway 1 and Mission Street, (0.7 mile southwest of the San Lorenzo River bridge) go east on Mission Street for 0.15 mile, then turn north (left, at the plaza) onto Emmet Street and find a place to park; the historic building is on School Street, a few yards east of the plaza. (Note: westerly from the major intersection described above, Highway 1 is also Mission Street; at the intersection, Mission Street splits off on its own and goes east.)

Day Use Facilities: Mission Plaza city park, nearby; streetside parking.

Overnight Facilities: None; nearest public campground is in New Brighton State Beach.

Activities & Attractions: Restoration of an adobe originally part of Mission Santa Cruz in 1791; annual fiesta in October.

Natural Features: Located in-town; the mission area is landscaped with hardwoods, pines and lawns; park area is 1 acre; elevation 50´.

Season & Fees: Open all year; (no fee).

Mail & Phone: c/o CDPR Pajaro Coast District Office, 101 Madeline Drive, Aptos, CA 95003; ☎(408) 688-3241.

Park Notes: *Mision la Exaltacion de la Santa Cruz*, the twelfth Franciscan mission, was founded by Padre Lasuen in 1791. In 1793 the adobe church was built on the north side of the plaza (on the site of the present Holy Cross Catholic Church). The mission was damaged by several earthquakes and finally collapsed in 1857. A beautiful scale replica of the mission church was built in 1931, across the street from the first site. The mission contained 32 buildings at the time it was secularized in 1834. (Also see La Purisima Mission SHP). The last remaining adobe is the focal point of the park.

▲ California 74

THE FOREST OF NISENE MARKS
State Park

Location: Central California coastal area east of Santa Cruz.

Access: From California State Highway 1 at Seacliff Beach/Aptos Exit near milepost 10 +.5, turn north/east onto State Park Drive and go 0.2 mile; turn southeast (right) onto Soquel Drive and proceed 0.5 mile; a few yards after crossing the Aptos Creek bridge, turn north (left) onto Aptos Creek Road (paved for the first 0.8 mile, then graded) and travel north for 0.8 mile to a medium-sized parking lot and the end of the pavement; continue ahead for 1.1 mile to the first picnic area, another 0.5 mile to the West Ridge Trailhead parking lot, then 0.4 mile to a second picnic area and a final 0.6 to the last picnic site. (Note: motorhomes and trailers are discouraged from using the park road.)

Day Use Facilities: 3 small picnic areas; vault facilities; small parking areas.

Overnight Facilities: West Ridge Trail Camp, 6 miles north of the trailhead (available by reservation only).

Activities & Attractions: More than 30 miles of hiking trails and fire roads, limited use by mountain bikes and horses (a detailed brochure/map with trail use regs is available).

Natural Features: Located in Aptos Creek Canyon and on the southwest slopes of the Santa Cruz Mountains; vegetation consists of second-growth redwoods and very dense undergrowth; park area is 10,000 acres; elevation 100´ to 2500´.

Season & Fees: Open all year; (no fee).

Mail & Phone: c/o CDPR Santa Cruz Mountains District Office, 101 North Big Trees Park Road, Felton, CA 95018; ☎(408) 335-9145 or☎(408) 335-4598.

Park Notes: Walkers and joggers typically park their vehicles in the lot at the end of the pavement and then travel the very gently sloped main road upstream through the tunnel of trees which shrouds the roadway. In one respect, The Forest is a 'monument' to logging and clear cutting. The square miles of redwoods which once brushed the sky in this region were leveled in the late nineteenth and early twentieth centuries during what has been described as a "forty-year logging frenzy". Some evidence of logging operations still remains, but most of the structures themselves have been leveled by storms in turn. The park is named for Nisene, mother of the local Marks family which purchased the original, major tract of land to establish the park and to re-establish the forest which once stood here.

▲ California 75 ♿

NEW BRIGHTON
State Beach

Location: Central California Coast east of Santa Cruz.

Access: From California State Highway 1 at the Capitola/ Park Avenue Exit near milepost 12 (2 miles east of the Santa Cruz city limits), go southwest on Park Avenue for 0.15 mile; turn southeast (a hairpin left) onto a frontage road for 0.1 mile, then swing sharply right to the park entrance station; at a fork 0.1 mile beyond the entrance, take the right fork for 0.1 mile to the beach parking lot; or take the left fork for 0.3 mile to the picnic area and camp ground.

Day Use Facilities: Medium-sized picnic area; large ramada (sun shelter); drinking water; restrooms; small parking area at the picnic ground; large parking lot serves the beach.

Overnight Facilities: 112 campsites; (hike-bike sites are also available); sites are small+ to medium-sized, level, with minimal to fair separation; parking pads are paved, short+ to medium-length straight-ins; adequate space for medium to large tents in most sites; fire rings; firewood is usually for sale, or b-y-o; water at faucets throughout; restrooms with showers;

holding tank disposal station; paved driveways; complete supplies and services are available in Santa Cruz.

Activities & Attractions: Swimming; fishing; steps and trail down to the beach from the blufftop.

Natural Features: Located on the beach, and in a stand of tall conifers on a bluff (picnic and camp grounds); picnic and camp sites are lightly to moderately shaded/sheltered; park area is 95 acres; sea level to 50´.

Season & Fees: Open all year; please see Appendix for reservation information, park entry and campground fees.

Mail & Phone: New Brighton State Beach, 1500 Park Avenue & Highway 1, Capitola, CA 95010; ☎(408) 475-4850.

Park Notes: The beach area is locally known as "China Beach" or "China Cove" in reference to a small village made of scrap lumber and driftwood which stood here in the 1870's and 80's. The village was built by Chinese fishermen who net-fished these sheltered waters. Without knowing that the ocean was at the front door, you might think the picnic area and campground were in a forest many miles inland. There's tall timber here, and ocean views through the trees from most picnic sites and a dozen or so campsites on the edge of a bluff.

▲ **California 76** ♿

SEACLIFF
State Beach

Location: Central California Coast east of Santa Cruz.

Access: From California State Highway 1 at Seacliff Beach/Aptos Exit near milepost 10 +.5, turn south/west onto State Park Drive and proceed 0.5 mile to the park entrance station; just past the entrance, turn left into the upper parking lot, or swing right and go down to the bottom of the hill, then left to the picnic area or right to the campground.

Day Use Facilities: Large picnic area; ramadas (sun shelters) for many sites; drinking water; restrooms; large parking lot along the beach and also on top of the bluff.

Overnight Facilities: 26 full-hookup campsites; sites are very small, level, with nil separation, arranged in a parallel row; parking slots are paved, short to medium+ straight-ins; enough space for a small tent between sites; fire rings; firewood is usually for sale, or b-y-o; water at sites; restrooms with showers; paved driveways; adequate supplies are available in Aptos.

Activities & Attractions: Stairs from the upper parking lot down to the beach; visitor center with ocean-oriented exhibits; 'wreck' of the *Palo Alto*; fishing; fishing pier.

Natural Features: Located on a short shelf just above beach level and on a blufftop; the high, wooded bluff forms the backdrop for the picnic and camping area below; park area is 85 acres; sea level to 50´.

Season & Fees: Open all year; please see Appendix for reservation information, park entry and campground fees.

Mail & Phone: Seacliff State Beach, Highway 1 & State Park Drive, Aptos, CA 95003; ☎(408) 688-3222.

Park Notes: The story behind the *Palo Alto*? It was a concrete tanker built in the Oakland Shipyard during WWI, but the war ended before it sailed and the Navy brass decided it wasn't worth keeping a cement-hulled ship in commission or in mothballs. The ship was sold to a stock company which had her towed here in 1929. The *Palo Alto* was scuttled at the end of the pier so it would settle onto the sandy bottom. It was completely re-outfitted, this time as a 'cruise ship' of sorts, complete with a dance floor, a cafe, carny booths and a 54-foot swimming pool. The vessel took its 'maiden voyage' in 1930, but the honeymoon cruise lasted only two years before the company went belly-up, and the ship's fittings were plundered. You can go still aboard the *Palo Alto* by just walking out to the end of the pier. So, when you come right down to it, you can come to Seacliff and explore a sunken ship without even getting wet.

California 77 ♿

MANRESA
State Beach

Location: Central California Coast southeast of Santa Cruz.

Access: From California State Highway 1 near milepost 6 +.5 (6.5 miles north of the Santa Cruz-Monterey County Line near Watsonville, 12 miles southeast of Santa Cruz), take the Mar Monte Avenue/La Selva Exit and proceed southwest on Mar Monte Avenue for 1 mile to its intersection with San Andreas Road; turn south (left) onto San Andreas Road and continue for 0.7 mile; just after the railroad underpass, turn west (a hard right) into the park. (Note: from Santa Cruz, you might save a minute and a few 10ths of a mile by taking the San Andreas Road Exit off of Highway 1, then go straight down San Andreas Road for 2.1 miles to the park.)

Day Use Facilities: Small picnic area; drinking water; restrooms; large parking lot.

Overnight Facilities: None; nearest public campground is in Sunset State Beach.

Activities & Attractions: Fishing; walkway down to the beach; guarded swimming, seasonally.

Natural Features: Located on a beach and on a medium-high bluff; some vegetation has been planted around the parking lot; park area is 83 acres; sea level to 50′.

Season & Fees: Open all year; please see Appendix for park entry fees.

Mail & Phone: Mail c/o Sunset State Beach; park phone ☎(408) 724-1266.

Park Notes: There are some really good views of Santa Cruz Bay from up on the bluff.

California 78 ♿

SUNSET
State Beach

Location: Central California Coast southeast of Santa Cruz.

Access: From California State Highway 1 (southbound) near milepost 8, at the San Andreas Road/Seascape Exit (1 mile east of Aptos), head south on San Andreas Road for 5.2 miles to Sunset Beach Road; turn west onto Sunset Beach Road and proceed 0.8 mile to the park entrance; turn south (left) for 0.7 mile to the campground; continue past the campground for a final 0.3 mile to the day use area. **Alternate Access:** From Highway 1 (northbound) at milepost 0.9 (just north of the Santa Cruz-Monterey county line) take the Watsonville/State Highway 129 Exit, go to the west side of the freeway, then north on a frontage road for 0.3 mile to a 'T' intersection; turn southwest (left) onto Beach Road and proceed 1.4 miles; turn northwest (right) onto San Andreas Road and travel 2 miles; turn west (left) onto Sunset Beach Road and continue as above.

Day Use Facilities: Medium-sized picnic area; drinking water; restrooms; large parking lot; concession stand.

Overnight Facilities: 90 campsites in 3 loops; (hike-bike sites and a medium-sized group camp are also available); sites are small, with minimal to nominal separation; parking pads are paved, mostly short to short+ straight-ins, plus a few pull-offs; many pads will require a little additional leveling; adequate space for large tents in most sites; fire rings; firewood is usually for sale, or b-y-o; water at several faucets; restrooms with showers; paved driveways; complete supplies and services are available in Watsonville.

Activities & Attractions: Beach trails over the dune; campfire center.

Natural Features: Located along an ocean beach and in slightly hilly/rolling terrain just east of a long dune; vegetation consists of short grass, some small bushes, and large, full conifers that provide a fairly generous amount of shelter/shade in many sites; bordered by farm fields to the east; park area is 324 acres; sea level.

Season & Fees: Open all year; please see Appendix for reservation information, park entry and campground fees.

Mail & Phone: Sunset State Beach, 201 Sunset Beach Road, Watsonville, CA 95076; ☎(408) 724-1266.

Park Notes: A dune separates the camp loops from the ocean, so there are no ocean views. Don't let that stop you. The campground is in a very nice 'piney' setting. It's one of the nicer-looking state beach camps.

Park Notes: Zmudowski, Moss Landing, and their sister beach, Salinas River, are used quite a bit by equestrians. There's enough room for about a dozen rigs with horse trailers at Zmudowski and Salinas River, but for only a few outfits at Moss Landing. Horseback riding is allowed on the signed trails and on the beach, (subject to change, so check the brochure or posted 'regs').

▲ California 79

Zmudowski & Moss Landing
State Beaches

Location: Central California Coast northeast of Monterey.

Access: From California State Highway 1 (for Zmudowski SB), from milepost 97 +.6 (4 miles north of Castroville) turn north (right, if heading downcoast on Cal 1) onto Struve Road and proceed 0.2 mile, then turn west (left) onto Giberson Road and go 2 miles (around a half-dozen right-angle turns) to the parking lot; for Moss Landing SB, from Highway 1 at milepost 97 (1 mile north of the Moss Landing Power Plant), go west on a park access road for 0.3 mile to the parking lot.

Day Use Facilities: Vault facilities; small parking lot at Moss Landing, medium-sized parking lot at Zmudowski.

Overnight Facilities: None; nearest public campground is in Sunset State Beach.

Activities & Attractions: Hiking-equestrian trail (a trail guide is available, or on display, at the parks); beach access; fishing.

Natural Features: Located on the edge of a coastal plain; a long, medium-high, plant-anchored dune parallels the beach along this stretch of coast; park area at Zmudowski is 177 acres, Moss Landing is 55 acres; sea level.

Season & Fees: Open all year; (no fee).

Mail & Phone: Mail c/o CDPR Monterey District Office, 20 Custom House Plaza, Monterey, CA 93940; phone c/o Marina State Beach, ☎(408) 384-7695 or ☎(408) 384-6932.

▲ California 80

Salinas River
State Beach

Location: Central California Coast northeast of Monterey.

Access: From California State Highway 1 at milepost 95 +.2 (near the settlement of Moss Landing), go west on Potrero Road for 0.4 mile to the parking lot.

Day Use Facilities: Vault facilities; medium-sized parking lot.

Overnight Facilities: None; nearest public campground is in Sunset State Beach.

Activities & Attractions: Hiking and equestrian trail (a trail guide is available, or on display, at the parks); beach access; fishing.

Natural Features: Located on the edge of a coastal plain, at the Salinas River's entry to the sea; a medium-high dune parallels the beach; park area is 246 acres; sea level.

Season & Fees: Open all year; (no fee).

Mail & Phone: Mail c/o CDPR Monterey District Office, 20 Custom House Plaza, Monterey, CA 93940; phone c/o Marina State Beach, ☎(408) 384-7695 or ☎(408) 384-6932.

Park Notes: Since this is prime agricultural country, you could say that the trio of similar beaches in this area are like three peas in a pod. (Almost.) This beach, however, has the moderately wide, flat-running Salinas River and its bordering greenery as a bonus.

California 81

MARINA
State Beach

Location: Central California Coast northeast of Monterey.

Access: From California State Highway 1 near milepost 86 +.5 in the city of Marina, (8 miles northeast of Monterey) proceed west on Reservation Road for 0.3 mile to the park.

Day Use Facilities: Small picnic area; drinking water; restrooms; medium-sized parking lot; glider concession.

Overnight Facilities: None; nearest public campground is in Sunset State Beach.

Activities & Attractions: Hang glider launch ramp; fishing.

Natural Features: Located on the beach and on a short bluff above Monterey Bay; park area is 131 acres; sea level to 50´.

Season & Fees: Open all year; (no fee).

Mail & Phone: Mail c/o CDPR Monterey District Office, 20 Custom House Plaza. Monterey, CA 93940; park phone ☎(408) 384-7695 or ☎(408) 384-6932.

Park Notes: This might be the only state beach with a hang glider launch ramp. Even if you don't fly, you can get some terrific views of the Bay from the ramp, as long as no aircraft have been cleared for takeoff.

California 82

MONTEREY
State Beach

Location: Central California Coast in Monterey.

Access: From California State Highway 1 at the north Monterey city limit, take the Seaside/Del Rey Oaks/State Highway 218 Exit, then from the west side of the freeway, go south on Sand Dunes drive for 0.1 mile to the park. **Additional Access:** From Highway 1 at the Del Monte Avenue Exit on the north end of Monterey, head southwesterly on Del Monte Avenue into downtown for 1.3 miles to the "harbor" section of the state beach, one short block north (to your right).

Day Use Facilities: Several picnic tables, vaults, medium-sized parking area in the "dunes" section; small picnic area in the "harbor" section; (drinking water and restrooms in a nearby city park, streetside parking along Del Monte Avenue).

Overnight Facilities: None; nearest public campground is in Laguna Seca county park, 11 miles east on State Highway 68.

Activities & Attractions: Hike/bike trail in the "harbor" section.

Natural Features: Located along Monterey Bay; the "sand dunes" section has grass-covered dunes; the "harbor" section has scattered large hardwoods and cypress and sections of grass; total park area is 14 acres; sea level.

Season & Fees: Open all year; (no fee).

Mail & Phone: CDPR Monterey District Office, 20 Custom House Plaza, Monterey, CA 93940; ☎(408) 649-2836.

Park Notes: Great views of Monterey Bay from the "dunes" beach; some really good views of Fisherman's Wharf from the "harbor" beach. (There's also a fabulous city park just across Del Monte Avenue from the "harbor" beach, so if you tire of sand, sea and sailboats, check it out.)

California 83 ♿

MONTEREY
State Historic Park

Location: Central California Coast in Monterey.

Access: From California State Highway 1 (southbound) at the north end of Monterey, take the Del Monte Avenue Exit and travel southwesterly on Del Monte Avenue for 1.8 miles; turn north (right) onto Washington Street to the parking lots closest to the center of the park and the park office. **Alternate Access:** From State Highway 1 (northbound) at the south city limit of Monterey, take the Munras Avenue Exit and proceed 1.7 miles, first on Munras, then pick up Abrego, which shortly merges with

Washington, in downtown Monterey and Washington's intersection with Del Monte Avenue; continue straight across Del Monte Avenue to the parking lots.

Day Use Facilities: Sitting benches and picnic tables in several local parks/plazas; drinking water; restrooms; metered streetside parking, plus several large city parking lots and garages within 5 blocks of the waterfront.

Overnight Facilities: None; nearest public campground is in Laguna Seca county park, 11 miles east on State Highway 68.

Activities & Attractions: Self-guided walking or driving tour of historic homes, businesses and government buildings.

Natural Features: Located along and near Monterey Bay; very nicely landscaped gardens and courtyards are scattered throughout the historic area; (you might even get to see that silly seal who likes to catch some sun on the decks of sailboats berthed along the wharf); park area is 7 acres; sea level.

Season & Fees: Open all year; (no fee).

Mail & Phone: Monterey State Historic Park, No. 20 Custom House Plaza, Monterey, CA 93940; ☎(408) 649-7118.

Park Notes: The easiest approach to finding your way around is to (a) get here before noon on a weekday; (b) park your vehicle as close to the wharf as you can; and (c) find one of the large maps on display at key locations in the historic district. As an alternative to (b) and (c), you can just cruise the entire downtown neighborhood looking for historic buildings, all of which should be signed and most of which are in modern use. If you're an individual who likes beautiful, century-old, traditional Spanish and colonial American buildings preserved in first-class condition, with tastefully landscaped gardens, courtyards, plazas, parks, and tree-lined walks, near an historic waterfront, look no farther. Strictly speaking, only a dozen buildings scattered over a couple-dozen square blocks of downtown are in the state park system. But from a practical standpoint, it might be unwise to break the synergism of Old Monterey by separating the parts from the whole.

▲ **California 84** ♿

ASILOMAR

State Beach and Conference Grounds

Location: Central California Coast northwest of Monterey.

Access: From California State Highway 1 at its junction with State Highway 68 (at the north edge of Carmel, 3 miles southwest of Monterey), travel northwest on Highway 68 for 3.1 miles to the intersection of Sunset Drive and Asilomar Boulevard; continue ahead on Sunset for 0.1 mile to the beach, or turn right onto Asilomar into the conference grounds. (Note: '68 starts out as Holman, then curves and becomes Sunset, then finally turns into Asilomar.)

Day Use Facilities: Parallel parking along Sunset Drive.

Overnight Facilities: Meeting rooms and lodging for individuals or "almost any size convention or conference" on the grounds. (And when you see this setup, you'll believe it. Ed.)

Activities & Attractions: Boardwalks and numerous paths to the beach.

Natural Features: Located adjacent to a mile-long section of ocean beach and on a short bluff above the beach; the rocky shoreline is backdropped by grass-covered dunes; conference grounds are fully landscaped; park area is 105 acres; sea level.

Season & Fees: Open all year; Conference Grounds operated by a concessionaire; it is suggested that you contact the concessionaire for current brochures, rate cards, and reservation information.

Mail & Phone: Asilomar Conference Grounds, Asilomar State Beach, 800 Asilomar Boulevard, Pacific Grove, CA 93950; ☎(408) 372-8016; beach info only☎(408) 372-4076.

Park Notes: A long time ago, this complex started out as a YMCA summer camp. Well, sort of. The 'Y' reportedly began building this retreat back in the early 1900's and expanded it beyond the point of no return. (From a fiscal standpoint, it was mostly outflow, and no net return.) In the mid 1950's, the property was sold to the state and subsequently turned into a unit of the state park system. (This isn't an uncommon event. Scores of state parks all over the country have sprung into existence in the aftermath of purchases or gifts from public, quasi-public and private entities which could no longer pick up the tab for the property's upkeep and/or taxes.) The buildings and grounds are fully in keeping with what could be termed an atmosphere of "maintained naturalness" of the Monterey Peninsula. *Asilomar* is a Spanish phrase for "seaside refuge".

California 85

CARMEL RIVER
State Beach

Location: Central California Coast south of Monterey.

Access: From California State Highway 1 at a point 3 miles south of Carmel: the beach is located approximately between mileposts 71 and 72.

Day Use Facilities: Vault facilities; roadside parking; a small parking lot is located at the northwest corner of the beach, near the intersection of Scenic Road & Carmelo Street in the southwest corner of Carmel.

Overnight Facilities: None; nearest public campground is in Pfeiffer-Big Sur State Park.

Activities & Attractions: Beachcombing; surf fishing; toe-dipping in the lagoon.

Natural Features: Located between the Carmel River on the north and San Jose Creek on the south; wide spot on the river (the lagoon) is a few yards upstream of the river's ocean entry point and draws birds and and other visitors to its shallow waters; park area is 100 acres; sea level.

Season & Fees: Open all year; (no fee).

Mail & Phone: c/o Point Lobos State Reserve.

Park Notes: Most people avoid parking along the highway. Instead, they find a spot on a side street at the south end of town and then walk down a block or three to the beach.

California 86 ♿

POINT LOBOS
State Reserve

Location: Central California Coast south of Monterey.

Access: From California State Highway 1 at milepost 70 +.5 (4 miles south of Carmel, 22 miles north of Big Sur), turn west into the park; from the entrance, the main park road goes west for a half mile, then curves south for three quarters of a mile to a small turnaround.

Day Use Facilities: Several small picnic areas; drinking water; restrooms; several small parking areas.

Overnight Facilities: None; nearest public campground is in Pfeiffer-Big Sur State Park.

Activities & Attractions: Foot trails crisscross the reserve; designated scuba diving area can be used by certified pairs or teams of divers, (park permit required); (a detailed brochure/map, a walker's guide, flower and bird booklets, etc. are available).

Natural Features: Located along and under the Pacific Ocean; vegetation consists of tall conifers, hardwoods and brush, cypress, and open meadows; watching for gray whales during their annual December to May migration, best in mid-winter; sea otters, harbor seals, sea lions and deer are among the resident critters; park area includes 550 land acres and 750 undersea acres; sea level.

Season & Fees: Open all year; no motorhomes, trailers or dogs (especially Greyhounds) allowed; please see Appendix for park entry fees.

Mail & Phone: Point Lobos State Reserve, Route 1 Box 62, Carmel, CA 93923; ☎(408) 624-4909.

Park Notes: More than a quarter-million visitors come here each year to reflect on what has been hyperbolically described as "the greatest meeting of land and water in the world". (That same verbal sketch has also been used to illustrate Monterey's world-renowned 17-Mile Drive.) With less than a square mile of area, the number of people allowed in the reserve at any given time during busy periods is tightly regulated, so you might have a bit of a wait outside the gate on a sunny Saturday in August. *Precious little time.....precious little space.....*

California 87

GARRAPATA
State Park

Location: Central California Coast south of Monterey.

Access: From California State Highway 1: the park boundary extends along both sides of the highway approximately between mileposts 63 and 67 (7 to 11 miles south of Carmel, 17 to 21 miles north of Big Sur).

Day Use Facilities: None; (many small highwayside pull-offs).

Overnight Facilities: None; nearest public campground is in Pfeiffer-Big Sur State Park.

Activities & Attractions: Hiking trails; limited beach access; fishing.

Natural Features: Located on a mountainous section of coastline; vegetation consists mostly of grass and brush; park area is 2800 acres; sea level to 200´.

Season & Fees: Open all year; (no fee).

Mail & Phone: c/o Pfeiffer-Big Sur State Park.

Park Notes: The coastal slopes steeply drop to meet the sea, and deep canyons have been cut into the mountainsides. The coastal headlands are very impressive. The park is said to be a good spot for winter whale-watching. One of the better watch points reportedly is near milepost 66.

California 88

POINT SUR
State Historic Park

Location: Central California Coast south of Monterey.

Access: From California State Highway 1 at milepost 54 (20 miles south of Carmel, 8 miles north of Big Sur), turn west onto the park access road and proceed 0.6 mile to the parking area.

Day Use Facilities: Small parking lot.

Overnight Facilities: None; nearest public campground is in Pfeiffer-Big Sur State Park.

Activities & Attractions: Guided tours (only) of Point Sur Light Station.

Natural Features: Located on a forested hill at the end of an isthmus/sand spit which connects the hill to the mainland; sea level to 300´

Season & Fees: Open all year; very limited weekend hours, please contact the park for a current tour schedule.

Mail & Phone: mail c/o Pfeiffer-Big Sur State Park; park phone ☎(408) 625-4419.

Park Notes: The Coast Guard operates this now-automated lighthouse which has been in service since 1889. There's a half-mile hike from the parking lot to the historic area included in the tour package. Other lighthouse-site park areas on the central coast are the Point Montara Light Station, and Pigeon Point Lighthouse, which are operated by American Youth Hostels Association. Formerly Coast Guard barracks, they can provide overnight sleeping and light cooking facilities for groups of up to 30 and 50 persons, respectively. Both are on the San Mateo Coast south of San Francisco. For reservations call Point Montara at ☎(415) 728-7177 or Pigeon Point at ☎(415) 879-0633.

▲ **California 89**

ANDREW MOLERA
State Park

Location: Central California Coast south of Monterey.

Access: From California State Highway 1 at milepost 51 +.2 (23 miles south of Carmel, 5 miles north of Big Sur), turn west onto a park access road and proceed 0.2 mile to the parking lot; from the lot, trails along either side of the river can be followed, with connections to other park trails.

Day Use Facilities: Small picnic area adjacent to the parking lot; drinking water; vault facilities; large parking lot.

Overnight Facilities: Approximately 50 primitive campsites along the River Trail; drinking water; vault facilities.

Activities & Attractions: 15 miles of hiking trails to the coast, through the river thickets, and into the hills (a detailed brochure/map with contour lines is available); several foot bridges spanning the river are installed in summer.

Natural Features: Located on generally hilly terrain along a coastal bluff, in lowland on the banks of the Big Sur River, and in the mountains upland of the coastal area; vegetation consists of sections of open grass, a considerable quantity of brush and twiggy hardwoods, large hardwoods and conifers; park area is 4800 acres; sea level to 2600′.

Season & Fees: Open all year; please see Appendix for reservation information and campground fees.

Mail & Phone: c/o Pfeiffer-Big Sur State Park.

Park Notes: One small section of beach is relatively accessible from the parking lot. The trail follows the river to its exit at the ocean. The remaining two miles of the park's beach property is awash at high tide. Most of the park isn't sand and booming surf but river bottom and rolling hills. The park land formerly was *Rancho El Sur*, established by a sea captain in 1840, which was passed down to the descendants of the original owner until 1968. The park was named after one of the last members of the founding family.

▲ **California 90** ♿

PFEIFFER BIG SUR
State Park

Location: Central California Coast south of Monterey.

Access: From California State Highway 1 at milepost 46 +.8 in Big Sur (27 miles south of Carmel, 67 miles north of San Simeon), turn east onto the park access road to the entrance station; just beyond the entrance at a fork, take the left fork to the picnic areas or the right fork to the campground.

Day Use Facilities: Several small or medium-sized picnic areas; 3 reservable group picnic areas with shelters; drinking water; restrooms; several medium to large parking lots.

Overnight Facilities: 218 campsites; (bike sites and 2 hike-in group camps are also available); sites are small to small+, level, with separation varying from none to good; parking pads are gravel/dirt, short to medium-length straight-ins; excellent tent-pitching possibilities; fireplaces; b-y-o firewood; water at several faucets; restrooms with showers; holding tank disposal station; paved driveways; Big Sur Lodge has cabin rentals and a restaurant (operated by concessionaire); small store and laundry in the park; gas and groceries along the highway; nearest source of complete supplies and services is in Monterey.

Activities & Attractions: Nature trails; hiking trails; fishing; ball field; small nature center; campfire center; the 165,000-acre Ventana Wilderness in Los Padres National Forest, lies just east of the park.

Natural Features: Located on a large, densely forested flat along the Big Sur River and on bordering slopes near the west edge of the Santa Lucia Mountains; park vegetation consists of a wide variety of hardwoods, conifers, including some 1200-year-old redwoods, brush and ferns; some picnic and camp sites are in dense forest, others are in more open sections; the picnic and camp grounds stretch for a mile along the river, picnics on one bank, camps on the other; park area is 821 acres; elevation 200´.

Season & Fees: Open all year; please see Appendix for reservation information, park entry and campground fees.

Mail & Phone: Pfeiffer-Big Sur State Park, Big Sur, CA 93920; ☎(408) 667-2315.

Park Notes: Named *El Pais Grande del Sur* by the Spanish, "The Big Country of the South" is just "Big Sur" to everybody now. The dense, rain forest-like environment along the river makes the park appear as if it were actually hundreds of miles to the north—in Northwest California, or even Oregon or Washington. Life in Big Sur is a flashback to the 60's. There probably are more vintage VW bugs and vans, with appropriately attired, suitably hirsute occupants to match, than in any other region in the West, with the possible exception of Boulder, Colorado.

▲ **California 91** ♿

JULIA PFEIFFER BURNS
State Park

Location: Central California Coast south of Monterey.

Access: From California State Highway 1 at milepost 35 +.9 (11 miles south of Big Sur, 41 miles south of Carmel, 57 miles north of San Simeon), turn east onto the McWay Canyon access road and proceed 0.1 mile to the entrance station, then another 0.1 mile to the parking lots.

Day Use Facilities: 2 small picnic areas; drinking water; restrooms; small and medium-sized parking lots.

Overnight Facilities: 2 hike-in environmental campsites (check-in at Pfeiffer-Big Sur State Park first); nearest standard campground is in Pfeiffer-Big Sur SP.

Activities & Attractions: Trails to an ocean overlook point, and a waterfall, and upstream along a creek; designated scuba access area for groups of divers only (contact Pfeiffer-Big Sur State Park for information).

Natural Features: Located on oceanside bluffs and in a canyon above the Pacific Ocean; vegetation consists of a dense mixture of hardwoods, conifers and other evergreens, including a redwood grove; high, steep, brushy hills and mountains border the canyon; park area is 3600 acres; sea level to 400´.

Season & Fees: Open all year; please see Appendix for reservation information, park entry and campground fees.

Mail & Phone: c/o Pfeiffer-Big Sur State Park.

Park Notes: McWay Canyon is only one of several separate pieces of property that make up the park, but virtually all of the facilities and trails are accessed from it. Three other wild tracts border both sides of the highway north and south of here. The park land was given to the public by the former owners of the Saddle Rock Ranch, which for several years in the early 1900's had been operated from its headquarters at McWay Canyon by the park's namesake, "a true pioneer" of the Big Sur country.

▲ **California 92**

PORTOLA
State Park

Location: Western California southwest of Palo Alto.

Access: From California State Highway 84 (La Honda Road) at milepost 8 +.3 (8 miles east of the junction of Highway 84 & State Highway 1, 7 miles south of the junction of Highway 84 & State Highway 35), turn southwest onto Pescadero Road and proceed 1.1 miles, then pick up Alpine Road and travel another 4 miles; turn south (right) onto Portola Park Road (curvy and very steep on some sections) and proceed 3 miles to the park entrance station; continue for 0.2 mile, then turn right into the Sempervirens picnic area; go past Sempervirens for 0.3 mile, turn left into the Huckleberry picnic area, or just beyond, the Madrone picnic area, also on the left; or go a final 0.4 mile (past the visitor center) to the campground. **Alternate Access:** From State Highway 35 (Skyline Boulevard) at milepost 3 +.3 (at the junction of Highway 35 & Page Mill Road & Alpine Road), head southwest on Alpine Road for 3.4 miles, then turn south onto Portola Park Road and continue as above.

Day Use Facilities: Small or medium-sized picnic areas with matching parking lots; restrooms in the Madrone area; group picnic area with a medium-sized ramada (rain/sun shelter); (group area is available only by reservation).

Overnight Facilities: 52 campsites; (a trail camp and a group campground are also available, group area by reservation only); sites are small to small+, with nominal to good separation; parking pads are paved, most are short to medium-length straight-ins; some additional leveling will be required on many pads; generally small to medium-sized tent areas, many are sloped; storage cabinets; fire rings; firewood is usually for sale, or b-y-o; water at several faucets; restrooms with showers; paved, narrow driveways; limited groceries in La Honda, 9 miles northwest.

Activities & Attractions: Hiking trails (a brochure/map with contour lines and trail profiles is available); Sequoia Nature Trail (0.75 mile loop, trail guide is printed in the park brochure); visitor center; campfire center.

Natural Features: Located in a deep, densely forested canyon and its bordering ridges; redwoods and other tall conifers are the featured trees, hardwoods and dense undergrowth fill in the remaining available space; portions of the developed areas are rimmed with rail fences; Pescadero and Peters Creeks flow through the park; park area is 2400 acres; elevation 400´ at the visitor center to 1400´ on the ridgetops.

Season & Fees: Open all year; please see Appendix for reservation information, park entry and campground fees.

Mail & Phone: Portola State Park, Star Route 2, La Honda, CA 94020; ☎(415) 948-9098.

Park Notes: All of the picnic areas are nice, but Sempervirens might be just a wee bit nicer than the others. The visitor center is reasonably large and looks like it might be a comfortable spot for brief gatherings. Pescadero Creek is generally an all-year stream, (thanks to some springs) and when the water is up during the winter rains, some small (12-16 inches) steelhead and salmon can occasionally be seen making their uphill runs.

California 93

CASTLE ROCK
State Park

Location: Western California southwest of San Jose.

Access: From California State Highway 35 (Skyline Boulevard) at milepost 11 +.6 (2.5 miles south of the junction of Highway 35 & State Highway 9 at Saratoga Gap), turn west into the Castle Rock (main) parking lot. (Note: this is one of at least 18 possible entrances to the park, but it offers by far the largest parking area; other access points, a few of them with small roadside pullouts, are available along Skyline Drive and Highway 9; watch out for "no parking" signs.)

Day Use Facilities: Large parking lot.

Overnight Facilities: Castle Rock Trail Camp, 2.8 miles from the Castle Rock parking lot; Waterman Gap Trail Camp, 0.5 mile northeast of the junction of State Highways 9 & 236; drinking water and vault facilities in both camps.

Activities & Attractions: Skyline to the Sea Trail from this trailhead to the Pacific Ocean in the Rancho del Oso unit of Big Basin Redwoods State Park; hiking along entire length, equestrian use along designated segments (a detailed brochure/map with contour lines is available); guided nature walks, 2-5 miles, spring through fall (contact the park office for a current schedule).

Natural Features: Located on generally densely forested, fairly rugged terrain in the Santa Cruz Mountains; majority of the park is semi-wilderness; elevation 1000´ to 3200´.

Season & Fees: Open all year; no dogs on trails; reservations required from the park office for trail camps other than Castle Rock Camp (subject to change); please see Appendix for park entry and campground fees.

Mail & Phone: Castle Rock State Park, 15000 Skyline Boulevard, Los Gatos, CA 95030; ☎(408) 867-2952.

Park Notes: If you're just up for the day, short hikes to Castle Rock (0.3 mile), Castle Rock Falls (0.8 mile), or around one of the short, local loops can be accomplished leisurely. At the opposite end of the hiking/backpacking spectrum is the 38-mile, all-out trek to Waddell Beach. These hikes were made possible by the unprecedented effort of 2500 volunteers who built the first segment of the trail connecting Castle Rock and Big Basin Redwoods State Parks in a single weekend in 1969.

California 94

BIG BASIN REDWOODS
State Park

Location: Western California northwest of Santa Cruz.

Access: From California State Highway 236: the northeast park boundary crosses near milepost 13, the southeast boundary is near milepost 7 +.5; visitor center is 9 miles northwest of the city of Boulder Creek. Individual access points: visitor center and a picnic area are at milepost 9 +.3; a paved side road leads north from the visitor center for 0.3 mile to 2 other picnic areas; campground turnoffs are within 0.9 mile south of the visitor center, along either side of the main highway.

Day Use Facilities: 3 medium-sized picnic areas; drinking water; restrooms; small or medium-sized parking lots for picnic areas and trailheads; snack bar and small store.

Overnight Facilities: *Standard campsites*: 152 sites in 3 major sections; sites are generally small, with nominal to fairly good separation; parking pads are gravel, short to medium-length straight-ins; most pads in hillside loops will require additional leveling; small to medium+ areas for tents; storage cabinets; fire rings; firewood is usually for sale or b-y-o; water at several faucets; restrooms with showers; holding tank disposal station; paved driveways; (6 trail camps are also available). *Tent cabins*: 36 cabins in the Huckleberry section; cabins are small, woodframed, with wood siding to about 4´ above ground level and all-around window screening; peaked, open-frame roof is covered by canvas, with a storm flap to enclose the screening; 2 bunks with foam pads in each unit (i.e., cozily sleeps four if they're on really good terms); each cabin has a parking pad, table, fire ring, plus a small table and wood stove inside; adequate supplies and services are available in Boulder Creek.

Activities & Attractions: 100 miles of trails for hiking or for hiking/equestrian use; (a detailed brochure/map with contour lines is available); Redwood Nature Trail leads to one of the most impressive stands of redwoods in the park (a guide booklet is available).

Natural Features: Located in a densely forested, deep and steep region of the Santa Cruz Mountains; picnic areas, Sempervirens and Blooms Creek camp areas are located along the creek bottoms, other camp areas are on hillsides; all picnic and camp sites are moderately shaded/sheltered by redwoods and hardwoods; total park area is 19,000 acres; sea level to 1600´ (1000´ at the visitor center).

Season & Fees: Open all year; please see Appendix for reservation information, park entry and campground fees.

Mail & Phone: Big Basin Redwoods State Park, 21600 Big Basin Way, Boulder Creek, CA 95006; ☎(408) 338-6132.

Park Notes: The highway winds through just the southeast corner of the park, so autobound visitors catch only a narrow glimpse of the park's total majesty, but it's still an exceptionally nice drive. But most people who've been here agree that the true way to see the park is to get out onto a trail. The tent cabins here are unique for this part of the country. (The only other state parks in the West with anything similar are Mount Tamalpais in California and a couple-dozen parks in Texas.) The canvas roofs of the cabins can be flipped back for sky-watching. Most of the cabin sites are quite private, too. For an excellent perspective of the triad of state parks in this region—Big Basin Redwoods, Portola, and Castle Rock—take a good look at the large, 3D map in the visitor center. Big Basin Redwoods is the grandparent of all California state parks. It was established in 1901 as California Redwood Park in the Big Basin, the first park created by the citizens of California.

▲ California 95

Henry W. Coe
State Park

Location: Western California southeast of San Jose.

Access: From U.S. Highway 101 in Morgan Hill, take the East Dunne Avenue Exit and travel east on Dunne Avenue for 12 miles to the park boundary, then another 0.5 mile to the ranch yard, museum, picnic and camp areas. (Note: the trip up from the freeway involves going up and over a couple of hills on a paved, narrow, often steep road with a fair number of switchbacks and other tight turns; the route is straightforward as long as you watch the road signs while passing through the subdivisions leaving Morgan Hill; if you cross a major bridge high above a reservoir 4 miles out, you're on the right road.)

Day Use Facilities: Small picnic area and restrooms at the museum; medium-sized picnic/camp area with shared facilities; small parking lot.

Overnight Facilities: 20 camp/picnic sites; (about the same number of individual backpacking sites, and 11 backpacking group camps, are also available; no fires in the backcountry); sites are small to small+, with nominal separation; parking pads are gravel/earth, short to medium-length straight-ins; most pads will require a bit of additional leveling; large areas for tents; small ramadas (sun shelters) for about half of the sites; fireplaces; b-y-o firewood; water at central faucets; vault facilities; gravel driveways; complete supplies and services are available in Morgan Hill.

Activities & Attractions: Hiking and horse trails; (detailed maps are available in the museum); small museum with ranch life exhibits; barn, stables, sheds with antique farm equipment; possible fishing for small trout in streams at lower elevations.

Natural Features: Located on the ridges bordering Coyote, Pacheco and Orestimba Creeks and their canyons; vegetation consists of mostly oak woodland with ponderosa pine forest on the western ridges, plus large grasslands and oak savannah; streams flow nicely in spring, but most dry up in summer (nearly all rain falls November through March); the park is noted for it's dazzling wildflower blooms; total park area is 67,000 acres, including a 22,000-acre wilderness; elevation 1100´ to 2500´.

Season & Fees: Open all year; please see Appendix for park entry and campground fees.

Mail & Phone: Henry W. Coe State Park, P.O. Box 846, Morgan Hill, CA 95038; ☎(408) 779-2728.

Park Notes: California's second-largest state park originally was called Pine Ridge Ranch, started in the mid-1800's by Henry Coe. At one time, many homesteaders lived back in the hills, too. But not many could survive in this dry country for long, so gradually they sold out to ranchers like Coe who could run enough cattle to make it pay. The open, grassy slopes throughout much of the area around the ranch are inviting—the kind of spot that makes you want to park your car and just take off over the hill to see what you can see. Most people who come here do so to hike, and occasionally they catch a glimpse of a mountain lion, a bobcat or an eagle. The grizzly which once roamed California is gone, but if the Silvertip ever did come back, this is the kind of country he would come back to first.

California 96 ♿

San Juan Bautista
State Historic Park

Location: Western California south of San Jose.

Access: From California State Highway 156 at milepost 3 in the city of San Juan Bautista (3 miles south of the junction of Highway 156 & U.S. Highway 101 northeast of Salinas, 8 miles northwest of Hollister), turn east onto The Alameda and proceed 0.2 mile into downtown (The Alameda becomes Third Street); at the corner of Third and Washington Streets, turn right onto Washington and go up 1 block to the plaza and the center of the park.

Day Use Facilities: Small picnic area; drinking water; restrooms; streetside parking.

Overnight Facilities: None; nearest public campground is in Fremont Peak State Park.

Activities & Attractions: Self-guided tours of some of the buildings and grounds of the original section of the town of San Juan Bautista, including a hotel, residence of a prominent family, community hall, blacksmith shop and stage line stable; the stable houses a collection of carriages and wagons; interpretive programs.

Natural Features: Located on a hill above the San Benito Valley; the buildings, small and large gardens, are situated around the edge of a large, grassy plaza; beautiful views to the east across the valley; park area is 6 acres; elevation 200´.

Season & Fees: Open all year; please see Appendix for park entry fees.

Mail & Phone: San Juan Bautista State Historic Park, P.O. Box 1110, San Juan Bautista, CA 95045; ☎(408) 623-4881.

Park Notes: The park's theme covers the Indian, Spanish and early American periods in regional history, and the structures, elegant furnishings, and Spanish gardens have been maintained at a high level of quality. Just about every visitor is at least equally impressed with the Mission San Juan Bautista which faces the plaza opposite the park's section of town. Although the mission isn't an official part of the state park, it's unofficially 'adopted' by nearly everybody. Part of the mission property, including the historic church, can be toured. Even though it has been damaged by earthquakes more times than anyone knows, the church has been in continuous use since July 1, 1812 and there's still a daily Mass schedule. The bell tower of the church literally stands on the brink of the San Andreas Rift.

California 97

Fremont Peak
State Park

Location: Western California south of San Jose.

Access: From California State Highway 156 at milepost 3 in the city of San Juan Bautista (3 miles south of the junction of Highway 156 & U.S. Highway 101 northeast Salinas), turn west onto Salinas Road/San Juan Canyon Road/San Benito County Road G1 and go 0.3 mile, then take a quick left-right jog and stay on San Juan Canyon Road/G1; travel southerly for 10.5 miles to the park boundary; continue ahead on the main park road for another 0.5 mile to the picnic and camp area, on the right, or for a final 0.1 mile to the trailhead parking lot. (Note: the road is paved all the way to the park, but the last 5 miles are very steep and curvy.)

Day Use Facilities: Small picnic area; small and medium-sized parking lots; drinking water; vault facilities.

Overnight Facilities: 17 (primitive) campsites; (several group camps and a horse camp are also available); sites vary from small to large, with nominal to good separation; parking pads are sandy gravel, short to medium-length straight-ins; some additional leveling may be needed; large tent areas; fire rings; b-y-o firewood; water at several faucets (b-y-o extra water 'just in case'); vault facilities; hard-surfaced driveways; limited supplies and services are available in San Juan Bautista.

Activities & Attractions: Trail to the summit of 3169´ Fremont Peak; nature trail.

Natural Features: Located on grassy slopes dotted with hardwoods and some conifers; (but the mountainsides below the park look like a battalion of berserk bulldozers once played a frenzied game of tic-tac-toe across their mid-sections); park area is 244 acres; elevation 2800´ to 3169´.

Season & Fees: Open all year; please see Appendix for reservation information, park entry and campground fees.

Mail & Phone: Mail c/o CDPR Gavilan District Office, P.O. Box 1110, San Juan Bautista, CA 95045; park phone ☎(408) 623-4255.

Park Notes: Fremont Peak was called "Gavilan Peak" (from the Spanish word for "Hawk") in early California. In March of 1846, Captain John Charles Fremont of the U.S. Army Corps of Engineers was conducting his third exploration of California. His presence with an armed force in a settled area was unsettling to the Mexican authorities and they ordered him out. Instead, Fremont and his troops ascended Gavilan Peak and built a log fort. A sapling was cut for a flagpole and on March 6th, Fremont raised a United States flag—the first American flag to fly over California. The Mexican forces were mobilized down in San Juan Bautista. Before any shots were traded, though, the flagpole blew down on the afternoon of March 9th. Fremont took this as a bad sign, and moved on toward the San Joaquin Valley. An American-Mexican military confrontation was avoided, for the time being anyway, and Gavilan Peak once again became the meeting place of the hawks.

Northern Inland

California 98 ♿

CASTLE CRAGS
State Park

Location: North-central California north of Redding.

Access: From Interstate 5 near milepost 63 +.5 (6 miles south of Dunsmuir, 50 miles north of Redding), turn west onto Castle Creek Road; proceed 0.3 mile and turn north (right) to the park entrance station; turn east (right) and proceed 0.7 mile to the campground loops; continue beyond the campground for an additional mile up a steep, narrow winding road to the vista point; or from the east side of the freeway exit, go northeast on a frontage road for 0.2 mile, then turn southeast (right) into the riverside day use area.

Day Use Facilities: Medium-sized picnic area, drinking water, restrooms and medium-sized parking lot along the river; small picnic area and small parking lot at the vista point.

Overnight Facilities: 64 campsites in 3 loops; (3 environmental camps and enroute/overflow sites are also available); sites are small to medium-sized, with fair to fairly good separation; parking pads are paved, short to medium-length straight-ins; many pads will require a strong dose of additional leveling; tent spots are mostly sloped; large, stone fireplaces; firewood is usually for sale, or b-y-o; water at several faucets; restrooms with showers; paved driveways; gas and groceries at the freeway interchange.

Activities & Attractions: Terrific views from the vista point; 18 miles of hiking and equestrian trails, including 7 miles of the Pacific Crest Trail along the base of the Crags; self-guided nature trail; guided nature walks; campfire center for scheduled summer evening programs; trout fishing (said to be good); swimming/wading in the river and in Castle Creek.

Natural Features: Located between the Coast Range and the Cascades a few miles north of the Sacramento Valley, at the base of an unusual geological feature, Castle Crags; another prominent volcanic feature, Mt. Shasta, is clearly visible from points in the park; the Sacramento River flows through a canyon past the day use area and is within a short walk of most campsites; tall pine, oak and light underbrush predominate; park area is 6200´; elevation ranges from 2000´ at the river to 6000´ at the summit of the Crags.

Season & Fees: Open all year; please see Appendix for reservation information, park entry and campground fees.

Mail & Phone: Castle Crags State Park, P.O. Box 80, Castella, CA 96017; ☎(530) 235-2684.

Park Notes: On a reasonably clear day, not only are the comely Castle Crags visible from the vista point, but 14,100 foot Mount Shasta can be viewed in all its glory from the same advantageous perch hundreds of feet above the canyon floor. Unlike volcanic Mount Shasta, Castle Crags were formed when heated granite thrust its way up through the surface of the earth, much like a set of lower molars push their way through a toddler's gums. The block of exposed raw material was then carved to its present multi-peaked form by wind, rain and ice.

▲ California 99

WEAVERVILLE JOSS HOUSE
State Historic Park

Location: Northern California west of Redding.

Access: From California State Highway 299 in midtown Weaverville, at the corner of Highway 299 & Oregon Street, 0.1 mile east of the junction of Highway 299 & State Highway 3, turn south into the parking lot.

Day Use Facilities: Sitting benches; drinking water; restrooms; medium-sized parking lot; streetside parking is also available.

Overnight Facilities: None; nearest public campground is Junction City (BLM), 1 mile west of Junction City, 10 miles west of Weaverville.

Activities & Attractions: Guided walks through the oldest continuously used Chinese temple in California; interpretive center with Chinese art objects, photos, mining tools.

Natural Features: Located in-town in the Coast Range; park area is 1 acre; the park is landscaped with impeccable oriental-style gardens; elevation 2000´.

Season & Fees: Open all year, with limited hours, October to April.

Mail & Phone: Weaverville Joss House State Historic Park, P.O. Drawer 1217, Weaverville, CA 96093; ☎(530) 623-5284.

Park Notes: Hundreds of Chinese miners came to Weaverville in the 1850's and prospered despite hardships, discrimination, and a tax on foreign labor. Their first house of worship burned in 1873. The Chinese continued their Taoist religious traditions, which teaches serenity through harmony with Nature, in this, "The Temple Amongst the Forest Beneath the Clouds", dedicated in 1874. The landscaping here is what you might expect—modest and yet elegant, unpretentious but dignified. There is a cluster of sitting benches in a semicircle around a fountain with a small image, Quan Yin, "One Who Listens".

▲ California 100

SHASTA
State Historic Park

Location: Northern California west of Redding.

Access: From California State Highway 299 near milepost 18 +.5 (4 miles west of Redding, 32 miles east of Douglas City), the park lies along both sides of the highway.

Day Use Facilities: Medium-sized picnic area; drinking water; restrooms; highwayside parking.

Overnight Facilities: None; nearest public campground is Oak Bottom, in Whiskeytown National Recreation Area, 6 miles west; (reservations are usually needed in summer).

Activities & Attractions: Self-guided tours of the ruins and restorations of a historic mining town; (a 20-page guide booklet is available from the park office); courthouse museum.

Natural Features: Located on the far eastern slopes of the Coast Range; picnic area is on a large lawn well-dotted with tall conifers and hardwoods; bordered by hardwood and conifer dotted hills; park area is 13 acres; elevation 1000´.

Season & Fees: Open all year, with limited hours November to March; please see Appendix for park entry fees.

Mail & Phone: Shasta State Historic Park, P.O. Box 2430, Shasta, CA 90687; ☎(530) 243-8194.

Park Notes: Founded in 1849 as "Reading's Springs", the town was named "Shasta" in 1850. A one-time county seat, Shasta (or "Shasta City") was the metropolis of Northern California during the 1850's. Unlike many other mining boom towns, Shasta wasn't here and gone in a year or three. The town's geographical and economic advantages were slowly weakened by changes in stage routes and the placement of the railhead in what Shastans referred to as a "hot, malarious, stinkhole", a little local burg known as "Poverty Flat". (Poverty Flat was later renamed for a Central Pacific RR exec, B.B. Redding.) There's not much effort involved in seeing this park—almost all of it is visible from the highway. It is possible, and very enjoyable, to just wander about the town using the *laissez faire* method of historical exploration. But getting a copy of the helpful park tour booklet to find your way around is the serious way do it. More than a dozen buildings and sites are within the historic district, most of them right along the main drag. The picnic area is a good one—one of the best on the highway between Redding and Arcata/Eureka.

▲ California 101 ♿

McARTHUR-BURNEY FALLS
Memorial State Park

Location: Northeast California northeast of Redding.

Access: From California State Highway 89 at milepost 27 +.55 (5.8 miles north of the junction of State Highways 89 and 299 near Burney, 52 miles southeast of the junction of Highway 89 and Interstate 5 near Dunsmuir), turn north/west and proceed 0.1 mile to the park entrance station; a small picnic area and the museum are just beyond the entrance; continue ahead for 0.1 mile past the entrance to the camping areas; a second picnic area is on the shore of Lake Britton, at the end of the main park road 1.1 miles north of the entrance.

Day Use Facilities: Small picnic areas; drinking water; restrooms nearby; several medium-sized parking lots; concession stand.

Overnight Facilities: 118 campsites in 2 sections; (a small environmental/walk-in camp is also available); overall, sites are medium to large, essentially level, with fair to good separation; parking pads are paved or earth/gravel, short to medium-length straight-ins, many are extra wide; large tent areas; storage cabinets; fireplaces or fire rings; b-y-o firewood; water at several faucets; restrooms with showers; holding tank disposal station; paved driveways; gas and groceries 1 mile south.

Activities & Attractions: Hiking trails, including a 1-mile Falls Trail and a 1.5-mile Rim Trail from the falls/camping area to Lake Britton; amphitheater for evening campfire programs; museum; fishing for warm water species, boating, boat launch and sandy beach at Lake Britton; good to excellent trout fishing in local streams, especially wide, deep, fast, beautiful (and world-famous) Hat Creek.

Natural Features: Located on a large, forested flat along the rim of Burney Creek Gorge, at the southern end of the Cascade Range; Burney Falls is within the gorge; picnic and camp sites are sheltered/shaded by moderately dense, tall conifers and some smaller hardwoods; park area is 875 acres; elevation 3000´.

Season & Fees: Open all year; please see Appendix for reservation information, park entry and campground fees.

Mail & Phone: McArthur-Burney Falls Memorial State Park, Route 1 Box 1260, Burney, CA 96013; ☎(530) 335-2777.

Park Notes: A fascinating feature of the falls, which is the focal point of the park, is that its water supply originates in an aquifer (underground lake), and the falls flows all year, even when the creek is bone dry a half-mile upstream. Lake Britton shouldn't be overlooked. It's a fairly nice-looking, 4000-acre power company reservoir on the Pit River. No wonder this is a popular park—there's elbow room here. Because it is some distance from Northern California's major metro areas, and because of its cool (but relatively dry) weather during much of the year, the park doesn't see a lot of use except in summer. But both spring and fall are superb times to visit here.

California 102

Ahjumawi Lava Springs
State Park

Location: Northeast California northeast of Redding.

Access: From California State Highway 299 in the small community of McArthur (21 miles northeast of Burney, 29 miles southeast of Adin) at the northeast corner of town, head north on a gravel/dirt road for 3.7 miles to the embarkation point at Rat Ranch on the shore of Horr Pond; access to the state park on the north shore is via small craft.

Day Use Facilities: Open picnicking.

Overnight Facilities: None; nearest public campground is in McArthur-Burney Falls Memorial State Park.

Activities & Attractions: Fishing (said to be good); limited boating; the park is laced with old roads and trails.

Natural Features: Located in an extensive area of lava beds along the north shores of a chain of small, shallow lakes called Eastman Lake, Tule Lake, Horr Pond and Big Lake, at the headwaters of the Tule and Little Tule Rivers; Timbered Crater rises above the lava fields 3 miles northwest of the park; park area is 6000 acres; elevation 3000´.

Season & Fees: Open all year, subject to weather conditions.

Mail & Phone: c/o McArthur-Burney Falls State Park.

Park Notes: A half-dozen dirt roads lead to possible embarkation points (some of which are on private land) on the south shores of the small lakes. The easiest spot to find (which is also the 'official' one) is at Rat Ranch. (The place is also called "Rat Farm Landing", and it's bordered by McArthur Swamp and Mud Swamp, if you can believe all of that.) If you have some sort of an easily launchable, shallow-draft vessel at your disposal, the place might be worth a look.

California 103 ♿

William B. Ide Adobe
State Historic Park

Location: North-central California north of Red Bluff.

Access: From Interstate 5 (southbound) take the northernmost exit in Red Bluff for Business I-5/California State Highway 36 and travel south on Biz 5/Main Street for 1 mile; turn east (left) onto Adobe Road and proceed 0.9 mile, then turn south (right) into the park. **Alternate Access:** From Interstate 5 (northbound) in midtown Red Bluff, take the Antelope Boulevard/Highway 36 Exit and go west on Antelope Boulevard for 0.5 mile; turn north (right) onto Main Street and proceed 0.9 mile; turn east (right) onto Adobe Road and continue as above.

Day Use Facilities: Small picnic area; drinking water; restrooms; medium-sized parking lot.

Overnight Facilities: None; nearest public campground is in Woodson Bridge State Recreation Area.

Activities & Attractions: Restoration of a small adobe house and other farm buildings owned by William B.Ide.

Natural Features: Located on a short shelf above the west bank of the Sacramento River; the grounds are lightly to moderately shaded by large hardwoods, a few conifers, evergreen and hardwood shrubs, on mown grass; park area is 3 acres; elevation 300´.

Season & Fees: Open all year; please see Appendix for park entry fees.

Mail & Phone: William B. Ide Adobe State Historic Park, 3040 Adobe Road, Red Bluff, CA 96080; ☎(530) 527-5927.

Park Notes: "Who was William B. Ide?", you ask. The gentleman who made a home for his family in this simple adobe cabin was the first, and only, President of California. It was 1833 when William and Susan Ide packed up their family and belongings and left Massachusetts. They headed west, stopping to live in Kentucky, Ohio, and Illinois for a few years before joining an Oregon-bound wagon train in 1845. Along the way, they were talked into changing course for the Sacramento Valley by one of John Sutter's sales reps (see Sutter's Fort SHP). Less than a year after putting down roots in California, Ide and the other American settlers were threatened with deportation by the Mexican government, which then ruled the territory. The American ex-patriots joined forces and started what became known as the "Bear Flag Revolt". Since the group had no official U.S. support, they declared the independence of the Republic of California on June 14, 1846 and elected Ide their President. The Republic was short-lived. Unbeknownst to the rebels, the U.S. and Mexico had been at war for a month, and the American flag was raised in Sonoma on July 9, 1846, ending the California Republic and the presidency of William B. Ide.

▲ **California 104** ♿

Woodson Bridge

State Recreation Area

Location: North-central California south of Red Bluff.

Access: From Interstate 5 near milepost 7 +.5 at the South Avenue Exit on the south edge of Corning (17 miles south of Red Bluff) travel east on South Avenue for 4.3 miles, then pick up Tehama County Road A9 and continue easterly for another 1.8 miles; turn north (left) onto the park access road and proceed 0.25 mile, then go east (right) for 0.15 mile; turn north (left) to the picnic and river access areas, or continue east or south into the campground. **Alternate Access:** From California State Highway 99 at milepost 4 +.5 (23 miles southeast of Red Bluff, 18 miles northwest of Chico), turn southwest onto Tehama County Road A9 and proceed 3.2 miles to the park turnoff and continue as above.

Day Use Facilities: Small picnic area.

Overnight Facilities: 46 campsites; sites are small+ to medium-sized, most are level, with fair to very good separation; most parking pads are paved, medium to long straight-ins, plus a few pull-offs; plenty of tent space; fire rings and barbecue grills; b-y-o firewood; water at central faucets; restrooms with showers; holding tank disposal station; paved driveways; adequate supplies and services are available in Corning.

Activities & Attractions: Fishing; limited floating/canoeing; nature trail.

Natural Features: Located on a large flat along the east bank of the Sacramento River; vegetation consists of very tall valley oaks and other hardwoods, sections of dense undergrowth, areas of mown grass and tracts of waist-high grass; surrounded by orchards; the Coast Range can be seen in the west and the foothills of the Sierra can be glimpsed to the east; park area is 428 acres; elevation 200´.

Season & Fees: Open all year; please see Appendix for reservation information, park entry and campground fees.

Mail & Phone: Woodson Bridge State Recreation Area, 25340 South Avenue, Corning, CA 96021; ☎(530) 839-2112.

Park Notes: Probably only a bull rider, a nitro driver, or a Louisiana 'gator who lost her way home would really *want* to spend a midsummer night here. It can become more than a bit still and steamy along this densely vegetated riverbank after sundown; and the locals make good-natured wise cracks about the 'skeeto population. All kidding aside, there's a generous amount of grass and shade, and the acres and acres of orchards in the valley add a touch of cultivated class to the park's naturally nice simplicity.

California 105

Bidwell-Sacramento River
State Park

Location: North-central California west of Chico.

Access: From California State Highway 32 at milepost 10 +.6 (Glenn County) near the west end of the Sacramento River bridge, (1 mile east of Hamilton City, 8 miles west of Chico), turn south into the Irvine-Finch area; or at milepost 1 +.4 (Butte County), (1.4 miles east of the river bridge, 6 miles west of Chico), turn south onto River Road and proceed 2.3 miles, then turn west (right) into the Indian Fishery day use area; or continue past Indian Fishery for 0.8 mile to the boat launch.

Day Use Facilities: Small picnic area, drinking water, restrooms and large parking lot at Irvine-Finch; small picnic area, vault facilities and medium-sized parking lot at Indian Fishery.

Overnight Facilities: None; nearest public campground is in Woodson Bridge State Recreation Area.

Activities & Attractions: Limited boating and canoeing; boat launch; fishing.

Natural Features: Located on the banks of the Sacramento River; park areas are lightly to moderately shaded by large hardwoods on a grassy surface and bordered by orchards; total park area is 180 acres; elevation 150´.

Season & Fees: Open all year; (no fee).

Mail & Phone: Bidwell-Sacramento River State Park, 12105 River Road, Chico, CA 95926; ☎(530) 342-5185.

Park Notes: This property was deeded to the state in 1908 by Annie Bidwell (see Bidwell Mansion SHP), who called it "General Bidwell Park". Plans call for utilizing the Irvine-Finch section as the principal public use area. Reportedly, this stretch of the Sacramento is very popular with the area's 30,000+ university students for rafting, tubing and other wet pursuits.

California 106 ♿

Bidwell Mansion
State Historic Park

Location: North-central California in Chico.

Access: From California State Highway 99 near midtown Chico, take the California State Highway 32/Chester/Orland Exit and go southwest on Highway 32/Eighth Street for 1.1 miles; turn northwest (right) onto Main Street and go 0.7 mile through downtown Chico to a traffic triangle; just past the triangle, pick up The Esplanade and continue northerly for 1 long block, then turn southwest (left) into the park.

Day Use Facilities: Medium-sized parking lot.

Overnight Facilities: None; nearest public campground is in Woodson Bridge State Recreation Area.

Activities & Attractions: Guided tours of the home of nineteenth century pioneer General John Bidwell.

Natural Features: Located in-town in the Sacramento Valley; the mansion grounds are landscaped with large lawns, tall conifers, huge hardwoods, palms, decorative shrubs, flowers and a gazebo in the front yard; park area is 5 acres; elevation 200´.

Season & Fees: Open all year; please see Appendix for park entry fees.

Mail & Phone: Bidwell Mansion State Historic Park, 525 The Esplanade, Chico, CA 95926; ☎(530) 895-6144.

Park Notes: An agricultural enterprise which once covered 26,000 acres, *Rancho Arroyo Chico* was started in 1850 by John Bidwell, who purchased the first plot of land with his earnings from the gold fields. Bidwell's most noteworthy contributions were in the field of agriculture, introducing plants from all over the world (like the casaba melon) to California. Bidwell was an agricultural management genius, but he lost most of his half-dozen forays into the seedy and greedy arena of California politics. Bidwell was elected to Congress once, but his high-principled approach to public service didn't fit in with most political motives of the day. He was a prohibitionist, an advocate of women's suffrage, an anti-monopolist, and pro-conservationist in a time when none of these were popular causes. (The "General" in his title came from his appointment by Governor Leland Stanford as a brigadier general in the California Militia.) In 1865, Bidwell began constructing the 26-room pink mansion here, which he shared with his wife Annie for 35 years, and in time it became the social and cultural center of the Upper Sacramento Valley. The mansion's guest register included friends and influentials from the couple's social and political ties. (Susan B. Anthony slept here.) The Bidwells were philanthropic as well. As you drive through Chico, you'll see several parcels of land donated to the public by them—the original townsite, the spacious park along Chico Creek, and the turf for Chico State University.

▲ California 107 ♿

LAKE OROVILLE:
BIDWELL CANYON
State Recreation Area

Location: Northeast California north of Sacramento.

Access: From California State Highway 162 at milepost 22 +.85 (8 miles east of the junction of State Highways 162 & 70 in Oroville), turn north onto Kelly Ridge Road; proceed north for 1.6 miles; at a fork in the road, take the right fork and continue east and north for 0.5 mile to the entrance station; camp loops are within a mile of the entrance station. (Highway 162 is an extension of Olive Highway in Oroville.)

Day Use Facilities: Community center (available by reservation).

Overnight Facilities: 75 full-hookup campsites in 2 loops; (primitive and boat-in camps are also available, at scattered spots around the lake shore); sites are small to small+, with nominal separation; parking pads are paved, medium to long straight-ins; many pads will require additional leveling; tent spots are mostly small and many are sloped; fire rings; firewood is usually for sale, or b-y-o; water at sites; restrooms with showers; paved driveways; gas and groceries at the marina; complete supplies and services are available in Oroville.

Activities & Attractions: Boating; boat launch; fishing; nearby visitor center has interpretive displays, audio-visual presentations and a 47′ observation tower for views of the lake.

Natural Features: Located in the foothills of the Sierra Nevada on a hill above the south shore of Lake Oroville; the campground's lightly wooded slopes are dotted with manzanita, oak, pine and planted hardwoods; wooded/grassy hills surround the lake; total park area is 31,000 acres, including 16,000 acres of land and 15,000 acres of water; elevation 900′ to 1100′.

Season & Fees: Open all year; please see Appendix for reservation information, park entry and campground fees.

Mail & Phone: Lake Oroville State Recreation Area, 400 Glen Drive, Oroville, CA 95966; ☎(530) 538-2200 or ☎(530) 538-2218; or ☎(530) 538-2219 (visitor center).

Park Notes: Considering the slope of this hillside, most of the campsites here are very well leveled. Although there are spots for tents here, the campground clearly is far more suitable for rv's. Nearby Loafer Creek Campground has a lot of very nice sites better-suited to tenters.

▲ California 108 ♿

LAKE OROVILLE:
LOAFER CREEK
State Recreation Area

Location: Northeast California north of Sacramento.

Access: From California State Highway 162 at milepost 24 +.5 (10 miles east of the junction of California State Highways 70 and 162 in Oroville), turn north onto a paved park access road; proceed north for 0.2 mile to the entrance station; continue for 0.7 mile (down) and turn east (right) into the campground. (Highway 162 is an extension of Olive Highway in Oroville.)

Day Use Facilities: Large picnic area; drinking water; restrooms; large parking lot.

Overnight Facilities: 137 campsites in 2 loops; (6 small or medium-sized group camp areas are also available); sites are medium to medium+, with fairly good to very good separation; parking pads are paved, mostly level, medium to medium+ straight-ins or pull-throughs; some tent spots may be sloped, but most are excellent; fire rings or fireplaces; firewood is usually for sale, or b-y-o; (only driftwood may be gathered); water at several faucets; restrooms with showers; holding tank disposal station; paved driveways; complete supplies and services are available in Oroville.

Activities & Attractions: Boating; boat launch; fishing mostly for rainbow trout, largemouth and smallmouth bass, catfish; swimming beach; Maidu Interpretive Trail; scheduled interpretive programs in summer.

Natural Features: Located in the foothills of the Sierra Nevada on an oak-covered hill overlooking the south shore of Lake Oroville; fairly dense vegetation of oak, conifers, manzanita, with a few open grassy areas; total park area is 31,000 acres; elevation 900´ to 1100´.

Season & Fees: Day use area open all year; campground open May to October; please see Appendix for reservation information, park entry and campground fees.

Mail & Phone: Lake Oroville State Recreation Area, 400 Glen Drive, Oroville, CA 95966; ☎(530) 538-2200; Loafer Creek phone ☎(530) 538-2217 (seasonally).

Park Notes: The best seasons to enjoy the recreational opportunities at Lake Oroville are spring and early summer. Like many large reservoirs, the water level typically drops considerably later in the year. There are many pleasant, private camp sites here at Loafer Creek, (known locally as Coyote Campground in order to distinguish it from the group camp areas). Loafer Creek has the only sanctioned swimming area on the main lake.

▲ **California 109**

LAKE OROVILLE: NORTH FOREBAY

State Recreation Area

Location: North-central California southeast of Chico.

Access: From California State Highway 70 at milepost 16 +.6 just north of the Oroville city limit, take the Garden Drive Exit and go west for 0.1 mile to the park.

Day Use Facilities: Large picnic area; some sites have ramadas (sun shelters); group picnic areas with ramadas; drinking water; change house; vault facilities; large parking lot.

Overnight Facilities: None; nearest public campgrounds are in the park's Loafer Creek and Bidwell Canyon areas.

Activities & Attractions: Designated swimming beach; limited boating (canoeing, windsurfing, sailboating); boat launch; fitness course; fishing for rainbow trout, black bass, catfish.

Natural Features: Located on a very large flat along North Forebay, (also called Thermalito Forebay North), an impoundment on a power plant diversion canal below Lake Oroville; acres of watered and mown lawns are sprinkled with large hardwoods and conifers; bordered by grassy plains and hills; park area is 300 acres; elevation 150´.

Season & Fees: Open all year; please see Appendix for park entry fees.

Mail & Phone: Lake Oroville State Recreation Area, 400 Glen Drive, Oroville, CA 95966; ☎(530) 538-2200; North Forebay phone ☎(530) 538-2221 (seasonally).

Park Notes: North Forebay is a bit of a bonus, thrown in for good measure with the large picnic/camp areas on the main lake. This is one of only two designated swim spots in the entire Lake Oroville SRA. North Forebay is reserved for swimming and quiet boating, but power boats are OK on Thermalito Forebay South, just below this area. There's a boat launch at the South area. Lake Oroville itself is subject to deep summer drawdown, but there's a better chance that the water level here will remain reasonably constant.

▲ California 110 ♿

PLUMAS-EUREKA
State Park

Location: Northeast California northeast of Oroville.

Access: From California State Highway 89 at milepost 7 +.8 (0.9 mile south of the junction of State Highways 89 & 70 at Blairsden, 8 miles north of the Plumas-Sierra county line), turn west onto Plumas County Road A14 (paved) and travel westerly for 5 miles to the Jamison Creek picnic area; or continue ahead for another 0.15 mile, then turn south (left) to the museum; or continue south/southwest past the museum on a paved park road (narrow with pullouts) for an additional 1.2 miles, then turn east (sharply left, at the end of the road) into Upper Jamison Campground.

Day Use Facilities: Small picnic area; drinking water; restrooms; small parking lot.

Overnight Facilities: *Upper Jamison Campground*: 70 campsites; sites are small to medium-sized, with good to very good separation; parking pads are paved, short to medium-length straight-ins; some pads may require a little additional leveling; generally enough space for small to medium-sized tents in most sites (some will take larger canvas); storage cabinets (bear boxes); fireplaces; some firewood may be available for gathering on surrounding national forest lands, b-y-o to be sure; water at several faucets; restrooms with showers; paved driveways; gas and groceries+ in Blairsden.

Activities & Attractions: Museum with displays relating to mining and early pioneer life; hiking trails; nature trail; stream fishing for small trout; interpretive talks for groups (available by reservation, contact the park office); campfire center; cross-country skiing; the park surrounds the old mining town of Johnsville, which includes a partially restored stamp mill.

Natural Features: Located on the east slope of the Sierra Nevada; picnic and camp sites are on gently rolling and sloping terrain along Jamison Creek in a super dense forest of conifers and some low hardwoods; park area is 6750 acres; elevation 4000′ to 7500′.

Season & Fees: Principal season is May to October, with limited services in winter; please see Appendix for reservation information, park entry and campground fees.

Mail & Phone: Plumas-Eureka State Park, 310 Johnsville Road, Blairsden, CA 96103; ☎(530) 836-2380.

Park Notes: Although it's many miles from the coast, this park might remind you very much of Redwood Country. It's just *that* kind of place—towering trees, tranquility, environmental orientation, and so forth. (On a trip through the park, you might be tempted to turn off the ignition and quietly coast past the picnic and camp sites.) The campsites are surprisingly private (compared to most state parks). Although some are relatively closely spaced, you'll still see only two or three of your neighbors at any one time. If you spend a night here, it might rapidly become one of your favorite camps in the California state park system. The park's historical side relates not only to the diggings in the region, but also to a singularly significant event which had long-term, far-reaching effects: the first sport ski area in the western hemisphere was established in the Sierra Nevada near here in the 1850's. Ski clubs and annual races were sponsored by mining towns like Whiskey Diggings, Poker Flat, Port Wine, and Onion Valley.

▲ California 111 ♿

COLUSA-SACRAMENTO RIVER
State Recreation Area

Location: North-central California northwest of Sacramento.

Access: From the junction of California State Highways 20 & 45 in midtown Colusa, proceed northeast on Levee Road for 0.2 mile to the park entrance. (Note: from Interstate 5, take the Colusa-Clear Lake exit, then drive east on State Highway 20 for 8.6 miles to Colusa.)

Day Use Facilities: Medium-sized picnic area with ramadas; drinking water; restrooms; medium-sized parking lot.

Overnight Facilities: 22 campsites; sites are small, level, with minimal separation; parking pads are paved, short to medium-length straight-ins, some are extra wide; large, grassy tent areas; storage cabinets; barbecue grills; firewood is usually for sale, or b-y-o; water at central faucets; restrooms with showers; paved driveways; limited supplies and services are available in Colusa.

Activities & Attractions: Trail to a river beach; fishing for a variety of fish, depending upon the season, including salmon, trout, striped bass, shad; fishing from a boat is recommended; boat launch; Colusa Levee Scenic Park (city) is adjacent.

Natural Features: Located on the west bank of the Sacramento River in the great Sacramento Valley; park vegetation consists of 5 acres of watered and mown lawns, and hardwoods which provide some shade/shelter in most picnic and camp sites; lots of large trees in the surrounding area; park area is 67 acres; elevation 50´.

Season & Fees: Open all year; please see Appendix for reservation information, park entry and campground fees.

Mail & Phone: Colusa-Sacramento River State Recreation Area, P.O. Box 207, Colusa, CA 95932; ☎(530) 458-4927

Park Notes: This place is a dump! Or, rather, it was when the state acquired the first of several pieces of property on the edge of Colusa and turned it into a park. They've really performed a beautiful job of landscaping this former riverfront junkyard. The campground is located between the entrance station and the day use facility, so thru traffic may be a minor concern. In summer, bring the skeeter stuff, 'cause the wee beasties might bug you at times.

 *California* 

North Central Inland

California 112

Woodland Opera House
State Historic Park

Location: Central California northwest of Sacramento.

Access: From Interstate 5 (northbound) in Woodland at the Main Street/California State Highway 113 Exit, proceed west on Main Street for 1.5 miles into midtown Woodland; the park is located on the north side of Main Street at Second Street.

Day Use Facilities: Small sitting area in the courtyard; streetside parking, plus several nearby parking lots.

Overnight Facilities: None; nearest public campground is in Colusa-Sacramento River State Recreation Area.

Activities & Attractions: Completely renovated performing arts center originally built in 1885; public performances are scheduled regularly; the building may also be reserved for meetings, productions, weddings and other special events.

Natural Features: Located in the Sacramento Valley; the courtyard is landscaped with grass, flowers and small hardwoods; elevation 60´.

Season & Fees: Open all year; (it is suggested that you contact the office directly for current visitor hours and a performance schedule); operated by the city of Woodland.

Mail & Phone: The Woodland Opera House, P.O. Box 1425, Woodland, CA 95695; ☎(916) 666-9617.

Park Notes: As the first opera house to serve the vast agricultural regions of the Sacramento Valley, in the late nineteenth and early twentieth century, the elegant Woodland Opera House played host to a series of stars and future stars of music, stage and screen: John Philip Sousa's oom-pah band; George M. Cohan's song-and-dance troupe; pugilists Gentleman Jim Corbett and John L. Sullivan; Sidney

Greenstreet (who played the portly antagonist opposite Humphery Bogart in the film classic *The Maltese Falcon*); Oscar-winner Walter Huston (who starred in another "Bogey" classic, *Treasure of Sierra Madre*); and more than 300 touring companies. After nearly eight decades of decay and neglect following its closure in 1913 (it had become a victim of the popularity of the motion picture), the opera house was meticulously renovated into the handsome structure it is today. The state owns the property; the sign says "State Historic Park"; but the operation is entirely financed and managed by a local not-for-profit organization. Classical music, ballet, big band sounds, folk dances, musicals, comedies and melodrama have all been on the showbill of the re-opened opera house.

California 113 ♿

OLD SACRAMENTO

State Historic Park

Location: Central California in Sacramento.

Access: From Interstate 5 (northbound) near milepost 23 on the west edge of downtown Sacramento, take the J Street/ Downtown Exit onto Third Street (Third St. parallels the freeway on the east side of I-5); go down Third for a few yards to Capitol Avenue, then west (left) over the Interstate; get in the right lane and just after crossing over I-5, hang a right into the park. **Alternate Access:** From Interstate 5 (southbound) take the J Street Exit, pass under the freeway (west to east) to Third Street; turn south (right) onto Third, go 0.1 mile to Capitol, then turn west (right), and continue as above. (Note: Old Sacramento is sandwiched between I-5 and the river; there are a number of parking lots in the area; considering the traffic and parking congestion inside Old Sacramento during busy periods, you might save time and fuel in the long run by just quickly finding an open spot soon after exiting the freeway and walking a couple of blocks into the park.)

Day Use Facilities: Several benches along the river; drinking water; restrooms inside the railroad museum and near the parking garage; parking lots (including a designated rv lot north of the railroad museum), parking garage, limited streetside parking.

Overnight Facilities: None; nearest public campgrounds are in Folsom Lake State Recreation Area.

Activities & Attractions: Reconstructions, renovations and replications of the original downtown Sacramento waterfront district; California State Railroad Museum has restored railroad cars and more than 40 exhibits about railroading; Sacramento History Center; Pony Express monument (Sacramento was the western terminus of the 1860-1861 2000-mile Pony Express route which originated in St. Joseph, Missouri.)

Natural Features: Located along the east bank of the Sacramento River; riverside day use area is landscaped with small sections of grass and a few trees; park area is 14 acres; elevation 20´.

Season & Fees: Open all year; please see Appendix for reservation information, park entry and campground fees.

Mail & Phone: Old Sacramento State Historic Park, 111 I Street, Sacramento, CA 95814; ☎(916) 445-7387 (office); ☎(916) 445-7373 (railroad museum).

Park Notes: There are dozens of interesting historical buildings and sites here, as well as the many tourist-oriented shops, pubs, restaurants and cafes inside them. The local visitor information center on Front Street can provide you with a free map and "walking tour" guide. But the park's *primo* attraction is the railroad museum. Inside the 100,000-square foot brick building are more than 20 locomotives and cars—each of them restored to a spit-shine level of perfection. The exhibits—all from the Golden State's Golden Age of Railroading—collectively constitute what is billed as "the finest railroad museum in North America". They're probably right. Old Sacramento is the place where the Pony Express and the Iron Horse meet on common ground.

▲ California 114

LELAND STANFORD MANSION

State Historic Park

Location: Central California in Sacramento.

Access: From Interstate 5 (northbound) near milepost 24 +.5 on the west edge of downtown Sacramento, take the J Street/ Downtown Exit onto Third Street; go south on Third to N Street (1 block south of Capitol Avenue); turn east onto N Street and proceed 0.8 mile; the park is located on the southeast corner of N Street & Eighth Street.

Day Use Facilities: Small picnic area; drinking water and restrooms inside the building; limited, metered streetside parking; (the small lot next to the house is for handicapped and official vehicles only).

Overnight Facilities: None; nearest public campgrounds are in Folsom Lake State Recreation Area.

Activities & Attractions: Home of Leland Stanford, California's eighth governor, oldest house in Sacramento open to the public; individual and group tours on a limited basis (contact the reservations office); special holiday events during Christmastime and in mid-May.

Natural Features: Located in the Sacramento Valley; the grounds are landscaped with large hardwoods, small sections of grass and assorted bushed and flowers; elevation 30´.

Season & Fees: Open all year, with limited availability during restoration; (it is suggested that you call the park for current days and hours of operation); please see Appendix for park entry fees.

Mail & Phone: Stanford House State Historic Park, 800 N Street, Sacramento, CA 95814; ☎(916) 324-0575.

Park Notes: In 1861, as President of the Central Pacific Railroad, Leland Stanford was looking for an appropriate residence for a man of his social stature and ambitions when he purchased this property from a prominent Sacramento merchant. Stanford served one term as governor of California and then went back to work full-time as a railroad magnate. The original two-story house was re-worked into a 19,000-square foot, 44-room domicile worthy of the man whose company's rails were to link with those of the Union Pacific at Promontory, Utah in May of 1869, thus establishing the first transcontinental railroad. After Stanford's death, his widow gave the house to the Diocese of Sacramento in 1900 for use as a home for friendless children. In 1978 the property was purchased by the state; in the late 1980's, it was handed over to the state parks department for renovation. Plans call for a complete facelift and earthquake-stabilization of the Stanford Mansion, as it is often called. State government has grown up around the Mansion, and the park is now surrounded by state office buildings.

While you're in the Capitol neighborhood, you might want to visit two other operations run by the state parks office. Although they're not actually state parks, both the Governor's Mansion (323-3047) and the California State Capitol Museum (324-0333) may be of interest to anyone who delves into California history. Tours of the mansion are given daily; the museum has tours and exhibits about the legislative process. (In deciding upon a visit to the halls of government, you may want to ponder the words of President John Adams, who cautioned: "There are two things in life which you should not watch being made: sausage.....and the law." Ed.)

▲ California 115 ♿

SUTTER'S FORT

State Historic Park

Location: East-central California in Sacramento.

Access: From Interstate 80 Business Route (eastbound) in downtown Sacramento (0.7 mile north of the junction of Business I-80 & U.S. Highway 50), take the N Street Exit; at the bottom of the ramp, continue ahead (north, parallel to the freeway) for 0.2 mile to L Street; turn west (left) onto L Street, and proceed 0.2 mile; the park is located on the north side of L Street, between 28th & 26th Streets. **Alternate Access:** From Biz I-80 (westbound) in downtown Sacramento (1 mile south of the American River), take the J Street Exit; at the bottom of the ramp, continue south on 29th Street (parallel to the freeway) for 0.2 mile; turn west (right) onto L Street and continue as above.

Day Use Facilities: Small picnic area; drinking water; restrooms; metered streetside parking in the surrounding area.

Overnight Facilities: None; nearest public campgrounds are in Folsom Lake State Recreation Area.

Activities & Attractions: Restoration of an adobe fort originally built in the 1840's by Swiss-German adventurer and entrepreneur John Augustus Sutter; extensive and impressive exhibits depict pioneer life in early California; self-guided tours of the fort for individuals; guided tours for groups and special presentations, including an "Environmental Living" program, for elementary school children by reservation; costumed staff and volunteers demonstrate pioneer baking, spinning, weaving, candle-making, blacksmithing, etc; activities include re-enactments of events in the history of the fort and the Sacramento Valley.

Natural Features: Located in the Sacramento Valley; park vegetation consists of mown lawns lightly shaded in some areas by large hardwoods; a pair of ponds add an aquatic touch to the grounds and attract small wildlife; park area is 6 acres; elevation 20´.

Season & Fees: Open all year; please see Appendix for park entry fees.

Mail & Phone: Sutter's Fort State Historic Park, 2701 L Street, Sacramento, CA 95814; ☎(916) 445-4422; for group reservations, contact the state park district reservations office at ☎(916) 445-4209.

Park Notes: John Sutter figured prominently in the history of Mexican California and in early American California. He built this 50,000-square-foot fort to serve as the headquarters for his agricultural and commercial empire. Sutter's biography reads like a nineteenth century update of Homer's *Odyssey* or Virgil's *Aeneid*: it is a tale of exceptional achievement coupled with extraordinary misfortune. Few other historic parks in California equal or surpass the extensiveness of displays, scope of programs and level of community involvement as this one. Overshadowed (literally and figuratively) by the immensity of Sutter's Fort and the scale of its presentations is the State Indian Museum, which lies a few feet north of the fort on the same block. (The museum faces K Street to the north, but the visitors' entrance is on the south side of the long, low, white building.) The museum, also operated by the state parks department, houses a collection of California Indian artifacts and periodically features demonstrations of Indian crafts and wood lore.

▲ California 116 ♿

BRANNAN ISLAND
State Recreation Area

Location: West-central California southwest of Sacramento.

Access: From California State Highway 160 at milepost 7 +.3 (14 miles northwest of Antioch, 3.4 miles south of the junction of Highway 160 and State Highway 12), turn east and proceed 0.1 mile to the park entrance station; continue for 0.1 mile and turn south (right) into the camping area.

Day Use Facilities: Large picnic area; drinking water; restrooms with freshwater rinse showers; 2 large parking lots; concession stand (open in summer).

Overnight Facilities: 102 campsites in 2 loops; (32 slips in the Delta Vista area on Three-Mile Slough are available for overnight on-boat camping or adjacent walk-in camping; also, 6 primitive small group areas are available by reservation); sites are fairly spacious, level, with reasonable separation for most sites; parking pads are paved, short to long straight-ins, some are double wide; very nice large, grassy, tent spots; storage cabinets; fireplaces and fire rings; firewood is usually for sale, or b-y-o; water at each site; restrooms; holding tank disposal station;

paved driveways; adequate+ supplies and services are available in Antioch.

Activities & Attractions: Boating; sailing; large boat launch, boat-in camping slips; fishing for striped bass, black bass, sturgeon, catfish and panfish; swimming beach on Seven Mile Slough; campfire circle; visitor center with interpretive displays; recreational vehicle rally site.

Natural Features: Located on the Sacramento-San Joaquin Delta between the main channel of the Sacramento River and backwaters known as Three Mile Slough and Seven Mile Slough; waves of green and golden grass are dotted with a wide a variety of large hardwoods and evergreens trees throughout the picnic and camp areas; from a knoll nearby, the river and delta are visible; typically breezy, with mild temperatures year round; park area is 336 acres; elevation 25´.

Season & Fees: Open all year; please see Appendix for reservation information, park entry and campground fees.

Mail & Phone: Brannan Island State Recreation Area, 17645 State Highway 160, Rio Vista, CA 94571; ☎(916) 777-6671.

Park Notes: The Delta provides a thousand miles of opportunities for water-oriented recreation. If you have a boat, you can also explore nearby Franks Tract State Recreation Area, 5 miles southeast of Brannan Island. Franks Tract is quite large, about 3500 acres, though all but 300 of them are under water. The lake there was created when a levee burst and the island was flooded. The area is said to have exceptionally productive fishing waters.

▲ **California 117** ♿

BETHANY RESERVOIR

State Recreation Area

Location: Central California Southwest of Stockton.

Access: From Interstate 580 at the Grant Line Road/Byron Exit (0.6 mile west of the junction of Interstates 580 & 205 west of Tracy, 13 miles east of Livermore) proceed north on a local road for 0.5 mile to a 'T' intersection; turn northeast (right) onto Grant Line Road and go 0.8 mile (over the aqueduct) to a 3-way intersection; turn north (left) onto Mountain House Road and head north for 3.1 miles; turn west (left) onto Kelso Road and proceed 1.5 miles; turn south (left) onto Bruns Avenue for 0.5 mile, then the road curves to the west and becomes Christenson Road; go west on Christenson for another 0.5 mile, the swing south (left) for 0.25 mile to the main park area. (Note: If you're approaching from the Stockton-Tracy vicinity via Interstate 205, you can save a few miles by taking the Grant Line Road/J4 Exit just west of Tracy, then travel County Road J4 northwest for 5.7 miles to Kelso Road; go west on Kelso for 3 miles to Bruns Avenue and continue as above.)

Day Use Facilities: 2 small picnic areas with ramadas (sun shelters); vault facilities; medium-sized parking lots.

Overnight Facilities: None; nearest public campground is in Durham Ferry State Recreation Area.

Activities & Attractions: Limited boating; boat launch and dock; fishing for warm water species; northern terminus of the California Aqueduct Bikeway.

Natural Features: Located in a small basin surrounded by grass-covered, virtually treeless hills; park vegetation consists of open grassy areas and scattered hardwoods and conifers; park area is 300 acres; elevation 250´.

Season & Fees: Open all year; please see Appendix for park entry fees.

Mail & Phone: CDPR Diablo District Office, 4180 Treat Boulevard, Concord, CA 94521; ☎(415) 687-1800.

Park Notes: Hundreds and hundreds, acres and acres, miles and miles of white windmills cover the hills surrounding the park. The two-and-three-bladed 'mills are the harvesting implements of giant 'wind farms' which have been 'homesteaded' here.

California 118

DURHAM FERRY
State Recreation Area

Location: Central California west of Modesto.

Access: From Interstate 5 at the California State Highway 33 Exit (5 miles south of the junction of Interstates 5 & 205 east of Tracy, 6 miles north of the junction of Interstates 5 & 580 southeast of Tracy), proceed southeast on State Highway 33 for 1.3 miles; turn east (left) onto Durham Ferry Road and travel 3 miles, then the road becomes Airport Way; continue northeasterly on Airport Way for 1.7 miles; turn northwest (left) onto a paved park access road and proceed 0.5 mile to the park entrance station; continue ahead for 0.3 mile to the day use area, on the left, or a final 0.25 mile to the campground.

Day Use Facilities: Picnic area with several small and medium-sized ramadas (sun shelters); drinking water; restrooms; medium-sized parking lot.

Overnight Facilities: 60 campsites, some with electrical hookups; sites are small, level, with minimal separation; parking pads are gravel, short to short+ straight-ins, some are extra wide; adequate space for small tents on designated areas; small ramadas (sun shelters) over table areas; fire rings and/or barbecue grills; a limited amount of firewood may be available for gathering in the general vicinity, b-y-o to be sure; water at several faucets; restrooms with showers; holding tank disposal station; gravel driveways; gas and groceries 2 miles southwest.

Activities & Attractions: Equestrian area; archery range; limited fishing.

Natural Features: Located on a riverside plain near the east bank of the San Joaquin River, a mile downstream of the confluence of the San Joaquin & Stanislaus Rivers; park vegetation consists of large, open grassy areas dotted with a few trees, plus stands of hardwoods along the river; elevation 30´.

Season & Fees: Open all year; park entry fee $2.00 ($3.00 weekends/holidays); standard site $7.00, hookup site $9.00, pet $1.00, $3-$4 for extra vehicles (subject to change); campsite reservations accepted (see phone, below); operated by San Joaquin County.

Mail & Phone: County of San Joaquin, Department of Parks & Recreation, Stockton, CA 95201; (209) 953-8800.

Park Notes: The developed areas of the park are protected from flooding by a high dike along the river, so there aren't any easy river views. A short scramble up and over the embankment and through the woods will take you to the San Joaquin. The 'ridgetop' trail along the dike is often used by hikers.

California 119

CASWELL MEMORIAL
State Park

Location: Central California northwest of Modesto.

Access: From California State Highway 99 at the Ripon Exit (10 miles northwest of Modesto) go west into midtown Ripon and travel west on Main Street through downtown; at the west edge of town, Main Street becomes West Ripon Road; continue on West Ripon Road for another 2 miles (a total of 3.3 miles from '99); turn south (left) onto Austin Road and proceed 2.8 miles to the park entrance station; just past the entrance, turn east (left) into the campground; or continue for an additional 0.4 mile to the day use areas.

Day Use Facilities: 2 small-medium-sized picnic areas; group picnic area (available by reservation); drinking water; restrooms; medium-sized parking lots.

Overnight Facilities: 66 campsites; (a group camp is also available, by reservation); sites are small to medium-sized, reasonably level, with fair to excellent separation; parking pads are paved, very short straight-ins. some are extra wide; enough space for small to medium-sized tents in most sites, large in some; storage cabinets; fire rings; b-y-o firewood; water at several faucets; restrooms with showers; paved driveways;

adequate supplies and services are available in Ripon.

Activities & Attractions: Fishing for bass, catfish, bluegill; seasonal rafting/floating; designated wading beach; nature trail; great blue heron rookery (available for field study at a distance); campfire center; annual Tule Fog Fete in February.

Natural Features: Located along the north bank of the Stanislaus River; much of the park is within a woodland consisting mostly of tall valley oaks and very dense undercover; bordered by farmland which includes hundreds of acres of orchards; park area is 258 acres; elevation 40´.

Season & Fees: Open all year; please see Appendix for reservation information, park entry and campground fees.

Mail & Phone: Caswell Memorial State Park, 28000 South Austin Road, Ripon, CA 95366; (209) 599-3810.

Park Notes: The Central Valley's legendary winter ground cloud is celebrated during the park's annual Fog Fete—a contest to decide which cook has the tastiest or thickest pea soup. The one-day fest (for the benefit of the Great Valley Museum) draws quite a crowd. In summer, the woods are as thick and green as the pea soup they brew up in the winter. The locals like to boast that Caswell Memorial is the only state park in the Great Central Valley. The catch? All of the other places are state *historic* parks, state *recreation areas*, state *reserves*, etc.

California 120

GEORGE J. HATFIELD

State Recreation Area

Location: Central California northwest of Merced.

Access: From Interstate 5 near milepost 5 +.5 at the Stuhr Road/Newman Exit (5.5 miles north of the junction of I-5 & State Highway 140 west of Gustine) travel east on Stuhr Road/Stanislaus County Road J18 for 4.8 miles; cross over State Highway 33 and continue east on Stuhr Road for another 1.9 miles to a 'T' intersection; turn northeast (left) onto Hills Ferry Road and proceed northeast for 2 miles, then bear north onto Kelly Road and go 0.1 mile, then swing east (right) to the park entrance station; just beyond the entrance at a fork, bear left for a few yards to another fork, then bear right to the main camp/picnic area.

Alternate Access: From California State Highway 165 near milepost 30 at the south end of the Merced River bridge (8 miles south of Turlock, 3 miles south of Hilmar, 2 miles north of Stevinson), turn west onto River Road/Merced County Road J18 and travel westerly (the road makes several sharp turns) for 7.1 miles to a 3-way intersection just west of another Merced River bridge (locally called the Stevinson Bridge); turn north (right) onto Kelly Road and continue as above. (It's great sport trying to find this park after dark. Ed.)

Day Use Facilities: Medium-sized picnic area; medium-sized parking lot; other facilities are shared with the campground.

Overnight Facilities: Approximately 12 park 'n walk campsites; (a group camp is also available, by reservation); sites are small, level, with nominal separation; parking areas are paved, short straight-ins or pull-offs; ample space for large tents; storage cabinets; fireplaces; b-y-o firewood; water at several faucets; restrooms; paved driveways; limited+ supplies and services are available in Hilmar.

Activities & Attractions: Fishing for warm water species, plus some salmon seasonally; limited floating/rafting; campfire center; interpretive displays about Indians and acorns, and about mosquitos.

Natural Features: Located in the San Joaquin Valley on a large flat on the north bank of the Merced River just upstream of the confluence of the Merced and San Joaquin Rivers; the park has large sections of open grassy areas plus stands of large oaks; park area is 47 acres, including 1.25 miles of river frontage and several sandy beaches; elevation 60´.

Season & Fees: Open all year; please see Appendix for reservation information, park entry and campground fees.

Mail & Phone: George J. Hatfield State Recreation Area, 4394 Kelly Road, Hilmar, CA 95324; (209) 632-1852.

Park Notes: Former California Lieutenant Governor and State Senator George Hatfield provided the land for this park in the early 1950's. There's another state rec area in the district if the fishin' or floatin' opportunities at Hatfield are at less than optimum levels. Great Valley Grasslands State Park has about 2800 essentially undeveloped acres located southeast of Hatfield SRA along the banks of the San Joaquin River. It's just off State Highway 140, six miles northeast of Gustine. Great Valley Grasslands also incorporates the 100 acres in what was formerly Fremont Ford SRA. You can contact the state parks' Four Rivers District office (209-826-1196 or 209-826-1197) for info about current river conditions.

California 121

TURLOCK LAKE

State Recreation Area

Location: East-central California east of Modesto.

Access: From California State Highway 132 at milepost 35+.9 (10 miles west of La Grange, 8 miles east of Waterford, 21 miles east of Modesto), turn south onto Roberts Ferry Road; proceed 1.1 miles to a 'T' intersection; turn east (left) onto Lake Road and go 1.2 miles, then turn south (right) into the day use area; or continue past the day use turnoff for another 1 mile to the campground access road; turn north (left), and go down 0.2 mile to the campground.

Day Use Facilities: 2 medium-sized picnic areas; drinking water; restrooms; several small to large parking lots; concession stand.

Overnight Facilities: 67 campsites; sites are small to medium-sized, level, with fair to very good separation; parking pads are gravel, short to medium-length, mostly extra-wide straight-ins; excellent, large tent spots; storage cabinets; fireplaces or fire rings; b-y-o firewood; water at faucets throughout; restrooms with showers; paved driveways; minimal supplies at a small store, 2 miles west; limited to adequate supplies and services are available in Waterford.

Activities & Attractions: Swimming beach on a small cove; fishing for catfish, bass, crappie, bluegill and rainbow trout in both the lake and the river; boating, boat launch and docks on the lake; short nature trail; artesian well; campfire circle; marina.

Natural Features: Located along the northwest shore of Turlock Lake in the San Joaquin Valley (day use area); located on bottomland along the south bank of the Tuolumne River (campground); vegetation consists of mown grass shaded by large hardwoods on the lake shore; large hardwoods, mown grass, berry bushes, wildflowers and other dense vegetation fills the campground; surrounding terrain is comprised of mostly treeless, rolling grassland and farmland; lake surface area varies from 1800 acres to 3500 acres, depending upon precip and drawdown; park area is 248 acres; elevation 250′.

Season & Fees: Open all year; please see Appendix for reservation information, park entry and campground fees.

Mail & Phone: Turlock Lake State Recreation Area, 22600 Lake Road, Star Route, La Grange, CA 95329; (209) 874-2008.

Park Notes: When you consider the nearly treeless surrounding terrain, this park is a lush, green surprise—the riverside campground more so than the lakeside day use area. Here's another oddity—the lake is above the level of the river, rather than being a mainstream impoundment, as you might expect. Diversion canals running parallel to the river feed and drain the shallow, upper basin in which the lake sits. Fishing is said to be good on either the lake or the river, but knowledgeable locals admit to heading directly for a streamside fishing spot when motorized traffic picks up on the lake.

▲ California 122

McCONNELL
State Recreation Area

Location: Central California southeast of Modesto.

Access: From California State Highway 99 at the Delhi Exit at milepost 34 +.4 (20 miles southeast of Modesto, 19 miles northwest of Merced), turn east off the freeway, then south onto Vincent Road; proceed 0.3 mile, then turn east (left) onto El Capitan; travel 3.1 miles on El Capitan, then turn south (right) onto Pepper Street; drive south 1 mile on Pepper to Second Avenue South; turn east (left) onto Second, proceed 0.5 mile, then the road curves to the right and becomes McConnell Road (just a little farther and you've got it made); continue for 0.1 mile to the park entrance, and a final 0.15 mile to the day use area and campground. (Whew.)

Day Use Facilities: Medium-sized picnic area; large group picnic area; drinking water; restrooms; medium-sized parking area.

Overnight Facilities: 17 campsites, plus a small overflow area; (a group camp is also available); sites are large, level, and fairly well separated; parking pads are paved, short, extra-wide straight-ins or long pull-offs; very nice, spacious tent spots; storage cabinets; fireplaces; firewood is usually for sale, or b-y-o; water at faucets throughout; restrooms with showers; paved driveways; limited supplies and services are available in Delhi.

Activities & Attractions: Limited fishing for bass, perch, catfish in the river; campfire center for Saturday evening programs in summer.

Natural Features: Located on a wooded flat along the bank of the Merced River in the San Joaquin Valley; fully developed hardwoods on watered and mown lawns provide light-medium to medium-dense shade for most picnic and camp sites; total park area is 74 acres; elevation 100´.

Season & Fees: Open all year; please see Appendix for reservation information, park entry and campground fees.

Mail & Phone: McConnell State Recreation Area, McConnell Road, Ballico, CA 95303; (209) 394-7755.

Park Notes: McConnell was the first state park unit established in the fertile San Joaquin Valley. The park is surrounded by nut farms. It's really an attractive little place.

▲ California 123 ♿

MALAKOFF DIGGINS
State Historic Park

Location: East-central California northeast of Sacramento.

Access: From California State Highway 49 at a point 0.4 mile northwest of the junction of Highway 49 & State Highway 20 at the north end of Nevada City, (0.2 mile west of the USDA Forest Service headquarters complex), turn north onto North Bloomfield Road and proceed 0.6 mile north, then bear northeast (right) onto North Bloomfield-Graniteville Road and travel another 14 miles to the park visitor center. **Alternate Access:** From State Highway 49 at a point 11 miles northwest of Nevada City, head northeast on Tyler-Foote Crossing Road and proceed 8 miles to a point just past the settlement of North Columbia; turn east (right) onto Lake City Road and proceed 6 miles to the visitor center. (Note: both routes involve a half-dozen miles of gravel travel as they approach the park; the Alternate Access is suggested for single vehicles larger than a crew cab pickup or for any vehicles with trailers; you'll pass The Diggins on the way to the visitor center.)

Day Use Facilities: 2 small picnic areas, (at The Diggins overlook and at the visitor center).

Overnight Facilities: 30 campsites; (a group camp and 3 rustic cabins are also available, by reservation); sites are small, with minimal separation; parking pads are mostly short straight-ins; additional leveling may be required; small to medium-sized tent areas; storage cabinets; water at central faucets; restrooms. plus auxiliary vault facilities; paved driveways; adequate supplies and services are available in Nevada City.

Activities & Attractions: Location of an hydraulic mining operation of the mid 1800's; museum with mining exhibits and a film about hydraulic mining; historic buildings.

Natural Features: Located in the high foothills on the west slope of the Sierra Nevada; bordered by meadows and conifer-dotted hills; park area is 3000 acres; elevation 2200´ to 4200´.

Season & Fees: Open all year, subject to weather conditions, with limited hours in winter; please see Appendix for reservation information, park entry and campground fees.

Mail & Phone: Malakoff Diggins State Historic Park, 23579 North Bloomfield Road, Nevada City, CA 95959; ☎(916) 265-2740.

Park Notes: Malakoff Diggins focuses on the third, and perhaps most impersonal, of the three major methods of gold mining used in this part of the Sierra. While Marshall Gold Discovery is centered around simple placer mining and Empire Mine was a hardrock operation, (see separate info on both of these state parks), hydraulic mining was employed at Malakoff Diggins. The miners used water cannons to blast the gold-bearing gravel from the hillsides and wash it into giant sluice boxes for separation. Hydraulic mining used incredible quantities of water (and did an incredible amount of damage to the local geography.) After a landmark court decision in 1884 which put the lid on wanton hydraulic mining, this method no longer proved profitable and it was entirely abandoned by the early 1900's. Nature has reclaimed a portion of The Diggins.

▲ California 124 ♿

EMPIRE MINE
State Historic Park

Location: East-central California northeast of Sacramento.

Access: From the junction of California State Highways 49 & 20 near the south end of the city of Grass Valley, proceed east on Empire Street for 0.6 mile to the park boundary; continue ahead for another 0.7 mile to the visitor center and the center of the park. (Note: from Highway 49 take the Empire Street Exit, then go east on Empire; from Highway 20 eastbound, just continue straight ahead over the freeway and onto Empire Street East.)

Day Use Facilities: 2 small picnic areas; drinking water; restrooms; several small and medium-sized parking lots.

Overnight Facilities: None; nearest public campground is White Cloud (Tahoe National Forest) 10 miles east of Nevada City on State Highway 20.

Activities & Attractions: Self-guiding or guided tours of the building and grounds of a gold mine dating back to 1850; visitor center with exhibits and a-v programs.

Natural Features: Located high in the foothills on the west slope of the Sierra Nevada; park vegetation consists mostly of grassy hills moderately forested with tall conifers; picnic sites are tucked in among the trees off the parking lots; park area is 788 acres; elevation 2600´.

Season & Fees: Open all year, subject to winter weather conditions; please see Appendix for park entry fees.

Mail & Phone: Empire Mine State Historic Park, 10791 East Empire Street, Grass Valley, CA 95945; ☎(916) 273-8522.

Park Notes: Hardrock mining lacks much of the 'glamour' and aesthetic appeal of the classic picture of the old prospector wearing a turned-up hat, panning for gold in a nugget-flecked creek. Hardrock miners probe the depths of the earth for gold in shafts and tunnels sometimes miles deep, getting cold, wet, dirty, tired, sick—and sometimes worse—in the process. Hardrock is just plain hard work. Nearly all of the men who worked the Empire Mine from the late 1800's until the mine folded in the mid-1950's came from Cornwall in England. These Cornishmen hailed from a millennium-long hardrock tradition in the copper and tin mines of their native region.

You can get a good idea of what it must have been like to work the Empire by taking a few hours to investigate the couple-dozen major buildings and displays here. There's a *lot* to look at. The many old stone buildings and walls, mine shaft, giant ore bin, shops, and yard full of heavy equipment are all in remarkably good condition. So is the 'Empire Cottage', the English-style, local home of one of the mine's owners. For an industrial project, the mine fits in remarkably well with its natural surroundings.

California 125

AUBURN
State Recreation Area

Location: East-central California east of Sacramento.

Access: From Interstate 80 near milepost 17 +.4 in Auburn, take the Grass Valley/Placerville Exit for California State Highway 49; travel southeasterly on Highway 49 through downtown Auburn for 1.6 miles, then swing north (left) to the park office (see below); or continue southeasterly for another 1.5 miles to the junction of Highway 49 and Foresthill Road at the river; from this point you can begin your exploration of the recreation area (see below). (Note: you can avoid Auburn's CBD by taking the Foresthill/Auburn Ravine Road Exit, 2 miles northeast of the Auburn Exit, if you'd prefer to go directly to the center of the park and right into the thick of it, so to speak.).

Day Use Facilities: Several small and medium-sized parking areas, some with vault facilities, throughout the park.

Overnight Facilities: 5 medium-sized, primitive, walk-in, or boat-in campgrounds, most with vault facilities but no drinking water, throughout the recreation area; gravel/dirt roads serve most camps; boat-in camp is on Lake Clementine; some campsites along the river trail are also available; adequate supplies and services are available in Auburn.

Activities & Attractions: More than 50 miles of hiking, equestrian and mountain bike trails; fishing; boating; boat launch at the dam on Lake Clementine.

Natural Features: Located in the forested foothills of the Sierra Nevada bordering the American River Canyon/Gorge, and along the North and Middle Forks of the American River; Lake Clementine backs up for several miles behind the dam on the North Fork; vegetation consists of a mixture of oaks and other hardwoods, pines and junipers; 42,000 acres; elevation 600′ to 2800′.

Season & Fees: Open all year; please see Appendix for camping fees.

Mail & Phone: Auburn State Recreation Area, P.O. Box 3266, Auburn, CA 95604; ☎(916) 885-4527.

Park Notes: Auburn is a roughcut rec area, albeit a large and popular one. The 20-mile-long, 5-mile-wide park stretches from a couple of miles southwest of Auburn northeast to a point just past the town of Colfax. Your best bet is to stop by the park office just east of Auburn in order to get your bearings, a detailed park map, and the current 'regs' for using the back country. From there, it's a mile-and-a-half down '49 to the confluence of the two forks of the American River which pass through the park. The river's gravel beaches and bars are a favorite spot of sunbathers, toe-dippers, and rock-ploppers.

California 126 ♿

MARSHALL GOLD DISCOVERY
State Historic Park

Location: East-central California northeast of Sacramento.

Access: From California State Highway 49 at milepost 23 +.2 in Coloma (8 miles northwest of Placerville, 19 miles southeast of Auburn), turn west onto Bridge Street to the park visitor center; or at a point 0.1 mile north of the visitor center turnoff, turn east into the Sutter's Mill area; or at a point 0.35 mile north of the v.c., turn east into the North Beach area; or from a point 0.4 mile southwest of the v.c., turn west onto Cold Springs Road and proceed 0.4 mile, then turn right onto Marshall Monument

Road (no buses, trucks, or trailers) for 0.3 mile to the Marshall Monument area.

Day Use Facilities: Medium-large picnic areas, drinking water, restrooms, large parking lots at North Beach and Sutter's Mill (picnic area at the Mill is on the west side of the highway, across from the parking lot); small picnic area, restrooms and small parking area near the Marshall Monument; group picnic area in the Beer Garden, a few yards off the highway, just south of the visitor center (available by reservation).

Overnight Facilities: None; nearest public campgrounds are in Auburn State Recreation Area.

Activities & Attractions: Replication of Sutter's Mill, site of the discovery which touched-off the California Gold Rush; hiking and interpretive trails; visitor center with interpretive displays (small parking lot at the v.c., so be prepared to park 'n walk from one of the other lots); mining exhibit contains examples of equipment used in different types of mining operations; grave site topped by a statue of James W. Marshall overlooks the valley from a hilltop; site of the celebrated Metropolitan Saloon and Bowling Alley (location of one of California's first 'strikes' of a different sort), and other historic buildings and sites in and around Coloma; interpretive and hiking trails; rafting/floating; recreational gold panning area.

Natural Features: Located in a narrow valley along the banks of the South Fork of the American River; park vegetation consists of conifer-and-hardwood-dotted, grassy flats along and near the river and lightly forested hills; park area is 280 acres; elevation 800´.

Season & Fees: Open all year; please see Appendix for reservation information and park entry fees.

Mail & Phone: Marshall Gold Discovery State Historic Park, P.O. Box 265, Coloma, CA 95613; ☎(916) 622-3470.

Park Notes: Little did James Marshall realize when he first glimpsed those flecks of 'something' glittering in the sunshine of the Sierra foothills that fateful January day in 1848 that his discovery was about to precipitate one of most extraordinary events in Western history. Marshall had been building a small sawmill on the bank of the South Fork of the American River for California entrepreneur John Sutter when he spotted what soon proved to be gold in the mill's tailrace. Word of the 'find' spread slowly at first; but by 1849 the rush was running full tilt as thousands of fortune-hunters from around the world walked, rode, sailed, begged, borrowed, bought and fought their way to the gold fields of the Sierra. But Marshall was left far behind in this race to riches and he never achieved the wealth which might have been expected from his singularly significant revelation. Marshall spent his remaining days embittered and lonely, living in a simple log cabin a few yards from the spot where the second history of California began.

California 127 ♿

FOLSOM LAKE:
BEAL'S POINT
State Recreation Area

Location: East-central California northeast of Sacramento.

Access: From U.S. Highway 50 near milepost 15 +.7 at the Hazel Avenue/Sacramento County Highway E3 Exit southwest of Folsom, travel north on Hazel Avenue for 2.4 miles; turn east (right) onto Madison Avenue and proceed 2 miles, then pick up Greenback Lane and continue east for another mile to a 3-way intersection at Greenback Lane and Folsom-Auburn Road; turn north (left) onto Folsom-Auburn Road and proceed 2.6 miles; turn east (right) onto the park access road and go 0.2 mile to the park entrance station; continue ahead for 0.1 mile to the campground or another 0.1 mile to the day use area.

(Note: if you're southwestbound on U.S. 50 from Placerville, you could take the Scott Road/Bidwell Road Exit near milepost 22 east of Folsom for 5 miles into Folsom on Scott Road; then you'll have to pick your way through downtown Folsom and north across the American River bridge in order to get northbound onto Folsom-Auburn Road).

Alternate Access: From Interstate 80 at the exit for Greenback Lane/Elkhorn Boulevard/Sacramento County Highway E14 (13 miles northeast of Sacramento, 4 miles southwest of Roseville) travel east on Greenback Lane/E14 for 8 miles to the intersection of Greenback Lane & Folsom-Auburn Road and continue as above.

Day Use Facilities: Large picnic area; about a dozen small to medium-sized ramadas (sun shelters); drinking water; restrooms; large parking lot; (another day use area with a medium-sized picnic area, vault facilities, a boat ramp and parking lot is located on the lake's south shore, 5 miles northeast of Folsom, then 0.4 mile north off of Green Valley Road).

Overnight Facilities: 49 campsites, including a number of park 'n walk units; sites are small to medium-sized, with nominal to fairly good separation; parking surfaces are paved, short to short+ straight-ins, some are double-wide and some will require a little additional leveling; adequate space for mostly small to medium-sized tents; fire rings; b-y-o firewood; water at several faucets; restrooms with showers; paved driveway; adequate+ supplies and services are available in the Folsom area.

Activities & Attractions: Large, sandy swimming beach; boating; boat launch; (another boat launch is located on the east side of Hazel Avenue near U.S. 50); American River Bikeway begins near here and ends at Old Town Sacramento, 32.8 miles downstream; state park staff-guided tours of the historic Folsom Powerhouse (groups by reservation only, contact the park office for info).

Natural Features: Located near the base of the foothills of the Sierra Nevada; day use area is along the shore and has large tracts of lawns lightly dotted with hardwoods; campground is on and around a grassy, lightly forested knoll; total park area is 17,700 acres; elevation 300´-450´.

Season & Fees: Day use area open all year, campground open April to October; please see Appendix for reservation information, park entry and campground fees.

Mail & Phone: Folsom Lake State Recreation Area, 7806 Folsom-Auburn Road, Folsom, CA 95630; ☎(916) 988-0205.

Park Notes: Much of the lake and its surrounding hills can be viewed from the day use area and beach. If you're camping ... no campfire sing-along would be complete without a soulful rendition of the ol' Country favorite "Folsom Prison Blues". (The slammer that's the song's namesake is near the lake's south shore.)

▲ **California 128** ♿

FOLSOM LAKE:
NEGRO BAR
State Recreation Area

Location: East-central California northeast of Sacramento.

Access: From U.S. Highway 50 near milepost 15 +.7 at the Hazel Avenue/Sacramento County Highway E3 Exit southwest of Folsom, travel north on Hazel Avenue for 2.4 miles; turn east (right) onto Madison Avenue and proceed 2 miles, then pick up Greenback Lane and continue east for another 0.7 mile; turn south (right) onto the park access road and go 0.1 mile to the park entrance station; just beyond the entrance (you'll now be heading east), swing south (right) to the principal day use area, or continue ahead (easterly) for 0.4 mile to the main section of the campground.

(Note: if you're southwestbound on U.S. 50 from Placerville, you could take the Scott Road/Bidwell Road Exit near milepost 22 east of Folsom, then 5 miles into Folsom on Scott Road; wind through downtown Folsom and north across the American River bridge to Greenback Lane; go west on Greenback Lane for 0.3 mile to the park turnoff.)

Alternate Access: From Interstate 80 at the exit for Greenback Lane/Elkhorn Boulevard/Sacramento County Highway E14 (13 miles northeast of Sacramento, 4 miles southwest of Roseville) travel east on

Greenback Lane/E14 for 8 miles to the park turnoff and continue as above.

Day Use Facilities: Medium-large picnic area with a couple of ramadas (sun shelters); drinking water; restrooms; large parking lot.

Overnight Facilities: 20 campsites, including a half-dozen park 'n walk units; (3 group camps are also available); most sites are along the perimeter of the parking lot and are very small to small, level, with nil separation; parking slots are paved, level, short, wide straight-ins; generally small tent areas; fire rings; b-y-o firewood; water at central faucets; restrooms; holding tank disposal station; paved driveways; adequate+ supplies and services are available in the Folsom area.

Activities & Attractions: Large, sandy swimming beach; boating; boat launch; American River Bikeway (goes 3 miles northeast to the park's Beal's Point area on Folsom Lake, or 30 miles southwest to Old Town Sacramento); equestrian trail, equestrian staging area and parking lot; hiking trail; state park staff-guided tours of the historic Folsom Powerhouse (groups by reservation only, contact the park office for info).

Natural Features: Located along the north shore of Lake Natoma, a long, slender, secondary impoundment on the American River downstream of the main dam on Folsom Lake; most picnic and camp sites receive light to light-medium shade from large hardwoods; large sections of grass in the day use area; total park area is 17,700 acres; elevation 250´.

Season & Fees: Open all year; please see Appendix for reservation information, park entry and campground fees.

Mail & Phone: Folsom Lake State Recreation Area, 7806 Folsom-Auburn Road, Folsom, CA 95630; ☎(916) 988-0205.

Park Notes: When the water level on the main lake is just on the high side of dry, (e.g. at the end of summer in a rain-short year), you may find the environment in the Negro Bar section of the park to be a little more to your liking. Lake Natoma essentially is kept at a constant level.

▲ California 129 ♿

INDIAN GRINDING ROCK

State Historic Park

Location: East-central California east of Sacramento.

Access: From California State Highway 88 at milepost 23 +.4 (in the small community of Pine Grove, 9 miles east of Jackson, 3.4 miles west of the junction of State Highways 88 & 26), turn north onto Pine Grove-Volcano Road (paved); proceed 1.3 miles northeast, then turn west (left) into the park; continue for 0.1 mile, and turn north (right) into the campground; or pass through the campground to the day use area and the interpretive exhibits.

Day Use Facilities: Small picnic area; drinking water and restrooms nearby; small parking lot.

Overnight Facilities: 21 campsites; (environmental/primitive sites with shelters are also available); sites are small to medium-sized, with generally good separation; parking pads are gravel, medium-length, mostly straight-ins, plus a few pull-throughs; some additional leveling may be necessary in many sites; good, private tent spots, adequate for medium to large tents; fire rings, plus a few barbecue grills; b-y-o firewood; storage cabinets; water at several faucets; restrooms; paved driveway; gas and groceries in Pine Grove; limited supplies and services are available in Jackson.

Activities & Attractions: Reconstructed Indian village with petroglyphs, displays and exhibits; interpretive programs; nature trail; museum with exhibits and Indian crafts demonstrations; guided group tours, available by reservation.

Natural Features: Located on forested flats and slopes in the western foothills of the Sierra Nevada; tall conifers, oaks, and a considerable amount of underbrush separate most of the campsites nicely; the park has some open meadows as well; park area is 136 acres; elevation 2400´.

Season & Fees: Open all year; please see Appendix for reservation information, park entry and campground fees.

Mail & Phone: Indian Grinding Rock State Historic Park, 14881 Pine Grove-Volcano Road, Pine Grove, CA 95665; (209) 296-7488.

Park Notes: The main grinding rock is a massive limestone table measuring about 25 yards by 60 yards. The rock contains nearly 1200 small holes, "mortar cups", which were worn into the soft stone by enthusiastic Miwok Indians grinding acorns and other seeds to make hot cereal or cake flour. The rock also is randomly marked with more than 350 petroglyphs. Within the reconstructed village are small, bark teepees used as family residences and a *hun'ge* or roundhouse, a domed, multi-sided, wooden structure used as a community center. Another small park on the west slope of the Sierra, Wassama Roundhouse State Historic Park, north of Fresno, also features a roundhouse as its principal point of interest. Wassama Roundhouse is near the village of Ahwahnee off State Highway 49, six miles northwest of Oakhurst. Tours are available on a limited basis. The San Joaquin Valley District Office (209-822-2332) probably can provide you with a current schedule. Both of these roundhouses are actively used by local Indians for dances and ceremonials.

▲ California 130 ♿

CALAVERAS BIG TREES
State Park

Location: East-central California northeast of Stockton.

Access: From California State Highway 4 at milepost 44 +.4 (23 miles east of Angels Camp, 27 miles southwest of Lake Alpine), turn south for 0.1 mile to the park entrance station; just past the entrance, turn right to the North Grove camp and picnic areas; or continue on the main park road for 3.8 miles to the Oak Hollow Campground turnoff, then another 0.5 mile to the campground; or go beyond the Oak Hollow turnoff for an additional 5.5 miles to several roadside picnic areas and the turnaround loop near South Grove.

Day Use Facilities: 5 small or medium-sized picnic areas; group picnic area at North Grove; drinking water; restrooms; medium to large parking lots.

Overnight Facilities: *North Grove Campground*: 74 campsites; (group camp area is also available nearby, by reservation); sites are small to medium-sized, with minimal to fair separation; parking pads are reasonably level, dirt/gravel straight-ins, plus a few pull-throughs; medium to large tent areas; some designated tent sites; *Oak Hollow Campground*: 55 sites; (3 environmental camp areas are located within several miles north and south of Oak Hollow); sites are small to medium-sized, with minimal to fair separation; parking pads are dirt/gravel, mostly short straight-ins, plus some extra-wide straight-ins and a few medium-length pull-offs; medium to large tent areas; *both campgrounds*: fireplaces; firewood is usually for sale, or b-y-o; water at several faucets; restrooms with showers; paved driveways; holding tank disposal station at North Grove; adequate supplies and services are available in Arnold, 3 miles west.

Activities & Attractions: Self-guided nature trail through North Grove; special Three Senses Trail; loop trail through a section of South Grove; several other, longer hiking trails through the park (a detailed brochure/map with contour lines is available); visitor center; rustic community building; campfire circle; trout fishing in the Stanislaus River.

Natural Features: Located in a conifer forest on the west slope of the Sierra Nevada; North Grove holds about 150 giant sequoias; much larger South Grove Natural Preserve protects a primeval sequoia forest; the North Fork of the Stanislaus River flows through the center of the park; park area is 6000 acres; elevation 3500´ to 5400´.

Season & Fees: Open all year, subject to brief closures during periods of heavy snow, with limited services October to May; please see Appendix for reservation information, park entry and campground fees.

Mail & Phone: Calaveras Big Trees State Park, P.O. Box 120, Arnold, CA 95223; (209) 795-2334.

Park Notes: When these trees were first seen in the early 1850's by a frontiersman running down a wounded bear, the discovery set off a global rush to see the "Big Trees of Calaveras County". It also touched off a rash of commercial ventures which exploited the trees in standard nineteenth century fashion. Road shows, featuring sequoias which were felled by unthinking promoters, traveled to the East Coast and to Europe. North Grove contains the most heavily promoted of the Calaveras trees, and is right along the main highway. (Calaveras County achieved worldwide fame for Mark Twain's "celebrated jumping frog" as well.) Suddenly encountering these trees while merely driving past the park is startling. South Grove, accessible only on foot, lies on the secluded slopes along Beaver Creek at the far southeast corner of the park. *Sequoiadendron giganteum* is the largest (though not quite the tallest) of the three species of redwoods left on the planet.

California 131

COLUMBIA

State Historic Park

Location: East-central California east of Stockton.

Access: From California State Highway 49 at milepost 20 +.3 (2.5 miles north of Sonora, 15 miles south of Angels Camp), turn northeast onto Parrotts Ferry Road/Tuolumne County Road E18 (paved) and proceed 1.6 miles to the park; the main parking lot is east (right) off the main road just as you enter the park; most of the midtown streets are closed to motor vehicles.

Day Use Facilities: Medium-sized picnic area (in and around the parking lot); drinking water; restrooms adjacent to the parking lot and at several other locations in town; large parking lot; limited streetside parking is also available.

Overnight Facilities: Restored 20-room City Hotel (operated by the local junior college, reservations suggested); nearest public campgrounds are in Stanislaus National Forest, northeast of Sonora.

Activities & Attractions: Well-preserved and/or renovated Gold Rush-era town, including more than 40 buildings within the historic district; 'living history' programs, festivals, parades, theater performances, contests and fly-ins are scheduled throughout the year; mining machinery exhibit; nature trail; concession/leased businesses provide food service, gifts, etc.; (also, a swimming pool at the local elementary school is open to the public in summer).

Natural Features: Located in the Sierra Nevada, closely bordered by forested hills and mountains; park area is 273 acres; elevation 2100′.

Season & Fees: Open all year; (no fee).

Mail & Phone: Columbia State Historic Park, P.O. Box 151, Columbia, CA 95310; (209) 532-4301.

Park Notes: It is somewhat possible to take a motor tour of Columbia by skirting the edge of downtown and glancing up the streets and alleys; but the fun starts when you get out from behind the dashboard and wander around. There are large signboards with detailed maps of the historic area posted at strategic points around town, so you should be able to find your way OK. (A detailed 'walking tour' guide/map is available from the museum and visitor center or from the park office). Gold was discovered in Columbia in the aftermath of an 1850 cloudburst and the population grew to over 6,000 in 6 weeks. In its heyday, the town was known as the "Gem of Southern Mines". Some $87 million (in nineteenth-century, non-inflated dollars) of gold was drawn from its veins. Columbia, which resembles the famous copper-mining boomtown of Jerome, Arizona in many respects, is also now one of the West's most lively ghost towns.

▲ California 132 ♿

RAILTOWN 1897
State Historic Park

Location: East-central California east of Stockton.

Access: From California State Highways 49 & 108 at the northeast edge of Jamestown (3 miles southwest of Sonora) turn east onto Fifth Avenue and proceed 0.4 mile to the park.

Day Use Facilities: Medium-sized picnic area; drinking water; restrooms; medium-sized parking lot (plus overflow parking); refreshment stand.

Overnight Facilities: None; nearest public campgrounds are in Stanislaus National Forest, northeast of Sonora.

Activities & Attractions: Restored depot, railyard, roundhouse, and car barns of the Sierra Railway of California; steam train excursions include 1-hour "Mother Lode Cannonball" trip to Chinese Station and back, plus several 2.5-hour "specials", e.g., "Keystone Special" round-trip to the town of Keystone, "Twilight Limited" evening train with a bbq at the end of the run, and a "New Year's Eve Party Train" (to who knows where?).

Natural Features: Located in the Sierra Nevada, bordered by forested hills and mountains; picnic sites are on a lightly shaded lawn; park area is 26 acres (plus all the scenery you can take in on the train trips); elevation 1400´.

Season & Fees: Open all year, with limited hours in winter; 1-hour excursions scheduled Saturdays, Sundays and holidays from April through November, "Specials" scheduled mostly June through September; passenger tickets for adults start at about $9.00 for the 1-hour rides and go to $34.00+ for certain "Specials"; children's tickets are 50-60 percent of the adult fare; "family plan" tickets are also available; reservations are highly recommended well in advance for the "Specials"; (it is suggested that you contact the park for current rates and a timetable).

Mail & Phone: Railtown 1897 State Historic Park, Sierra Railway Depot, P.O. Box 1250, Jamestown, CA 95327; (209) 984-3953 or (209) 984-3115.

Park Notes: Steam trains hauled the nation's passengers and freight from the 1830's to the 1950's when they were retired in favor of more efficient diesel-electric locomotion. Nowadays, the classic "choo-choos" run only in places like this park. (Railtown 1897 has a 'sister park' in a very different Western region: Rusk-Palestine State Park in the pine forest of East Texas operates half-day trips on the gleaming yellow Texas State Railroad.) All of the 'old timers' who lend a hand at Railtown help make this a special park.

▲ California 133 ♿

DONNER MEMORIAL
State Park

Location: Eastern California west of Reno, Nevada.

Access: From Interstate 80 near milepost 13 at the Donner Lake/Donner State Park Exit, 1 mile west of Truckee, from the south side of the freeway proceed west on Donner Pass Road (Old Highway 40) for 0.3 mile; turn south (left) into the park entrance and a 'T' intersection; turn left to the museum and historic area; or go west (right) to the day use area, 0.6 mile from the entrance, or the 3 camping sections, all within 0.8 mile south and west of the entrance.

Day Use Facilities: Large picnic area; drinking water; restrooms; a half-dozen medium-sized parking lots.

Overnight Facilities: 154 campsites in 3 loops; sites are small to medium-sized, with nominal to fair separation; parking pads are sand/gravel, short to medium-length straight-ins; some pads may require a little additional leveling; most tent spots are reasonably level and will accommodate good-sized tents; storage cabinets; fireplaces and fire rings; firewood may be available for gathering on national forest land in the vicinity, or b-y-o; water at several faucets; restrooms with showers; paved driveways;

adequate supplies and services are available in Truckee.

Activities & Attractions: Swimming and wading; short hiking trails; nature trail; (guide pamphlet available); cross-country skiing; campfire center for scheduled programs in summer; guided nature walks; Emigrant Trail Museum has information about building the railroad through Donner Pass, and about the Donner party's winter in the Sierra, including a slide presentation; boating (public boat launch at the northwest corner of the lake); lake and stream fishing (reportedly fair) for stocked trout and kokanee salmon.

Natural Features: Located in the Sierra Nevada along the northeast shore of Donner Lake in an open, conifer forest; tall pines, scattered underbrush and sparse grass are the predominant forms of vegetation; picnic sites are along the lake shore; park area is 353 acres; elevation 6000´.

Season & Fees: Museum and limited day use facilities open all year; campground open May to October; please see Appendix for reservation information, park entry and campground fees.

Mail & Phone: Donner Memorial State Park, P.O. Box 9210, Truckee, NV 95737; ☎(530) 587-3841.

Park Notes: Of all the Sierra's lakes, Donner Lake's beauty may be second only to Lake Tahoe's. (Many travelers would say that, in some ways, it's the other way around.) The park is surprisingly busy in winter because of the typically good x-c skiing conditions found here and the Sierra's beautiful winter scenery. While you're at the museum, you can read the tragic history of the 89-member Donner Party and its attempted crossing of the snowbound Sierra in 1846-47. It may give you new insight into the meaning of the expression "persistence in the face of adversity".

▲ California 135

KINGS BEACH

State Recreation Area

Location: Eastern California southeast of Truckee.

Access: From California State Highway 28 in the city of Kings Beach, 0.35 mile east of the junction of Highway 28 & State Highway 267 and 1.2 miles west of the California-Nevada border, turn south into the park.

Day Use Facilities: Medium-sized picnic area; drinking water; restrooms; large parking lot.

Overnight Facilities: None; nearest public campground is in Tahoe State Recreation Area.

Activities & Attractions: Swimming and wading; gravelly beach; boating; (boat launch, 0.1 mile east of the main park entrance); fishing; fishing pier; playground.

Natural Features: Located on the north shore of Lake Tahoe in the Sierra Nevada; picnic sites are lightly shaded by tall conifers and hardwoods; park area is 8 acres; elevation 6200´.

Season & Fees: Open all year, with limited services October to April; operated by the North Tahoe Recreation & Parks Department.

Mail & Phone: North Tahoe Recreation & Parks Department, Kings Beach, CA 95719; ☎(530) 446-7248.

Park Notes: From its strategic position at the head of the lake, the park commands a superior panorama of Lake Tahoe and its environs as far as the eye, and the curvature of the earth, will permit. A good stop just off a high-traffic thoroughfare.

▲ California 135

TAHOE

State Recreation Area

Location: Eastern California on the west shore of Lake Tahoe.

Access: From California State Highway 28 at milepost 0 +.7 on the northeast edge of Tahoe City (0.7 mile northeast of the junction of Highway 28 & State Highway 89, 10 miles southwest of the California-Nevada border), turn southeast into the park.

Day Use Facilities: Small picnic area; drinking water; restrooms; small parking area.

Overnight Facilities: 39 campsites; sites are generally small, with nominal separation; most parking pads gravel, short straight-ins; some pads may require a bit additional leveling; most tent spots are grassy and roomy enough for large tents; storage cabinets; fire rings and barbecue grills; b-y-o firewood; water at several faucets; restrooms with showers; paved driveways; limited+ supplies and services are available in Tahoe City.

Activities & Attractions: Boating; sailing; (boat ramp at Lake Forest, 2 miles east); fishing; fishing pier; floating on the Truckee River, nearby.

Natural Features: Located on a short bluff above the west shore of Lake Tahoe in the Sierra Nevada; many sites have views of the lake through the trees; sites receive light to light-medium shade/shelter from short to very tall conifers and light underbrush on a surface of sparse grass; park area is 12 acres; elevation 6300´.

Season & Fees: May to September; please see Appendix for reservation information, park entry and campground fees.

Mail & Phone: Tahoe State Recreation Area, P.O. Box 583, Tahoe City, CA 95730; ☎(530) 583-3074 or ☎(530) 525-7982

Park Notes: The setting for this park—on a grassy, tree-dotted bluff overlooking a beautiful mountain lake—is ideal. Most of the sites, however, are within a few yards of a very busy highway, and lake access is limited because of a residential strip between the park and the lake shore. But there are some views of the lake through the trees. Lake Tahoe's deepest hole, sounded at 1645 feet, is six miles east-southeast of this park, in the north third of the lake. The lake's other stats: 12 miles wide, 22 miles long, 19.6 square miles/122,600 acres in area, with 72 miles of shoreline. Just across the highway from Tahoe SRA is 2000-acre Burton Creek State Park, an undeveloped area which provides limited hiking and x-c skiing opportunities.

▲ **California 136** ♿

Sugar Pine Point
State Park

Location: Eastern California on the west shore of Lake Tahoe.

Access: From California State Highway 89 near milepost 26 (1 mile south of the El Dorado/Placer County line, 2 miles south of Tahoma, 18 miles north of South Lake Tahoe), turn east to the day use area and the visitor center; or near milepost 26 +.5, turn west onto the campground access road and proceed 0.1 mile to the entrance station, then continue for 0.2 mile to the camping area.

Day Use Facilities: Small picnic area; drinking water; restrooms; medium-sized parking area.

Overnight Facilities: *General Creek Campground*: 175 campsites in 4 loops; (group camps are also available, by reservation); sites are small to medium-sized, essentially level, with nominal to fairly good separation; many units are situated in clusters; parking pads are hard-surfaced, short to medium+ straight-ins; tent spots vary from small to large; assorted fire appliances; firewood is usually for sale, or b-y-o; storage cabinets; water at several faucets; restrooms with showers; (showers available in summer only); holding tank disposal station; paved driveways; groceries in Tahoma; adequate+ supplies and services are available in South Lake Tahoe.

Activities & Attractions: Fishing; fishing pier; day use area has a half-mile-long sandy beach; hiking trails; nature trail; amphitheater; visitor center; early settler's cabin.

Natural Features: Located in the Sierra Nevada, along and above the west shore of Lake Tahoe, where General Creek flows into the lake; vegetation consists of tall conifers, a small amount of underbrush, and some new growth timber; park area is 2011 acres; elevation 6300´.

Season & Fees: Open all year, with limited services September to May; please see Appendix for reservation information, park entry and campground fees.

Mail & Phone: Sugar Pine Point State Park, P.O. Drawer D Tahoma, CA 95733; ☎(530) 525-7982.

Park Notes: General Creek is named for "General" William Phipps, a Kentuckian who was one of the first permanent residents of the area. Phipps filed a homestead claim on The Point in 1860, and his second cabin is still standing near the lakeshore. In opulent contrast to the Phipps cabin is the park's visitor center, located inside what is locally called the "Ehrman Mansion". The granite-faced, turreted, three-story house was built in the late 1800's as a summer home for a West Coast banker. If the former residents of that decorous domicile only came here in summer, they missed three of Lake Tahoe's four best seasons. Sugar Pine Point is the only state park on Lake Tahoe with winter camping. Winter campers can expect to find deep snow pack, frequent snow storms, and nighttime lows near zero. However, it should also be noted that seeing Lake Tahoe and its snow-cloaked mountains in the crisp, clear, cold air following a frontal passage is one of the outdoors' most memorable occasions.

California 137

D.L. Bliss
State Park

Location: Eastern California on the west shore of Lake Tahoe.

Access: From California State Highway 89 at milepost 19 +.5 (7 miles south of the El Dorado/Placer county line, 11 miles north of the South Lake Tahoe area), turn northeast onto the park access road; proceed 1 mile down a curvy, narrow roadway to the park entrance station; campsites are in 3 sections within 1.3 miles of the entrance station; day use area is at the far north end of the park road, just beyond the last camp loop, 2.4 miles from the highway. (Note: there is limited maneuvering room in the park; only very short trailers are welcome.)

Day Use Facilities: Medium-sized picnic area; drinking water; restrooms; 2 medium-sized parking lots.

Overnight Facilities: 168 campsites in 3 sections; (a group camp is also available, by reservation); most sites are small, quite sloped, with fair to good separation; parking areas are mostly dirt, short to short+ straight-ins; many pads will require additional leveling; fairly good sized, sloped tent spots; storage cabinets; assorted fire appliances; b-y-o firewood; water at several faucets; restrooms with showers; paved driveways; adequate+ supplies and services are available in South Lake Tahoe.

Activities & Attractions: Swimming beach in the day use area; hiking (Rubicon Trail leads to Vikingsholm and to Eagle Creek Falls in adjacent Emerald Bay State Park); Lighthouse Trail to an old lighthouse; Balancing Rock Nature Trail; campfire center.

Natural Features: Located along and above the west shore of Lake Tahoe just north of Emerald Bay; day use area is adjacent to Lester Beach and Calawee Cove Beach; campsites are all situated on a forested slope; vegetation consists of light to medium-dense, tall conifers, including gnarled and stunted sugar pines, and a considerable amount of undergrowth; some campsites are near the lake shore; park area is 1237 acres; elevation 6300´ to 7000´.

Season & Fees: May to September; please see Appendix for reservation information, park entry and campground fees.

Mail & Phone: D.L Bliss State Park, P.O. Box 266, Tahoma, CA 95733; ☎(530) 525-7277.

Park Notes: D. L. Bliss has what is considered to be one of the two best beaches on the lake. (Also see Lake Tahoe Nevada State Park.) The area is named for a lumberman whose family donated the original tract for the park. This is one of the few state parks where a campsite might be available late in the day during the week without a reservation.

California 138

EMERALD BAY
State Park

Location: Eastern California on the west shore of Lake Tahoe.

Access: From U.S. 89 at milepost 15 +.3 (7 miles northwest of the South Lake Tahoe area, 12 miles south of the El Dorado/Placer county line), turn northeast into the park; proceed 0.1 mile to the entrance station; continue ahead for 0.4 mile to the upper camp area or another 0.8 mile to the lower camp area; or from near milepost 17 +.5, turn east into the Emerald Bay Overlook parking lot.

Day Use Facilities: Small picnic area at Vikingsholm; drinking water; restrooms; Vikingsholm Trail parking in the Emerald Bay Overlook parking lot

Overnight Facilities: *Eagle Point Campground*: 100 campsites; (20 primitive, walk-in or boat-in campsites on the middle north/west shore of the bay are also available); sites are small to small+, with minimal to nominal separation; parking pads are mostly short straight-ins, and many will require additional leveling; some parking pads are hard-surfaced, others are gravel/sand; tent spots are small to medium-sized and may be a bit sloped or rocky; storage cabinets; fire rings and barbecue grills; b-y-o firewood is recommended; water at several faucets; restrooms with showers; paved driveways; gas and groceries on Highway 89, 4 miles south; adequate+ supplies and services are available in the South Lake Tahoe area.

Activities & Attractions: Guided tours of Vikingsholm, a 38-room castle built in 1929; steep, 1 mile trail from the parking lot down to Vikingsholm; swimming beach and a short trail to Eagle Falls from Vikingsholm; trail to the beach from the lower camp loop; boating; sailing; dock and mooring buoys at the boat-in camp; (public boat launch in Camp Richardson, 5 miles southeast); shoreline fishing for small trout; boat fishing for Mackinaw trout and kokanee salmon; campfire center; Rubicon Trail leads 3.5 miles from near Vikingsholm to D.L. Bliss State Park.

Natural Features: Located around Emerald Bay on the southwest shore of Lake Tahoe; upper campsites are on a forested slope; lower sites are situated out on tree-dotted Eagle Point; vegetation includes tall conifers, moderate underbrush and sparse grass; Lake Tahoe's only isle, Fannette Island, lies near the southwest tip of the bay; park area is 593 acres; elevation 6300′ to 7000′.

Season & Fees: June to September; please see Appendix for reservation information, park entry and campground fees; extra charge for Vikingsholm tour.

Mail & Phone: Mail c/o CDPR Sierra District Office. P.O. Drawer D, Tahoma, CA 95733; park phone ☎(530) 541-3030.

Park Notes: Emerald Bay is shaped like an elongated 'U' with a narrow harbor entrance. The half-mile wide, 1.5-mile long bay is one of the best-sheltered spots on the lake. This part of Lake Tahoe's shoreline is indeed naturally beautiful. That was recognized when it was designated a National Natural Landmark in 1969. Vikingsholm is perhaps not quite 'naturally' beautiful, but it is considered by some to be the foremost example of Scandinavian architecture west of the North Sea. The granite castle, replete with towers and turrets and an authentic sod roof, was designed to replicate a Norse fortress of the ninth century A.D. It is said to have been built without disturbing a single tree on Lake Tahoe's shore. The Indians called Lake Tahoe "Lake of the Sky", and someone has yet to improve on that title.

California 139

LAKE VALLEY
State Recreation Area

Location: Eastern California south of Lake Tahoe.

Access: From U.S. Highway 50/California State Highway 89 at a point 3.4 miles south of the junction of U.S. 50 & State Highway

89 in the city of South Lake Tahoe, 1.5 miles north of the junction of U.S. 50 & State Highway 89 near the California ag inspection station, turn west into the park. (Note: the U.S. and state highways are merged into one road along this short section, hence the twin junctions listed above.)

Day Use Facilities: Drinking water; restrooms; large parking lot; concession stand.

Overnight Facilities: None; nearest public campground is in El Dorado city park in midtown South Lake Tahoe.

Activities & Attractions: 18-hole golf course; cross-country skiing and snowmobiling.

Natural Features: Located in Lake Valley near the banks of the Upper Truckee River; park vegetation consists of manicured fairways and greens dotted with trees; bordered by the lofty mountains of the Sierra Nevada; park area is 150 acres; elevation 6400´.

Season & Fees: Open all year; please contact the concessionaire for current greens fees and trail user fees; operated by the Lake Tahoe Country Club.

Mail & Phone: Mail c/o CDPR Sierra District Office, P.O. Drawer D, Tahoma, CA 95733; park phone ☎(530) 544-1583; golf info phone ☎(530) 577-0788.

Park Notes: This state recreation area is located on the grounds of the Lake Tahoe Golf Course. It takes no profound deduction to realize that (a) this is a swell place, and (b) you'll need to call well ahead or be really lucky to get a good tee time on a summer weekend. Another nearby park unit, 620-acre Washoe Meadows State Park, is an undeveloped piece of real estate which is op'ed in association with Lake Valley SRA. Hiking and x-c skiing opportunities are available at Washoe Meadows (trail fees required).

California 140 ♿

GROVER HOT SPRINGS
State Park

Location: Eastern California south of Carson City, Nevada.

Access: From California State Highways 89 & 4 at milepost 14 +.8 in midtown Markleeville, turn west onto Montgomery Street which becomes Hot Springs Road; proceed 3.5 miles; turn north (right) to the park entrance station; the picnic area is just inside the entrance; or continue for 0.2 mile to the "Quaking Aspen" camp loop or another 0.2 mile to the "Toiyabe" camp section; or, instead of turning into the park entrance station, continue west for 0.4 mile to the parking lot for the hot pools.

Day Use Facilities: Medium-sized picnic area; drinking water; restrooms; medium-sized parking area; large parking lot at the pools.

Overnight Facilities: 76 campsites in 2 sections; sites are medium to large with minimal to fair separation; parking pads are paved, short to medium-length, most are straight-ins, many pads may require additional leveling; tent spots are on grass or pine needle surfaces, some are sloped, many are spacious enough for large tents; storage cabinets; fireplaces; firewood is usually for sale, or b-y-o; water at several faucets; restrooms with showers; paved driveways; gas and groceries+ in Markleeville.

Activities & Attractions: Hot springs pools; nature trail; 3 hiking trails; stream fishing for small trout (stocked periodically as stream conditions permit); amphitheater for scheduled programs in summer; Nordic skiing.

Natural Features: Located in a valley on the east side of the Sierra Nevada, with mountains rising sharply on 3 sides; grassy slopes and meadows are interspersed with stands of aspens and conifers; park area is 519 acres; elevation 5800´.

Season & Fees: Open all year, with limited services (i.e., camping only in the picnic area, with no showers) October to May; pool hours vary seasonally; please see

Appendix for reservation information, park entry and campground fees; extra fee for pool use.

Mail & Phone: Grover Hot Springs State Park, P.O. Box 188, Markleeville, CA 96120; ☎(530) 694-2248.

Park Notes: Grover's mineral-rich waters leave the ground at 148°, but the temps in the water of the park's two pools run 102° to 105°. Unlike the water of most hot springs, the sulphur content of the water here is quite low. (A breakdown of the mineral content is available from the park office.) Many people believe that these waters, which percolate up from thousands of feet below the surface, are good for just about whatever ails you. You don't have to come here to use the pools, though. The alpine scenery is worth the trip.

California 141 ♿

BODIE
State Historic Park

Location: Eastern California southeast of Bridgeport.

Access: From U.S. Highway 395 at milepost 69 +.9 at the junction of U.S. 395 & California State Highway 270 (7 miles south of Bridgeport, 19 miles north of Lee Vining), travel east on Highway 270 for 13 miles (paved for the first 10 miles, then 3 miles of dirt/gravel) to the park. (It is suggested that you check on road conditions prior to venturing out to the park from September through May.)

Day Use Facilities: Small picnic area; drinking water; restrooms; large parking lot.

Overnight Facilities: None; nearest public campgrounds are 5 Toiyabe National Forest camps on Twin Lakes Road (paved), 8 to 11 miles west of Bridgeport.

Activities & Attractions: Self-guided walking tour along the streets of the well-preserved remains of more than 100 buildings of the gold mining town of Bodie (a detailed guide booklet is available).

Natural Features: Located on treeless, brushy, grassy, high desert terrain in the Bodie Hills near the east slopes of the Sierra Nevada; park area is 578 acres; elevation 8400′.

Season & Fees: Open all year, subject to weather conditions, principal season is May to October; please see Appendix for park entry fees.

Mail & Phone: Bodie State Historic Park, P.O. Box 515, Bridgeport, CA 93517; ☎(530) 647-6445.

Park Notes: In its prime, Bodie had a population of more than 10,000, including a cross-section of gold miners, saloon keepers, merchants, tavern tramps, swindlers, hooligans, and outlaws determined to cash in on the gold rush of the mid-1800's. Bodie survived a lengthy economic decline as the gold supply dwindled by the early 1880's, only to meet a swift and tragic death when a fire storm destroyed half of the town in the Depression year of 1932. The entire population escaped the blaze, leaving everything behind. No one returned after the fire, and Bodie became locked in time. Because of its remote, high-altitude location near the California-Nevada border, Bodie has remained virtually untouched for more than half a century. There are still tables set with dishes, schoolhouse desks piled with books, and bourbon on the bar—as if waiting for the specters of the owners to reclaim their belongings. As you turn off the main highway and head east across the seemingly limitless high desert, your mind may echo the words of the little pioneer girl who wrote in her diary: "Goodbye God, I'm going to Bodie".

California 142

MONO LAKE TUFA
State Reserve

Location: Eastern California south of Bridgeport.

Access: From U.S. Highway 395 near milepost 46 at the junction of U.S. 395 & California State Highway 120 (5 miles south of the town of Lee Vining), travel east on Highway 120 for 4.8 miles, then turn north (left) onto a park access road and proceed 0.4 mile to the South Tufa area. (Other viewpoints are located along U.S. 395, the principal ones are 2 miles north of Lee Vining near milepost 53, and in a Mono County park at the northwest corner of the lake.)

Day Use Facilities: Medium-sized parking area at South Tufa.

Overnight Facilities: Primitive camping is allowed in the Mono Basin Scenic Area outside of the state reserve, by permit from the Inyo National Forest ranger station in Lee Vining; nearest public campgrounds are in Inyo NF, east of Lee Vining on State Highway 120 (on the way to Yosemite).

Activities & Attractions: Viewpoints of enormous mineral formations rising above the surface of Mono Lake; 1-mile self-guided nature trail and guided nature walks at South Tufa; hiking trails; cross-country skiing; boating; swimming/wading in high-salinity, high-alkaline, high-buoyancy water.

Natural Features: Located in and around Mono Lake in the high desert Mono Basin near the east slopes of the Sierra Nevada; vegetation consists mostly of grass and some brush; park area is 17,000 acres; elevation 6400´.

Season & Fees: Open all year; (no fee).

Mail & Phone: Mono Lake Tufa State Reserve, P.O. Box 99, Lee Vining, CA 93541; ☎(530) 647-6331.

Park Notes: Mono Lake's massive tufa towers are deposits of calcium carbonate formed from the reaction of salty lake water with freshwater underground springs. The tufa (*too´-fah*) forms only underwater, but a steady drop in the lake level since the early 1940's has exposed the spires, columns and knobs of tufa, some of them nearly 40 feet high. Mono Lake is a classic case of serendipity coupled with ambivalence. On one hand is the alleged culprit, the City of Los Angeles, which has been diverting the waters of several major streams that feed Mono Lake, thus causing the low lake level. On the other hand, had it not been for L.A.'s heavy water usage, much of the tufa would still be under water, and unobservable by anyone except scuba divers and brine shrimp. (The situation is somewhat akin to the scenario of seeing an IRS agent in a brand new government car teetering on the edge of a cliff.)

Southern California

Red Rock Canyon State Park

California

South Central Coast

California 143

WILLIAM RANDOLPH HEARST
Memorial State Beach

Location: Central California Coast northwest of San Luis Obispo.

Access: From California State Highway 1 at milepost 57 +.7 (in the community of San Simeon, directly opposite the access road to Hearst San Simeon SHM, 8 miles north of Cambria), turn west onto San Simeon Road for 0.1 mile to the park.

Day Use Facilities: Medium-sized picnic area; drinking water; restrooms; 2 medium-sized parking lots.

Overnight Facilities: None; nearest public campground is in San Simeon State Beach.

Activities & Attractions: Beachcombing; fishing; fishing pier.

Natural Features: Located on a short bluff and along the beach; picnic area is on a grassy slope dotted with hardwoods and conifers; picnic sites are unshaded to very lightly shaded; park area is 8 acres; sea level.

Season & Fees: Open all year; please see Appendix for park entry fees.

Mail & Phone: Mail c/o Hearst San Simeon State Historical Monument; park info phone ☎(805) 927-2020.

Park Notes: W. R. Hearst's biography doesn't read like the standard up-from-poverty Horatio Alger story—his father had made millions in mining—but how he used his available capital to build a communications empire in the early twentieth century nonetheless makes good copy. Hearst was born in San Francisco in 1863. After expulsion from Harvard University because of a practical joke he played on the faculty, Hearst took over his father's newspaper, the *San Francisco Examiner*, in 1887. With his ever-increasing wealth resulting from the success of the *Examiner* and other newspapers, Hearst went on to own 26 major dailies at his peak. His circulation wars with Joseph Pulitzer's competing papers in the sensational days of 'yellow journalism' are legendary. (Hearst's and Pulitzer's editorial philosophy essentially was: All the news that's fit to print—and a lot that isn't.) Hearst's journals championed the cause of the underdog and often took on powerful industrial, governmental and political opponents.

Hearst's conglomerate also owned International News Service, which was sold to United Press to form the present-day United Press International (UPI); King Features Syndicate, the first major comic strip coalition; 13 magazines, including *Good Housekeeping*, *Cosmopolitan*, and *Harper's Bazaar*; a half-dozen radio stations; and several Hollywood motion picture companies. Hearst pioneered the use of telecommunications in business operation and "The Chief" frequently ran the empire from his San Simeon estate during 1925-1947. Hearst died in Beverly Hills in 1951. (It is widely believed that Orson Welles, who wrote, directed, produced and starred in the classic 1941 film, *Citizen Kane*, based the story and its egocentric principal character, Charles Foster Kane, largely on the life and times of William Randolph Hearst.)

▲ **California 144** ♿

HEARST SAN SIMEON
State Historical Monument

Location: Central California Coast northwest of San Luis Obispo.

Access: From California State Highway 1 at milepost 57 +.7 (in the community of San Simeon, 8 miles north of Cambria) turn northeast onto the park access road and proceed 0.5 mile to the parking lot; tour ticket sales windows are inside the visitor center.

Day Use Facilities: Small picnic area; drinking water and restrooms inside the visitor center; huge parking lot, including designated rv, bus and motorcycle parking sections; snack bar.

Overnight Facilities: None; nearest public campground is in San Simeon State Beach.

Activities & Attractions: Guided tours of "Hearst Castle", which includes a 130-room main residence "La Casa Grande", plus guest houses, pools, and 125 acres of formal gardens; four tours (each about 1 hour 45 minutes) are available; Tour 1 is the suggested first-time tour; elaborate visitor center features displays and audio-visual presentations about Hearst and the construction of this humble abode.

Natural Features: Located on a hill 2 miles east of the Pacific Ocean; landscaping defies description; sea level to 200´.

Season & Fees: Open all year, daily except certain major holidays; for guided tours: daytime $10.00 for adults and teens, $5.00 for children 6-12, evening $20.00 for adults and teens, $10.00 for children; (parking lot and visitor center are free of charge, subject to change); reservations strongly recommended; please see Appendix for additional reservation information.

Mail & Phone: Hearst San Simeon State Historical Monument, 750 Hearst Castle Road, San Simeon, CA 93452; ☎(805) 927-2020; reservation information ☎(800)-927-2020.

Park Notes: Communications magnate William Randolph Hearst (see the biographical brief in the Park Notes section of W. R. Hearst State Beach) began building *La Cuesta Encantata* ("The Enchanted Hill") in 1919. Designed by Hearst and architect Julia Morgan, the palatial estate was meant to be a kingly residence for one of the wealthiest and most influential private citizens of the period. Construction of the estate continued until 1947, when Hearst moved to Beverly Hills because of ill health. The only way to see the "castle" (except at a distance) is to take a guided tour. Reservations are strongly recommended. (About a million tourists come here each year, and the park is busy even on rainy Monday mornings in February.) One of many shuttle buses will take you up the hill from what must be the largest visitor center of any park in the country. Really, the place rivals Grand Central Station. Your friends who've been here can tell you about it, and you can look at countless photographs of this place, but until you actually walk the grounds of the estate, you'll still not believe it.

▲ California 145

San Simeon: San Simeon Creek & Washburn

State Park

Location: Central California Coast northwest of San Luis Obispo.

Access: From California State Highway 1 at milepost 52 +.8 (at the south end of the San Simeon Creek Bridge, 5 miles south of San Simeon, 3 miles north of Cambria), turn east into the main day use area; or at milepost 53 +.2 (at the north end of the San Simeon Creek Bridge), turn east onto San Simeon Creek Road and proceed 0.1 mile; turn south (right) for 0.2 mile to the park entrance station; continue ahead for 0.2 mile to a 'T' intersection, then turn right to San Simeon Creek Campground; or turn left and go up the hill for 1 mile to Washburn Campground.

Day Use Facilities: Small picnic area; drinking water; restrooms; medium-sized parking lot; (also a small day use and parking area on the west side of the highway).

Overnight Facilities: *San Simeon Creek Campground*: 131 campsites (2 hike/bike sites are also available); sites are small, generally level, with minimal to fair separation; most parking pads are paved, short to short+ straight-ins, some are extra-wide; adequate space for large tents; fire rings; b-y-o firewood; water at several faucets; restrooms with showers; holding tank disposal station; paved driveways; *Washburn Campground*: 69 (primitive) campsites; sites are small+, with nil separation; parking pads are packed gravel, medium-length straight-ins; a little additional leveling may be required; large tent areas; water at several faucets; vault facilities; packed gravel driveways; limited+ supplies and services are available in Cambria.

Activities & Attractions: Beach access across the highway; campfire center.

Natural Features: Located on a creekside flat and on a hillside (San Simeon Creek), and on an open hilltop (Washburn); park vegetation consists mostly of large, open grassy areas, plus trees and shrubbery which provide very light to light shade/shelter for some campsites in the San Simeon Creek area; Washburn campsites and picnic sites are unshaded; total park area is 540 acres, including 2.5 miles of ocean frontage; sea level to 150′.

Season & Fees: Open all year; please see Appendix for reservation information, park entry and campground fees.

Mail & Phone: Mail c/o Hearst San Simeon State Historical Monument; park info phone☎(805) 927-2020.

Park Notes: At San Simeon Creek, the view you get from most campsites is a good shot of the highway. (Most of the campground is below the built-up road.)

From the open hilltop at Washburn, there are vast views of the coastal hills and mountains and of the ocean. If you're self-contained, Washburn might be the way to go.

California 146

SAN SIMEON: LEFFINGWELL LANDING & SANTA ROSA CREEK

State Park

Location: Central California Coast northwest of San Luis Obispo.

Access: From California State Highway 1 (southbound) near milepost 52 (2 miles north of Cambria, 6 miles south of San Simeon) turn southwest onto Moonstone Beach Drive and proceed 0.3 mile to the scenic area and Leffingwell Landing; or continue south for another mile to several beach access areas and the Santa Rosa Creek area. **Alternate Access:** From Highway 1 (northbound) at milepost 51 (1 mile north of Cambria, 7 miles south of San Simeon) turn west onto Weymouth Street and go 0.2 mile to Moonstone Beach Drive; turn south (left) for 0.1 mile to the Santa Rosa Creek section, or go north along Moonstone Beach Drive for 1 mile to Leffingwell Landing or for a final 0.3 mile to re-access Highway 1.

Day Use Facilities: Small picnic area, drinking water, restrooms and medium-sized parking lot at Leffingwell Landing; medium-sized parking lot and vaults at Santa Rosa Creek; small parking areas and beach access/view points along Moonstone Beach Drive.

Overnight Facilities: See San Simeon State Beach—San Simeon Creek and Washburn Areas.

Activities & Attractions: Beachcombing; fishing.

Natural Features: Located on a short bluff and on sections of beach; vegetation consists of unsheltered grassy areas, plus a moderately wooded section at Leffingwell Landing; sea level.

Season & Fees: Open all year; (no fee).

Mail & Phone: Mail c/o Hearst San Simeon State Historical Monument; park info phone☎(805) 927-2020.

Park Notes: The Leffingwell Landing picnic area is one of the nicer ones along the Central Coast. This could be the spot of choice while you're waiting for your turn to tour Hearst Castle.

California 147

CAYUCOS

State Beach

Location: Central California Coast northwest of San Luis Obispo.

Access: From California State Highway 1 near milepost 36 at the north edge of Cayucos (5 miles north of Morro Bay), take the Cayucos Drive Exit west for 0.3 mile to North Ocean Avenue; turn north (right) onto North Ocean Avenue for 25 yards, then swing west (left) into the parking lot.

Day Use Facilities: Small picnic area; drinking water; restrooms; medium-sized parking lot.

Overnight Facilities: None; nearest public campground is in Morro Strand State Beach.

Activities & Attractions: Fishing; fishing pier.

Natural Features: Located along a sandy beach; park area is 5 acres; sea level.

Season & Fees: Open all year; operated by San Luis Obispo County.

Mail & Phone: San Luis Obispo County Department of Parks and Recreation, San Luis Obispo, CA 93401; ☎(805) 549-5200.

Park Notes: The picnic area looks like it would make a good place for a clambake or a fishbecue.

California 148

MORRO STRAND
State Beach

Location: Central California Coast northwest of San Luis Obispo.

Access: From California State Highway 1 at milepost 32 (at the north edge of the city of Morro Bay), turn west onto Yerba Buena Street and proceed 0.2 mile to the campground. **Additional Access** (day use area): From Highway 1 at milepost 34 +.5, at the 24th Street Exit near the south edge of the town of Cayucos (3 miles north of Morro Bay) turn southwest off the highway for a few yards, then angle left and go down 24th Street for 0.1 mile to Pacific Avenue and the parking lot.

Day Use Facilities: Small picnic area; drinking water; restrooms; medium-sized parking lot.

Overnight Facilities: 104 campsites in 2 rows parallel to the beach; sites are small, level, with nil separation; parking pads are paved, short straight-ins/pull-offs (depending upon how you park); enough space for very small tents in most sites (see Park Notes below); fire rings; firewood is usually for sale, or b-y-o; water at several faucets; restrooms with freshwater rinse showers; paved driveways; adequate supplies and services are available in Morro Bay.

Activities & Attractions: Fishing.

Natural Features: Located just above the beach and below a short bluff (campground); campground vegetation consists primarily of tall bushes and short trees between sites that provide some shelter from the wind, plus patches of grass for the table areas; day use area has a sandy beach; total park area is 117 acres; sea level.

Season & Fees: Open all year; please see Appendix for reservation information and campground fees.

Mail & Phone: c/o Morro Bay State Park.

Park Notes: There actually isn't a lot of room for a tent in most of the campsites, but the parking space could be used for a large, free-standing tent if your vehicle is small. The campground section of the park was formerly called Atascadero State Beach. Good views of 600´ Morro Rock and the ocean, especially from the campground, also from the day use area.

California 149 ♿

MORRO BAY
State Park

Location: Central California Coast northwest of San Luis Obispo.

Access: From California State Highway 1 at milepost 27 +.8 (11 miles northwest of San Luis Obispo, 1 mile south of the city of Morro Bay), turn south onto South Bay Boulevard; proceed 0.8 mile, then bear southwest (right) onto State Park Road (which gradually curves northwest and then north) for 0.75 mile to the campground and picnic area, or for an additional 0.4 mile to the museum.

Day Use Facilities: Medium-sized picnic area, drinking water, restrooms and parking area adjacent to the campground; a few picnic tables, drinking water, restrooms, medium-sized parking lot at the museum.

Overnight Facilities: 135 campsites, including 20 with partial hookups; (hike/bike sites and a reservable group camp are also available); sites are small to small+, level, with nominal to fair separation; parking pads are medium-length, gravel/dirt straight-ins in most of the sites; hookup units have paved pull-throughs; good-sized, level tent areas; storage cabinets; fireplaces or fire rings; firewood is usually for sale, or b-y-o; water at hookups and at several faucets; restrooms with showers; holding tank disposal station; paved driveways; adequate supplies and services are available in Morro Bay.

Activities & Attractions: Museum of Natural History features displays and audio-visual programs; guided nature walks and interpretive programs; 1.5 mile fitness trail; hiking trails, including trails to viewpoints on Black Hill; fishing; boating; public boat launch just north of the park; 18-hole public golf course and marina, operated by concessionaires.

Natural Features: Located primarily on a large wooded flat on the east shore of Morro Bay; tall conifers and some hardwoods provide a substantial amount of shelter/shade in most camp and picnic sites; Black Hill rises to 661´ east of the bayside section, another hill tops 900´; total park area is 2400 acres; sea level to 911´.

Season & Fees: Open all year; museum fee $2.00 for adults, $1.00 for children under 18 (subject to change); please see Appendix for reservation information, park entry and campground fees.

Mail & Phone: Morro Bay State Park, State Park Road, Morro Bay, CA 93442; ☎(805) 772-2560 or 772-9723 (office), or 772-2694 (museum).

Park Notes: There's little doubt that this is one of the nicer coastal parks. The natural history museum has an observation room from which you can look out to haystack-shaped Morro Rock and across Morro Bay through an array of large windows (bay windows, so to speak). Excellent picture-taking possibilities here. No single state park in California has it all; but if you were to take the combined facilities, activities, attractions, ease of access, and super scenery of Morro Bay and its neighboring sister park, Montana de Oro, they would probably come closest to presenting you with the whole enchilada.

▲ **California 150**

MONTANA DE ORO
State Park

Location: Southern California coastal area west of San Luis Obispo.

Access: From U.S. Highway 101 at milepost 25 +.8 on the south edge of San Luis Obispo, take the Los Osos/Baywood Exit and travel northwest on Los Osos Valley Road for 10.5 miles into Los Osos; pass through town, then west and south on Pecho Valley Road (paved) for 2 miles to the park boundary; continue for another 2.5 miles, then turn west (right) to the oceanside area, or east (left) for 0.2 mile to the campground. **Alternate Access:** From California State Highway 1 at milepost 27 +.8 (1 mile southeast of the city of Morro Bay, 11 miles northwest of San Luis Obispo), turn south onto South Bay Boulevard and travel 5 miles into Los Osos; turn west (right) onto Los Osos Valley Road/Pecho Valley Road and continue as above.

Day Use Facilities: Picnic area; vault facilities; parking lot.

Overnight Facilities: 50 campsites; sites are medium-sized, reasonably level (considering the terrain), with fair to fairly good separation; parking pads are mostly paved, short straight-ins, some are extra wide; adequate space for medium to large tents; fire rings; b-y-o firewood; water at a central faucet; vault facilities; paved driveways; adequate supplies and services are available in Los Osos.

Activities & Attractions: 50 miles of hiking and equestrian trails.

Natural Features: Located on hilly terrain above seven miles of Pacific Ocean shoreline; picnic area overlooks the sea; campsites are in a forested canyon and are sheltered by tall conifers plus some hardwoods, on a grassy surface; park area is 8400 acres; elevation sea level to 1600´.

Season & Fees: Open all year; please see Appendix for reservation information, park entry and campground fees.

Mail & Phone: Montana de Oro State Park, Los Osos, CA 93402; ☎(805) 528-0513.

Park Notes: *Montana de Oro* ("Mountain of Gold") refers not to the precious metal but to the natural springtime radiance of the mountainsides in this region. The four-mile-long sand spit which nearly encloses Morro Bay is an extreme northerly extension of the shorline in this park. Adjacent to Montana de Oro, just off the south side of Los Osos Valley Road at the east edge of the town of Los Osos, is Los Osos Oaks State Reserve. The 85-acre plot holds stands of weathered, intricately gnarled, centuries-old oak trees. A loop trail takes you through the reserve from a small parking lot.

California 151

PISMO: NORTH BEACH

State Beach

Location: Southern California Coast south of San Luis Obispo.

Access: From California State Highway 1 at its intersection with Grand Avenue in Grover City, proceed west on Grand Avenue for 0.15 mile to the day use area and the golf course; or at a point 0.75 mile north of the intersection of Highway 1 and Grand Avenue at the south edge of the city of Pismo Beach, turn west into the campground.

Day Use Facilities: Medium-sized picnic area; drinking water; restrooms with freshwater rinse showers; large parking lot; restaurant concession.

Overnight Facilities: 103 campsites; (hike-bike sites are also available); sites are generally medium-sized, level, with fair to very good separation; parking pads are paved, mostly long pull-throughs; excellent tent spots; storage cabinets; fire rings; firewood is usually for sale, or b-y-o; water at several faucets; restrooms; holding tank disposal station; paved driveways; adequate+ supplies and services are available within 1 mile.

Activities & Attractions: Short trails from the campground along a creek and to the beach; campfire center; golf course.

Natural Features: Located on a large, grassy flat (campground); tall hardwoods and evergreens provide very light to medium shelter/shade in most campsites; picnic area is located near the beach, tables are mostly unshaded; sea level.

Season & Fees: Open all year; please see Appendix for reservation information, park entry and campground fees.

Mail & Phone: Pismo State Beach, 555 Pier Avenue, Oceano, CA 93445; ☎(805) 489-2684.

Park Notes: If you want to camp at Pismo Beach, it's a tough choice between North Beach and Oceano (see info below). Both are quite nice. This one is in a more open setting, with less tall vegetation, but with large, grassy areas. Like Oceano, there are no ocean views, but the sea is only a short walk away.

California 152

PISMO: OCEANO

State Beach

Location: Southern California Coast south of San Luis Obispo.

Access: From California State Highway 1 in Oceano at a point 1.1 miles south of the intersection of Highway 1 and Grand Avenue in Grover City, turn west onto Pier Avenue and proceed 0.2 mile; turn north (right) into the campground entrance; or continue west for another 0.2 mile to the day use/beach access area.

Day Use Facilities: Restrooms; medium-sized parking lot.

Overnight Facilities: 82 campsites, including 42 with partial hookups, in 2 sections; sites are small to small+, level, with minimal to fair separation; hookup pads are paved, medium to long, parallel pull-throughs; standard pads are mostly short to medium-length straight-ins; excellent tent-pitching possibilities in the standard section; fire rings; firewood is usually for sale, or b-y-o; water at several faucets; restrooms with showers; paved driveways; groceries nearby; adequate+ supplies and services are available within 3 miles.

Activities & Attractions: Trails from the campground along the lagoon and to the beach; lagoon interpretive trail (a guide pamphlet is available); nature programs; beach access; Pismo Dunes SVRA, adjacent.

Natural Features: Located on a moderately to densely wooded flat (campground) or on an open beach (day use); campsites are lightly to moderately shaded/sheltered by large hardwoods, tall conifers, and bushes; Oceano Lagoon, adjacent to the campground, and high dunes provide added natural interest; total park area is 1050 acres; sea level.

Season & Fees: Open all year; please see Appendix for reservation information, park entry and campground fees.

Mail & Phone: Pismo State Beach, 555 Pier Avenue, Oceano, CA 93445; ☎(805) 489-2684.

Park Notes: When the tide is out, there are several square miles of sand that you can wander out onto. Don't forget to bring your clam gun. The beach is world famous for its Pismo clams and you might bag a 'keeper'. (The Pismo mollusks once were so plentiful that settlers plowed the beach to harvest them, then used the 'crop' as fertilizer and livestock feed.) Oceano Lagoon, from which this section of the park takes its name, is a man-made freshwater pond dredged from the marshlands in the early 1900's. There are a couple of disadvantages to camping in the sites adjacent to the lagoon, especially if you're easily 'bugged'. Nonetheless, those spots are some of the more naturally interesting ones in the campground. Unlike most state parks and beaches on this section of the coast, Pismo's Oceano and North Beach units are within moderate walking distances of plenty of goods and services. They're handy places to be if you run out of beans and wienies, or you're just "born to shop".

▲ California 153

POINT SAL
State Beach

Location: Central California Coast south of San Luis Obispo.

Access: From California State Highway 1 at milepost 47 +.2 (1.8 miles south of the junction of Highway 1 & State Highway 166 near Guadalupe, 8 miles northwest of Orcutt), head west on Brown Road for 9 miles (paved for the first 5 miles, then gravel/dirt) to the park.

Day Use Facilities: Small parking area.

Overnight Facilities: None; nearest public campground is in Pismo State Beach.

Activities & Attractions: Beachcombing; fishing.

Natural Features: Located on a cove backed by a bluff and bordered by rocky headlands; park area is 84 acres; sea level.

Season & Fees: Open all year, subject to weather conditions.

Mail & Phone: c/o La Purisima Mission State Historic Park, 2295 Purisima Road, Lompoc, CA 93436; ☎(805) 733-3713 or☎(805) 733-1303.

Park Notes: Point Sal is a lonely little spot on a wild section of coast at the north tip of Vandenberg AFB. The first half of the route is fairly easy going up a canyon. Most of the last four miles to the beach are on a gravel road which slithers up and over the steep slopes of Point Sal Ridge. During and just after any appreciable rainfall, the road is usually closed at a point only four miles from the highway, so taking off afoot would involve a long hike to the beach. If you want to see the place during a spell of good weather, the park people at La Purisima Mission may be able to apprise you of current road conditions.

▲ California 154 ♿

LA PURISIMA MISSION
State Historic Park

Location: Southern California northwest of Santa Barbara.

Access: From California State Highway 246 at a point 12.5 miles west of U.S. 101 at Buellton and 4.5 miles northeast of Lompoc, proceed northwest on Purisima Road for 0.8 mile, then turn north (right) into the park. **Alternate Access:** From California State Highway 1 at its junction with Santa Barbara County Road S20 (3 miles north of Lompoc) proceed southeast on Purisima Road for 2 miles to the park turnoff.

Day Use Facilities: Medium-sized picnic area; drinking water; restrooms; medium-large parking lot.

Overnight Facilities: None; nearest public campground is in Gaviota State Park.

Activities & Attractions: Complete reconstruction of an Early California Spanish mission; paved walkways throughout the grounds; visitor center with historical exhibits, including dioramas; historical and natural interpretive programs and guided tours scheduled regularly throughout the year (a calendar is available upon request).

Natural Features: Located in *La Canada de los Berros* (Canyon of the Watercress) in the Purisima Hills on the north edge of the Santa Ynez Valley; park vegetation consists of immense tracts of grass, and stands of hardwoods; picnic sites are nicely shaded; park area is 967 acres; elevation 100´.

Season & Fees: Open all year; please see Appendix for park entry fees.

Mail & Phone: La Purisima Mission State Historic Park, 2295 Purisima Road, Lompoc, CA 93436; ☎(805) 733-3713 or☎(805) 733-1303.

Park Notes: *Mission la Purisima Concepcion de Maria Santisima* was founded on December 8, 1787 (the Roman Catholic observance of the Immaculate Conception) by Franciscan Padre Fermin De Lasuen, as the eleventh of the twenty-one California missions. The original site was three miles south of here, but earthquakes destroyed the first buildings and the mission was re-established in the present location in 1812. The mission served the Chumash Indians and taught them not only religion but agricultural and industrial arts as well. But a 'secularization' (i.e., land grab) of the California missions by the Mexican governors in the 1830's led to the Franciscans' withdrawal from this mission in 1834. Exactly 100 years later, a consortium of private and religious organizations, plus local and state agencies, donated or purchased land for La Purisima's renewal; the CCC excavated the site and began to rebuild the structures as authentically as possible. The tens of thousands of square feet of church, courtyards, living quarters, workshops, gardens and orchards now make up what is said to be the only completely restored mission in the Western United States.

▲ **California 155** ♿

GAVIOTA
State Park

Location: Southern California Coast west of Santa Barbara.

Access: From U.S Highway 101 at milepost 46 +.3 (10 miles south of Buellton, 1 mile west of Gaviota, 32 miles west of Santa Barbara) turn southwest onto Gaviota Beach Road and proceed 0.3 mile to a fork; take the left fork for 0.1 mile to the beach and campground. (Note: if northbound on U.S. 101, you'll have to figure out an appropriate way to get into the southbound lanes on the 4-lane, undivided highway in order to get onto the park road.)

Day Use Facilities: Small picnic area; restrooms; large parking lot; concession stand.

Overnight Facilities: 59 campsites; (hike-bike sites are also available); most sites are very snug rectangles, level, in basically a parking lot-type arrangement in several parallel rows; parking areas are hard-surfaced, short straight-ins or short+ pull-offs; small tent areas in some sites, none in others; fire rings or barbecue grills; b-y-o firewood; water at central faucets; (b-y-o drinking water is recommended); restrooms with showers, plus auxiliary vaults; paved driveways; limited supplies and services are available in Buellton.

Activities & Attractions: Swimming beach; hiking and equestrian trails, including a short trail to a hot springs area and a trail which leads into adjacent Los Padres National Forest and to the summit of 2400´ Gaviota Peak; (trails are accessed from near the junction of Highways 101 & 1 at the upper end of the park); fishing; boat launch; pier.

Natural Features: Located at the lower end of a canyon (Canada de la Gaviota) on and near a small beach (day use area and campground); a small creek flows past the campground; rows of large hardwoods provide light to medium shade/shelter; remainder of the park is on rocky, grassy, tree-and-brush-dotted hills and low mountains; park area is 2776 acres; sea level to 800´.

Season & Fees: Open all year; please see Appendix for reservation information, park entry and campground fees.

Mail & Phone: c/o CDPR Gaviota District Office, #10 Refugio Beach Road, Goleta, CA 93117; ☎(805) 968-3294.

Park Notes: Seeing only this small beach with its close-quartered campground might lead you to wonder if Gaviota is little more than a state beach with a state park signboard. (Glancing skyward to the railroad trestle which looms over the place might raise a question or two, as well.) But the park's territory goes east from the beach for two miles to the junction of U.S. 101 & State Highway 1, and flanks Highway 101 for about a mile on either side of the road, so there's still room for a measure of seclusion here. If you're not very deep into beach play or hiking but still want to stick around for a while, you might consider taking a side trip to the unique city of Solvang, three miles southeast of Buellton. Solvang lays claim to the title "Danish Capital of America", and probably is the largest of the European-motif communities in the West. The town's architectural style is pure Scandinavian gingerbread. (Or is it Danish pastry?)

▲ California 156 ♿

REFUGIO
State Beach

Location: Southern California Coast west of Santa Barbara.

Access: From U.S. Highway 101 near milepost 36 +.5 (9 miles east of Gaviota, 22 miles west of Santa Barbara), take the Refugio Road Exit, then from the south side of the freeway, go southwest on Refugio Road for 0.4 mile to the park entrance station. (If you're northbound on U.S. 101, you'll need to take a freeway underpass to get onto the park road.)

Day Use Facilities: Large picnic area; drinking water; restrooms; large parking lot; concession stand

Overnight Facilities: 85 campsites in 2 sections; (hike-bike sites and a large group camp are also available); sites are very small to small, level, with minimal to fair separation; sites in the south section are perhaps a little larger and better-separated than those in the other loop; parking pads are gravel/dirt, mostly short straight-ins; small tent areas; fire rings; firewood is usually for sale, or b-y-o; water at several faucets; restrooms with showers; paved driveways; complete supplies and services are available in Santa Barbara.

Activities & Attractions: Swimming beach; surf fishing.

Natural Features: Located along and near a small cove on the Santa Barbara Channel; the park has lots of short and tall palms, big hardwoods, shrubbery, and open, expansive lawns; picnic sites are minimally to very lightly shaded, most campsites are well shaded and sheltered; bordered by the Santa Ynez Mountains to the north; park area is 85 acres; sea level.

Season & Fees: Open all year; please see Appendix for reservation information, park entry and campground fees.

Mail & Phone: Refugio State Beach, #10 Refugio Beach Road, Goleta, CA 93117; ☎(805) 968-3294.

Park Notes: Refugio is one of the best state beaches in terms of landscaping. On an off-season weekend, it would be a very nice place to spend some leisure time. All three beaches on this east-west segment of the coast benefit from direct southerly exposure and are fairly well sheltered from heavy seas when a norther' blows down the coast. The Channel Islands provide a measure of protection from southerly seas as well.

▲ California 157 ♿

EL CAPITAN
State Beach

Location: Southern California Coast west of Santa Barbara.

Access: From U.S. Highway 101 at milepost 34 (11 miles east of Gaviota, 20 miles west of Santa Barbara), turn south onto the park access road for 0.2 mile to the park entrance station; continue ahead to the day use area, or swing right, into the campground.

Day Use Facilities: Several small or medium-sized picnic areas; drinking water; restrooms; large parking lot; concession stand.

Overnight Facilities: 142 campsites in 4 loops; (hike-bike sites, enroute sites and 3 group camps are also available); sites are small or small+, generally level, with nominal to fair separation; parking pads are paved, short straight-ins, but many are extra wide; medium to large areas for tents; fire rings; firewood is usually for sale, or b-y-o; water at several faucets; restrooms with showers; holding tank disposal station; paved driveways; complete supplies and services are available in Santa Barbara.

Activities & Attractions: Beach access; swimming areas; surf fishing for perch, bass and halibut; small interpretive center.

Natural Features: Located along the beach and on a bluff overlooking the Santa Barbara Channel; medium-dense to dense hardwoods provide good to excellent shelter/shade for campsites; (like several other campgrounds along the coast, some sites are close to railroad tracks and to the highway, but you can't have everything); the Santa Ynez Mountains rise just north of the park; park area is 168 acres; sea level.

Season & Fees: Open all year; please see Appendix for reservation information, park entry and campground fees.

Mail & Phone: c/o CDPR Gaviota District Office, #10 Refugio Beach Road, Goleta, CA 93117; ☎(805) 968-3294.

Park Notes: El Capitan State Beach and the other two state park units near here (Refugio and Gaviota) were once part of *Rancho Nuestra Sonora del Refugio*, ('Our Lady of Refuge Ranch') which stretched from here westerly to near Point Conception, south of Lompoc. The 25-mile band of coastline, hills and innumerable canyons on the south slopes of the Santa Ynez Mountains was originally owned by Jose Francisco de Ortega, who was addressed as "*El Capitan*".

▲ **California 158**

CHUMASH PAINTED CAVE

State Historic Park

Location: Southern California northwest of Santa Barbara.

Access: From California State Highway 154 at milepost 24 +.4 (8 miles northwest of U.S. 101 in Santa Barbara, 16 miles southwest of Santa Ynez), go east on Camino Cielo (paved) for 2 miles; turn south (right) onto Painted Cave Road (paved) and proceed 0.7 mile and find a place to park in the hamlet of Painted Cave; continue on foot down Painted Cave Road for another 0.5 mile to the park. (Note: if you really *must* see the cave, it *probably* would be best to use the foregoing 'back door' approach and park your vehicle 'on top', then walk down Painted Cave Road to the cave, avoiding the locals as they whip around the curves on the one-lane track; you *could* drive north from Highway 154 milepost 26 +.7, *up* Painted Cave Road for 2 miles, but just remember that mountain driving protocol suggests that the vehicle coming *down* usually has the right-of-way.)

Day Use Facilities: Very small (cycle-size) roadside pull-off.

Overnight Facilities: None; nearest public campground is in Lake Cachuma county park, 10 miles northwest.

Activities & Attractions: Short trail to a shallow cave containing Chumash Indian petroglyphs.

Natural Features: Located on a hillside in the lightly forested Santa Ynez Mountains; park area is 7 acres; elevation 1800´.

Season & Fees: Open all year; (no fee).

Mail & Phone: c/o CDPR Gaviota District Office, #10 Refugio Beach Road, Goleta, CA 93117; ☎(805) 968-3294.

Park Notes: Chumash Indians were the original inhabitants of the Southern California coastal region and the cave contains a gallery of rock art left behind by imaginative aboriginal artisans.

California 159

El Presidio de Santa Barbara
State Historic Park

Location: Southern California in Santa Barbara.

Access: From U.S. Highway 101 near milepost 13 +.5 on the south/east side of Santa Barbara, turn northwest (i.e., right if coming upcoast) onto Santa Barbara Street and proceed 0.6 mile to the park, at the corner of Santa Barbara Street & Canon Perdido Street, on your left.

Day Use Facilities: Small sitting area in a courtyard; (limited streetside parking is available).

Overnight Facilities: None; nearest public campground is in El Capitan State Beach.

Activities & Attractions: Self-guided tour of the replicated structures or sites of the first buildings in Santa Barbara, founded in 1782, including 1 original building (comprehensive, illustrated guide booklets printed in English or Spanish are available); guided tours available by reservation.

Natural Features: Located in-town; landscaping is continuously undergoing restoration; park area is 2 acres; elevation 100´.

Season & Fees: Open all year; operated by the Santa Barbara Trust for Historic Preservation.

Mail & Phone: El Presidio de Santa Barbara State Historic Park, 123 East Canon Perdido Street, P.O. Box 388, Santa Barbara, CA 93102; ☎(805) 966-9719.

Park Notes: This ambitious project was undertaken by the local historical organization in order to preserve the deepest roots of the City of Santa Barbara. Only one small building of the original Royal Presidio remains, but the eventual reconstruction of the entire complex is planned. Already rebuilt are the chapel and adjacent structures. Because the original site straddles Santa Barbara and Canon Perdido Streets and modern businesses occupy these downtown blocks, a considerable amount of rerouting and relocating will have to be accomplished. Plans call for putting the completed buildings to use for interpretive, educational, civic and limited commercial purposes.

California 160 ♿

Carpinteria
State Beach

Location: Southern California Coast northwest of Ventura.

Access: From U.S. Highway 101 in Carpinteria, take the Casitas Pass Road/California State Highway 224 Exit at milepost 2 +.6; proceed west on Highway 224 to Carpinteria Avenue, north on Carpinteria Avenue to Palm Avenue, then west on Palm Avenue to the park, for a total of 0.75 mile from the freeway.

Day Use Facilities: Large picnic area; large group ramada (sun shelter); drinking water; restrooms; large main parking lot; secondary parking lot and good beach access at the far south end of the park.

Overnight Facilities: 262 campsites, including 86 with full hookups; (hike/bike sites are also available); sites are very small to small+, level, with zilch to nominal separation; most parking pads are paved, short to medium-length straight-ins; parking slots in the hookup section are very short, double-wide straight-ins; some pull-off/parallel parking for longer rv's; enough space for small to medium-sized tents; fire rings; firewood is usually for sale, or b-y-o; water at faucets throughout; restrooms with showers; holding tank disposal station; paved driveways; adequate+ supplies and services are available in Carpinteria.

Activities & Attractions: Beachcombing; swimming; fitness area; clamming; visitor center with displays about whale-watching, tide pools, Chumash Indians.

Natural Features: Located on level terrain at the edge of the beach; vegetation consists of very light to medium-dense, large hardwoods and conifers, a few palms, and large, grassy areas; park area is 84 acres; sea level.

Season & Fees: Open all year; please see Appendix for reservation information, park entry and campground fees.

Mail & Phone: Mail c/o CDPR Channel Coast District Office, 24 East Main Street, Ventura, CA 93001; park phone ☎(805) 684-2811.

Park Notes: The surroundings are generally quite nice, and thus the place is really packed most of the summer. Good views of the Channel Islands.

California 161

EMMA WOOD
State Beach

Location: Southern California Coast northwest of Ventura.

Access: From U.S. Highway 101 (northbound) near milepost 32 +.5 (3 miles northwest of Ventura), from the east side of the freeway proceed through the underpass to the west side, then go south on a frontage road for 0.7 mile to the park. **Alternate Access:** From U.S. 101 (southbound), the simplest access is just to drive past the park and get off the freeway at the next exit, 1 mile southeast of the park, then double-back northwest to the above-mentioned limited (north-off/south-on) exit. (Note: there's limited turnaround space at the south end of the park driveway.)

Day Use Facilities: Small parking lot; vault facilities.

Overnight Facilities: 61 campsites; (a group camp is also available); sites are very small, with nil separation; parking slots are paved, short straight-ins; enough space for small to medium-sized tents; no drinking water; vault facilities; holding tank disposal station; paved driveways; complete supplies and services are available in Ventura.

Activities & Attractions: Unrestricted ocean views.

Natural Features: Located on a narrow strip of land on a short shelf above a mile-long, rocky and sandy beach; sites are unsheltered.

Season & Fees: Open all year; $10.00 for an individual campsite; for individual campsite reservations, contact the local office listed below; for the group camp, please see Appendix for reservation information and campground fees; operated cooperatively by the county and the state.

Mail & Phone: Individual campsites operated by Ventura County: 800 South Victoria Avenue, Ventura, CA 93009; ☎(805) 654-3951; group camp operated by the state, phone ☎(805) 643-7532 or ☎(805) 654-4611.

Park Notes: The park land, which was originally donated to the state, served as an artillery site during WWII. At high tide, your trailer tongue will be lapping sea water. The freeway is fairly close behind and above the beach, but the railroad tracks between '101 and the park would probably block any misguided vehicles from dropping into your campsite. Camping is also available locally at three Ventura County beach parks: Faria, Rincon Parkway, and Hobson. Restrooms with showers are available there. All three parks are within six miles northwest of here.

California

Los Angeles Basin

California 162 ♿

SAN BUENAVENTURA
State Beach

Location: Southern California Coast in Ventura.

Access: From U.S. Highway 101 in midtown Ventura near milepost 28, take the Seaward Avenue Exit, proceed to the south/west side of the freeway then go southwest on Seaward Avenue and across Harbor Boulevard to the first intersection; turn northwest (right) onto Pierpont Drive and proceed 0.3 mile to the park.

Day Use Facilities: Very large picnic area; windbreaks for tables; drinking water; restrooms and freshwater rinse showers; very large parking lot; concession stand, large sun shelter.

Overnight Facilities: None; nearest public campground is in McGrath State Beach.

Activities & Attractions: Exercise course; bicycle path; swimming; fishing.

Natural Features: Located on an oceanside flat; park vegetation consists of several acres of lawns well-dotted with conifers and palms; a low dune lies between the beach and the day use area; hills and low mountains rise a few miles to the east; park area is 114 acres; sea level.

Season & Fees: Open all year; please see Appendix for park entry fees.

Mail & Phone: c/o CDPR Channel Coast District Office, 24 East Main Street, Ventura, CA 93001; ☎(805) 654-4611.

Park Notes: The beach is named for Mission San Buenaventura, located in midtown Ventura, the ninth and last mission founded by Padre Junipero Serra. The mission is known for its beautiful gardens, but if you don't have time to get there too, the beach park's surroundings will do nicely.

▲ **California 163** ♿

McGRATH
State Beach

Location: Southern California Coast west of Oxnard.

Access: From U.S. Highway 101 near milepost 28 +.5 in Ventura, take the Seaward Avenue Exit, then from the south/west side of the freeway, turn southeast (left) onto Harbor Boulevard and go southeast and south for 3 miles; turn west (right) onto the park access road and go 0.15 mile to the park entrance station; the first campsites are 0.15 mile beyond the entrance. **Alternate Access:** From California State Highway 1 (Oxnard Boulevard) in Oxnard, at a point 1 mile south of the junction of State Highway 1 & U.S. Highway 101 turn west onto Gonzales Road and travel 4.5 miles; turn north (right) onto Harbor Boulevard and proceed 0.6 mile; turn west (left) onto the park access road and continue as above.

Day Use Facilities: Medium-sized parking lot.

Overnight Facilities: 174 campsites; (a hike/bike site is also available); sites are small to small+, level, with nominal to fairly good separation; parking pads are paved, short to medium-length straight-ins; large, grassy areas for tents; fire rings; b-y-o firewood; water at central faucets; restrooms with showers; disposal station; paved driveways; complete supplies and services are available in Ventura and Oxnard.

Activities & Attractions: Beachcombing; trail to the beach; Santa Clara River Nature Trail; small visitor center; campfire center; Channel Islands NP visitor center, 1 mile north.

Natural Features: Located along and near an ocean beach; campground is on the lee side of a dune and has large expanses of grass bordered by dense bushes and medium-height trees; Santa Clara Estuary Natural Preserve, adjacent; park area is 295 acres; sea level.

Season & Fees: Open all year; please see Appendix for reservation information, park entry and campground fees.

Mail & Phone: McGrath State Beach, 2211 Harbor Boulevard, Ventura, CA 93001; ☎(805) 654-4744

Park Notes: McGrath's campground is unique among California camps. The sites are situated in six clusters or pods, with three perfectly circular cul-de-sacs within each pod. The parking pads radiate outward at an angle from each cul-de-sac. The entire campground, therefore, if you were to view it from above (or on the campground map), would resemble an assemblage of gears—for an 18-speed transmission, a Rube Goldberg contraption, or maybe a cuckoo clock.

▲ **California 164** ♿

POINT MUGU:
SYCAMORE
State Park

Location: Southern California Coast southeast of Oxnard.

Access: From California State Highway 1 at milepost 4 +.4 (14 miles southeast of Oxnard, 20 miles northwest of Malibu) turn north (i.e., left if approaching from Oxnard) and proceed 0.15 mile to the Sycamore Canyon Campground entrance station and the campground; or turn south into the Sycamore Cove day use area.

Day Use Facilities: Medium-sized picnic area; drinking water; restrooms with freshwater rinse showers; large parking lot.

Overnight Facilities: 58 campsites; (hike-bike sites in the campground, plus individual and group backcountry camps are also available); sites are small+, essentially level, with minimal to fair separation; parking pads are paved, mostly short straight-ins, some are extra wide; small to medium-sized tent areas; fire rings; b-y-o firewood; water at central faucets; restrooms with showers; holding tank disposal station; paved driveways; complete supplies and services are available in Oxnard.

Activities & Attractions: Swimming, surfing, windsurfing; more than 70 miles of hiking and equestrian trails; mountain bike travel on designated fire roads; (a large, detailed park brochure/trail map with contour lines is available); trailhead parking here for the Sycamore Canyon Trail, and also 2 miles north at the La Jolla Canyon trailhead; equestrian access and parking area is off of Potrero Road at Pinehill Street, in the northeast corner of the state park on the south edge of the community of Newbury Park.

Natural Features: Located at the mouth of Sycamore Canyon in the Santa Monica Mountains; picnic sites are along the beach; campsites are on the canyon floor, several hundred yards from the beach and are lightly to moderately shaded/sheltered by bushes and trees; canyon slopes are tree-and-brush-covered; Boney Mountain State Wilderness is adjacent to the east boundary of the park; total park area is 15,000 acres; elevation sea level (Sycamore) to 1500´ (highland areas).

Season & Fees: Open all year; please see Appendix for reservation information, park entry and campground fees.

Mail & Phone: c/o CDPR Santa Monica Mountains District Office, 2860A Camino Dod Rios, Newbury Park, CA 91320; ☎(818) 706-1310 or☎(805) 499-2112.

Park Notes: The park headquarters are at Sycamore Cove, so this would be a good place to stop and get in-depth info about the area's backcountry hiking and camping possibilities. Lower Sycamore Canyon's environmental conditions are nearly perfect for the wintering of monarch butterflies, and millions of the vividly marked and colored insects migrate here in early fall. Monarchs aren't the only noteworthy visitors to the park: California gray whales reportedly have demonstrated a certain preference for the shallow waters just offshore of the park's beaches and can often be seen during their annual December to May migration.

▲ **California 165**

POINT MUGU:
LA JOLLA BEACH
State Park

Location: Southern California Coast southeast of Oxnard.

Access: From California State Highway 1 at milepost 5 +.9 (13 miles southeast of Oxnard, 21 miles northwest of Malibu) turn south (i.e., right, if approaching from Oxnard) into the campground.

Day Use Facilities: None; nearest picnic area is in the park's Sycamore Cove section.

Overnight Facilities: 102 (semi-primitive) campsites in 2 sections; sites are very small with nil separation; parking surfaces are paved, short straight-ins or medium-length pull-offs; fire rings; b-y-o firewood; water at central faucets; vault facilities; outside, freshwater rinse showers; paved driveways; complete supplies and services are available in Oxnard.

Activities & Attractions: Swimming, surfing, windsurfing; La Jolla Canyon trailhead parking area, on the north side of the highway, 0.1 mile west of the campground entrance; please see additional backcountry info in the park's 'Sycamore' section.

Natural Features: Located along an open, ocean beach; campground vegetation consists of a small amount of brush and grass; the low, rocky and brushy Santa Monica Mountains rise just behind the beach; sea level.

Season & Fees: Open all year; please see Appendix for reservation information, park entry and campground fees.

Mail & Phone: c/o CDPR Santa Monica Mountains District Office, 2860A Camino Dos Rios, Newbury Park, CA 91320; ☎(818) 706-1310 or ☎(805) 499-2112.

Park Notes: Although the physical facilities in this section of the park are pretty basic, the local scenery is pretty good. A large, haystack rock adds interest to the shoreline at Point Mugu itself, at the northwest edge of the park, just up the coast from this beach. The park has a total of about five miles of ocean frontage, and you can see much of it from here. In fact, *Mugu* is derived from the Chumash Indian word *muwu*, meaning "beach".

▲ **California 166** ♿

LEO CARRILLO
State Beach

Location: Southern California Coast west of Santa Monica.

Access: From California State Highway 1 at milepost 62 +.2 (0.6 mile south of the Los Angeles-Ventura county line, 20 miles south of Oxnard, 28 miles northwest of Santa Monica,) turn east to the park entrance; Canyon section is to the east of the entrance; Beachside section is accessible via an underpass. (Vehicles must be less than 8 feet high to use the underpass.)

Day Use Facilities: Restrooms; large parking lot; concession stand.

Overnight Facilities: 50 campsites in the Beach section, 78 sites in the Canyon section; (hike-bike sites and a walk-in group camp are also available); sites in the Beach section are in a paved parking lot arrangement, with short, level, straight-in parking slots and fireplaces; Canyon section has conventional, small+, acceptably level, fairly well-separated sites with paved, short+ parking pads and fire rings; firewood is usually for sale, or b-y-o; water at several faucets; restrooms with showers; holding tank disposal station; paved driveways; nearest sources of adequate supplies are in Oxnard and Santa Monica.

Activities & Attractions: Swimming beach; surf fishing; several miles of hiking trails; guided nature walks.

Natural Features: Located on the beach and in a canyon a few hundred yards from the beach; very little vegetation or shelter in the beach section; large hardwoods, shrubs and grass in the canyon section; park area is 1600 acres; sea level to 900´.

Season & Fees: Open all year; please see Appendix for reservation information, park entry and campground fees.

Mail & Phone: c/o CDPR Santa Monica Mountains District Office, 2860A Camino Dos Rios, Newbury Park, CA 91320; ☎(818) 706-1310 or ☎(805) 499-2112 or ☎(805) 987-3303.

Park Notes: If you don't *have* to have a campsite with a continuous ocean view, the very nice, wooded, Canyon section might be considered the area of choice here. Leo Carrillo had many starring roles in the golden days of radio and motion pictures, and was active in civic affairs. But he may be best-known for his weekly performances with co-star Duncan Ranaldo in the early days of television as the jovial sidekick of the *Cisco Kid*. (Remember that exuberant exchange at the end of each show as the dashing duo rode off on horseback to new adventures in the Old West: "Oh, Pancho!" "Ohhhhh, Cisco!")

Special Section

STRING OF PEARLS
Los Angeles Coast State Beaches

Beginning near the Los Angeles-Ventura county line just northwest of Malibu and extending down to the Los Angeles-Orange county line near Long Beach is a string of day-use state beaches. Although the beaches vary in size, they are homogeneous in other respects. Most are accessible from

California State Highway 1, called the Pacific Coast Highway along this section of the coast. Most beaches have sizable parking lots and restrooms, plus ample sand and seawater. Many have volleyball courts and fire rings. A fee of four or five dollars is typically charged for parking.

Most of these units are operated by departments of city or county governments. The operating agreements between the state and the local entities are similar to a concession operation, but they are ongoing, essentially permanent arrangements. The rationale behind localization of management of the majority of these beach properties is evident: the beaches are used almost exclusively by residents of the local area and their guests. Because of these and other similarities, information about the L.A. beaches is provided in the following abbreviated listing. (Information about Malibu Lagoon State Beach, because of its unique offerings, is given in the standard text following this section.) The beaches are listed north to south.

California 167

Robert H. Meyer
State Beaches

Located at three points along Highway 1 near its junction with State Highway 23, 3 miles southeast of the L.A.-Ventura county line, 16 miles west of Malibu; CDPR Santa Monica Mountains District Office, ☎(818) 706-1310 or ☎(805) 499-2112.

California 168

Point Dume
State Beach

Located 0.3 mile south of Highway 1 near its junction with L.A. County Road N9, 8 miles west of Malibu; Los Angeles County Division of Beaches and Harbors, ☎(213) 305-9503.

California 169

Dan Blocker
State Beach

Located on Highway 1 between Corral Canyon Road and Latigo Canyon Road, 4 miles west of Malibu; L. A. County Division of Beaches and Harbors, ☎(213) 305-9503.

California 170

Las Tunas
State Beach

Located on Highway 1 at a point 1.3 miles west of the junction of Highway 1 & State Highway 27 in the community of Topanga Beach; L. A. County Division of Beaches and Harbors, ☎(213) 305-9503.

California 171

Topanga
State Beach

Located along Highway 1 at its junction with State Highway 27 in the community of Topanga Beach; L. A. County Division of Beaches and Harbors, ☎(213) 305-9503.

California 172

Will Rogers
State Beach

Located along Highway 1 between its junctions with Sunset Boulevard and Chautauqua Boulevard in Pacific Palisades; (4 miles west of I-10 in Santa Monica); L.A. County Division of Beaches and Harbors, ☎(213) 305-9503.

California 173

Santa Monica
State Beach

Located in Santa Monica along a 3-mile stretch of Ocean Avenue, north and south of Ocean's junction with Interstate 10; City of Santa Monica Parks & Recreation

Department, ☎(213) 305-9545 or ☎(213) 394-3266.

▲ California 174

Dockweiler
State Beach

Located along a 2.5 mile section of Vista Del Mar Boulevard between the cities of El Segundo and Marina Del Rey, 2 miles west of Highway 1; L. A. County Division of Beaches and Harbors, ☎(213) 305-9503.

▲ California 175

Manhattan
State Beach

Located along Highland Avenue in the city of Manhattan Beach, 0.2 mile west of Highway 1; L. A. County Division of Beaches and Harbors, ☎(213) 305-9503.

▲ California 176

Redondo
State Beach

Located along Highway 1 between the cities of Redondo Beach and Palos Verdes Estates; L. A. County Division of Beaches and Harbors, ☎(213) 305-9503.

▲ California 177

Royal Palms
State Beach

Located on Paseo Del Mar in San Pedro, 2 miles south of Highway 1, via Western Avenue; L. A. County Division of Beaches and Harbors, ☎(213) 305-9503.

An additional note:

Traffic on the Pacific Coast Highway moves along at a good clip, day or night, rain or shine. If you're unfamiliar with the territory and are headed upcoast, (i.e., on the opposite side of the highway from the beach), it might pay to scope out the beach access as you fly by, then find a good spot to do a '180' for another pass on the ocean side of the coast road. All of the above listed locations are approximate because mileposts and midtown fixes are scarce in this area.

▲ California 178 ♿

Malibu Creek
State Park

Location: Southern California northwest of Los Angeles.

Access: From U.S. Highway 101 (Ventura Freeway) at the Las Virgenes Road/Malibu Canyon Exit (7 miles east of Thousand Oaks, 6 miles west of Woodland Hills), travel south on Las Virgenes Road/L.A. County Road N1 for 3.5 miles; turn west (right) onto the park access road for 0.1 mile to the entrance station; proceed past the entrance for 0.25 mile, then turn left to the picnic area; or continue southwest and south for another 0.4 mile to the campground. **Alternate Access:** From California State Highway 1 at a point 2 miles west of Malibu, head north on Malibu Canyon Road/L.A. County Road N1 for 6 miles to the park access road and continue as above.

Day Use Facilities: Medium-sized picnic area; group picnic area; drinking water; restrooms; large parking lots for day users, visitor center and trail users.

Overnight Facilities: 63 campsites; (hike/bike campsites and 2 group camps are also available); sites are small+, with nominal separation; parking pads are hard-surfaced, short straight-ins; additional leveling will be required in some sites; enough space for just about any-size tent; fireplaces; charcoal fires only; water at several faucets; restrooms with showers; holding tank disposal station; paved driveways; complete supplies and services are available in Thousand Oaks and Woodland Hills.

Activities & Attractions: More than 15 miles of hike/horse trails and 15 miles of fire roads; mountain bikes are limited to designated fire roads; (a large, detailed park brochure/map with contour lines is available from the park office); nature trail for visually handicapped individuals; fishing for rainbow trout (stocked in cooler seasons), bass, bluegill, sunfish, bullheads; visitor center (accessible via a trail); campfire center.

Natural Features: Located in Malibu Canyon and in the craggy Santa Monica Mountains west of the canyon; the park land and its associated natural preserves lie along the banks of Malibu Creek (and one or both sides of Road N1) from near the Pacific Ocean to a point 2 miles north of the main park entrance, as well as extensively west of the creek; picnic sites are unshaded, campsites are unshaded to very lightly shaded; total park area is 6000 acres; elevation 100´ to 2300´.

Season & Fees: Open all year; please see Appendix for reservation information, park entry and campground fees.

Mail & Phone: c/o CDPR Santa Monica Mountains District Office, 2860-A Camino Dos Rios, Newbury Park, CA 91320; ☎(818) 706-1310 or ☎(805) 987-3303.

Park Notes: Malibu Creek prides itself as being "on the boundary of two worlds ... the freeways, people and pressures of the Los Angeles Basin ... and within an easy walk are rugged cliffs and shady canyons, brushy fields and bedrock pools, solitude and silence". And that, in a nutshell, is what the park is all about. A bit of Hollywood is associated with the park: Most of the outdoor "location" scenes for the long-running TV series M*A*S*H were filmed here.

California 179 ♿

Malibu Lagoon

State Beach

Location: Southern California northwest of Los Angeles.

Access: From California State Highway 1 near milepost 47 on the north edge of Malibu, at the south end of the Malibu Creek bridge, turn west to a picnic area and the Adamson House; or near the north end of the bridge, turn west to the picnic area and beach trailhead parking lot.

Day Use Facilities: Picnic areas; drinking water; restrooms; 2 medium-sized parking lots.

Overnight Facilities: None; nearest public campground is in Malibu Creek State Park.

Activities & Attractions: Wildlife observation; guided tours of the restored Adamson House, a Spanish-Moorish style home built in 1929; a museum with exhibits related to the early history of Malibu is associated with the house; trail to the swimming beach; nature trail; fishing.

Natural Features: Located on an ocean beach along the banks of Malibu Creek and Malibu Lagoon, which includes a 10-acre saltwater marsh; park area is 76 acres; sea level.

Season & Fees: Open all year for day use; Adamson House open limited days and hours (please contact the museum for a current schedule); please see Appendix for park entry fees.

Mail & Phone: c/o CDPR Santa Monica Mountains District Office, 2860-A Camino Dos Rios, Newbury Park, CA 91320; ☎(818) 706-1310; museum phone ☎(213) 456-8432.

Park Notes: Malibu Lagoon is one of the few remaining wetland estuaries in Southern California, and it is a residence or stopover point for waterfowl, including pelicans, egrets and herons. The attractive, bright-walled Adamson House is noted for its exclusive use of ceramic tile produced by a now-defunct local pottery firm.

California 180

Topanga

State Park

Location: Southern California northwest of Los Angeles.

Access: From California State Highway 27 at milepost 4 +.7 (8 miles south of the junction of Highway 27 & U.S. 101 in Woodland Hills, 5 miles north of the junction of Highway 27 & State Highway 1 in Topanga Beach), turn east (i.e., left if approaching from '101) onto Entrada Road and wind steeply up for 1.1 mile to the park entrance station; continue ahead for 0.1 mile to the main parking lots and trailheads.

Day Use Facilities: Several small picnic areas; drinking water; restrooms; small-medium and medium-large parking lots.

Overnight Facilities: Primitive trail camps for hikers, bicyclists and equestrians (register with the park office); drinking water, vaults, hitch rails and water troughs; complete supplies and services are available in Woodland Hills; nearest standard public campground is in Malibu Creek State Park.

Activities & Attractions: More than 30 miles of hiking and equestrian trails; mountain biking on designated fire roads; nature trail (a guide pamphlet is available).

Natural Features: Located in and above Topanga Canyon in the Santa Monica Mountains east of the canyon; park vegetation consists mostly of stands of hardwoods, brush and open grassy sections; majority of the park is near-wilderness; park area is 9200 acres; elevation 1400´ to 2100´.

Season & Fees: Open all year; please see Appendix for park entry and camping fees.

Mail & Phone: Mail c/o CDPR Santa Monica Mountains District Office, 2860-A Camino Dos Rios, Newbury Park, CA 91320; park phone ☎(213) 455-2465.

Park Notes: Much of the vegetation within the park is representative of the drought-resistant ecological community known as *chaparral* which occurs extensively in Southern California. Interpretive displays here describe how the local Indians, now called the *Gabrielino*, used all of the plants of the chaparral for the necessities of life. They found ways to make food, fuel, soap, baskets, medicine and arrows from oak, sage, yucca, chamise, even poison oak—sort of in the same way the Indians of the Great Plains used 'all of the buffalo'. A lot of people come in just to have a fine picnic, but the park is best enjoyed by obtaining a good map of the area and hitting the trails. There's a lot of rugged country around here.

▲ **California 181** ♿

Los Encinos
State Historic Park

Location: Southern California north of Los Angeles.

Access: From U.S. Highway 101 in Encino at the Balboa Boulevard Exit (2 miles west of the junction of U.S. 101 & Interstate 405), proceed south on Balboa Boulevard for 0.7 mile into midtown Encino; turn east (left) onto Moorpark Street and go 0.15 mile to the park entrance (walk-in entry).

Day Use Facilities: Picnic tables and benches in several locations throughout the grounds; drinking water; restrooms; streetside parking.

Overnight Facilities: None; nearest public campground is in Malibu Creek State Park.

Activities & Attractions: Self-guided tours (a comprehensive guide pamphlet is available) of the well-preserved buildings and grounds of the nucleus of a ranch dating back to 1849; guided tour of interior of the ranch house/museum; special programs are held throughout the year.

Natural Features: Located in-town; park landscaping consists of large lawns well shaded by a variety of mature hardwoods, shrubs, prickly pear and palms; park area is 5 acres; elevation 800´.

Season & Fees: Open all year, Wednesday through Sunday, guided tour $2.00 (subject to change).

Mail & Phone: Los Encinos State Historic Park, 16756 Moorpark Street, Encino, CA 91436; ☎(818) 784-4849.

Park Notes: The park covers about a city block right in the heart of town and was once the heart of a 4500-acre ranch called the *Encino*. When you enter the park, you might at first assume that the two-story building was the main house and the long, low adobe structure which resembles a small motel was a guest house or bunk house. Actually, the reverse is true. The limestone-lined pond was built for irrigation and livestock watering, but now provides accommodations for the resident waterfowl population. Los Encinos SHP serves as a focal point of local and regional history and has earned quite a lot of community support and sponsorship.

California 182 ♿

Will Rogers
State Historic Park

Location: Southern California west of Los Angeles.

Access: From Interstate 405 at the Sunset Boulevard Exit in the Brentwood-Bel Air area west of Los Angeles (6 miles south of the junction of I-405 & U.S. 101, 3 miles north of the junction of I-405 & I-10) travel southwest on Sunset Boulevard for 4.5 miles; turn northerly (a hairpin right) onto Will Rogers State Park Road and proceed 0.6 mile to the park entrance.

Alternate Access: From California State Highway 1 near Pacific Palisades (2 miles northwest of the junction of State Highway 1 & I-10 in Santa Monica), proceed northerly on Chautauqua Boulevard for 1 mile, then turn northeast (right) onto Sunset Boulevard and continue for another mile to the park access road and continue as above. (Note: Sunset Boulevard is narrow, curvy, steep, with fast traffic; if you're pulling a trailer, an early Sunday morning visit might be your best bet.)

Day Use Facilities: Small picnic area; drinking water; restrooms; large parking lot.

Overnight Facilities: None; nearest public campground is in Malibu Creek State Park.

Activities & Attractions: Home of the early 20th century entertainer, film star and home-spun philosopher, Will Rogers; biographical film; self-guided tours of the main house and grounds (audio tour of the grounds); group tours (by reservation, contact the park office); Inspiration Point Trail (2-mile loop); nature trail; nature center; visitor center; occasional matches are held on the ranch's polo grounds.

Natural Features: Located on hilly terrain on the south slope of the Santa Monica Mountains above Santa Monica Canyon; the park is landscaped with large sections of lawns, tall hardwoods, conifers, evergreens and shrubs; park area is 186 acres; elevation 700´.

Season & Fees: Open all year; please see Appendix for park entry fees.

Mail & Phone: Will Rogers State Historic Park, 14253 Sunset Boulevard, Pacific Palisades, CA 90272; ☎(213) 454-8212.

Park Notes: Born in a small house near Oologah in Northeast Oklahoma in 1879, Will Rogers first earned a living as a cowboy on ranches in the green and gold hills of the Cherokee. He started into show business early in life as a trick roper, and by the 1930's had risen to the top of his profession as a humorist, film star, newspaper columnist and radio commentator. Depression Era politics was a favorite target: "I won't run for President no matter how bad the country will need a comedian by that time"; and "I'm not a member of any organized political party—I'm a Democrat". In line with his unassuming personality, Rogers referred to this property as a "ranch"; just about anyone else might call it an "estate". He died in an airplane crash in Alaska in 1935 and is buried in Claremore, Oklahoma. Rogers' unembroidered philosophy "I never met a man I didn't like" is one of twentieth century America's most-often quoted principles.

California 183 ♿

Los Angeles Arboretum
State and County Arboretum

Location: Southern California northeast of Los Angeles.

Access: From Interstate 210 in Arcadia at the Baldwin Avenue Exit (6 miles east of the junction of I-210 & State Highway 134 in Pasadena, 5 miles west of the junction of I-210 & I-605 in Duarte), proceed south on Baldwin Avenue for 0.3 mile, then turn west (right) into the main entrance of the park.

Day Use Facilities: Picnic area; drinking water; restrooms; several medium-large parking lots along the west side of Baldwin Avenue.

Overnight Facilities: None; nearest public campgrounds are on State Highway 2 north of Pasadena in Angeles National Forest.

Activities & Attractions: Superlative botanical gardens and a horticultural research center; (a "bloom calendar" listing the peak viewing periods of major flowering species within the arboretum is available); open-air tram tours, guided walking tours or self-guided tours; demonstrations for home gardeners, environmental education programs, flower shows, etc. are held regularly (a calendar of upcoming events is available).

Natural Features: Located amid a display of flowers, trees, plants and shrubs from around the world; spectacularly landscaped grounds include fountains, pools, waterfalls, a gingerbread cottage, and bird life; plenty of plants, pines, palms ponds and peacocks; park area is 127 acres; elevation 450´.

Season & Fees: Open all year; park entry fee $3.00 for adults, 75 cents for children (subject to change).

Mail & Phone: Los Angeles State and County Arboretum, 301 North Baldwin Avenue, Arcadia, CA 91006; ☎(818) 446-8251.

Park Notes: One of the arboretum's principal objectives is to research and select plants from around the world which are suitable for growing in Southern California. Plants are chosen because of their attractiveness, their tolerance for disease and pests in order to minimize the need for pesticides, and their efficient use of water in an increasingly water-deficient region. Since this *is* Los Angeles, you would expect World Class botanical gardens—and you'll see no less than that here. Spend a day and then come back for more.

▲ California 184 ♿

Pio Pico
State Historic Park

Location: Southern California east of Los Angeles.

Access: From Interstate 605 (northbound) in Whittier at the Whittier Boulevard Exit, at the bottom of the freeway ramp, turn left onto Whittier Boulevard, pass under the Interstate to the west side of the freeway, then almost immediately turn left onto Pioneer Boulevard; the park is on the southwest corner of Pioneer & Whittier. **Alternate Access:** From Interstate 605 (southbound) at the Whittier Boulevard Exit, from the end of the freeway ramp, turn left onto Whittier Boulevard, go 100 yards, then turn right onto Pioneer Boulevard and to the park.

Day Use Facilities: Small picnic area; drinking water; restrooms; small parking lot (streetside parking is available along Pioneer Boulevard).

Overnight Facilities: None; nearest public campgrounds are in Bolsa Chica and Huntington State Beaches.

Activities & Attractions: Home of the last governor of California under Mexican jurisdiction.

Natural Features: Located in a residential area; landscaping includes lawns, large hardwoods, cactus and a fountain; park area is 3 acres; elevation 50´.

Season & Fees: Open all year, Wednesday through Sunday (subject to change); please see Appendix for park entry fees.

Mail & Phone: Pio Pico State Historic Park, 6003 Pioneer Boulevard, Whittier, CA 90606; ☎(213) 695-1217.

Park Notes: *Hacienda de Gobernador Pio Pico*, the governor's mansion, is a modest, single-story, adobe house. Modest, perhaps by modern standards, but Pico was one of the most influential men in early California history. The hacienda was badly damaged in an earthquake and is undergoing a lengthy renewal.

▲ California 185

Watts Towers of Simon Rodia
State Historic Park

Location: Southern California in south-central Los Angeles.

Access: From Interstate 710 in Downey, take the Imperial Highway Exit and travel west on Imperial Highway for 3.6 miles; turn north (right) onto Wilmington Avenue and proceed 0.7 miles to 108th Street; go west on 108th Street for 1 block to Graham Avenue, then north on Graham for 1 block to 107th Street; the park is at the east end of 107th Street. **Alternate Access:** From Interstate 110 near the northeast corner of the city of Gardena, take the El Segundo Boulevard Exit and travel east on El Segundo Boulevard for 2.7 miles; turn north (left) onto Wilmington Avenue and proceed 1.7 miles to Wilmington & 108th. (Note: there are a jillion ways of getting here, but these two routes should provide hassle-free alternatives for someone unfamiliar with the area.)

Day Use Facilities: Sitting benches nearby; several public parking lots in the area.

Overnight Facilities: None; nearest public campground is in Bolsa Chica State Beach.

Activities & Attractions: Massive, outdoor freestyle sculptures.

Natural Features: Located in-town; park area is 2 acres.

Season & Fees: Open all year; guided tours on weekends, $2.00; operated by Los Angeles County.

Mail & Phone: c/o Watts Towers Arts Center, 1765 East 107th Street, Los Angeles, CA; ☎(213) 569-8181.

Park Notes: Italian immigrant Simon Rodia, working with concrete and conduit, bits of glass and broken tile, seashells and shards, handcrafted a cluster of open-framework towers and related structures between 1921 and 1954. Rodia used only the simplest of tools (and a safety belt) to build the monument. The three main towers are arranged to symbolize the masts of a ship. (Rodia's art was strongly influenced by travelers and he called this his "Marco Polo Ship".) The tallest of the forms reaches to 100 feet and can be seen from a quarter-mile around. In some ways, the towers resemble the work of an imaginative giant experimenting with an erector set. Rodia was thought by many to be a crackpot and was often ridiculed for his work. Vigilante groups, using social, legal and mechanical force, unsuccessfully attempted to topple the massive structures. Rodia completed his work at age 75. "Tired of giving" his emotional and physical energy to the project, he then left the neighborhood to live with family members elsewhere in California. Later, a community group was formed to preserve the sculptures. When asked why he built the towers, Rodia is said to have replied "I wanted to do something big for America".

▲ California 186 ♿

BOLSA CHICA
State Beach

Location: Southern California Coast between Long Beach and Huntington Beach.

Access: From California State Highway 1 near its intersection with Warner Avenue (4 miles north of Huntington Beach, 10 miles south of Long Beach) turn west into the park.

Day Use Facilities: Large picnic area; drinking water; numerous restrooms with freshwater rinse showers; very large parking lots (parking for a total of about 2500 cars); concession stand.

Overnight Facilities: 50 enroute campsites for self-contained vehicles in a paved parking lot arrangement; parking slots are paved, short straight-ins; (no tents); water at central faucets; restrooms with freshwater rinse showers; complete supplies and services are available in Huntington Beach.

Activities & Attractions: Swimming, surfing, windsurfing; 8 miles of bicycle lanes; roller skating; beach volleyball; grunion gathering and whale watching, seasonally; interpretive programs.

Natural Features: Located on 100 acres (about 1.4 miles) of sandy beach; Bolsa Chica Ecological Preserve, 1000 acres of coastal wetlands set-aside for viewing and studying bird and marine life, is adjacent to the beach.

Season & Fees: Open all year; please see Appendix for reservation information, park entry and campground fees.

Mail & Phone: Mail c/o CDPR Orange Coast District Office, 18331 Enterprise Lane, Huntington Beach, CA 92648; park phone ☎(714) 846-3460.

Park Notes: This long, wide, open, windswept beach is a favorite spot of 'do-ers', but there's plenty of room for a few thousand onlookers as well.

▲ **California 187** ♿

HUNTINGTON
State Beach

Location: Southern California Coast south of Los Angeles.

Access: From California State Highway 1 at its intersection with Brookhurst Street just north of the Santa Ana River crossing (south entrance) or from Highway 1 at its intersection with Beach Boulevard/State Highway 39 (north entrance) in the city of Huntington Beach, turn west into the park.

Day Use Facilities: Open picnicking; fire rings; drinking water; restrooms with freshwater rinse showers; enormous parking lots; concession stand.

Overnight Facilities: 60 enroute campsites for self-contained vehicles in a paved parking lot arrangement; parking slots are paved, short straight-ins; (no tents); water at central faucets; restrooms with freshwater rinse showers; holding tank disposal station; complete supplies and services are available within 3 miles.

Activities & Attractions: Swimming; surfing; fishing; beach volleyball.

Natural Features: Located on a 2-mile-long beach on the edge of an ocean plain; some small areas are landscaped with grass, plants and palms; park area is 78 acres; sea level.

Season & Fees: Open all year; please see Appendix for reservation information, park entry and campground fees.

Mail & Phone: Mail c/o CDPR Orange Coast District Office, 18331 Enterprise Lane, Huntington Beach, CA 92648; park phone ☎(714) 536-1454 or ☎(714) 536-1455.

Park Notes: This is a 'ditto' of Bolsa Chica in most respects. Huntington is said to have "world famous" (although perhaps not truly 'world class') surfing.

▲ **California 188**

CRYSTAL COVE
State Park

Location: Southern California Coast south of Long Beach.

Access: From California State Highway 1 at the following points: at milepost 12 +.3, (3 miles northwest of Laguna Beach, 3 miles southeast of Newport Beach) turn northeast onto a park access road and proceed 0.2 mile to the El Moro/Moro Canyon areas and the park visitor center; coastal access points are located near mileposts 12 +.5, 13 +.5, and 14. (The park boundaries lie roughly at milepost 12 on the south and milepost 15 on the north.)

Day Use Facilities: Drinking water, restrooms, and large parking lots at El Moro and the coastal access points.

Overnight Facilities: None; nearest public campground is in Huntington State Beach.

Activities & Attractions: Trails to the beach and tide pools; scuba access; coastal trail; bikeway; hiking and mountain bike trails in the Moro Canyon area; Crystal Cove Historic District.

Natural Features: Located in 2 main divisions along the Pacific Ocean and in the hills east of the coast; vegetation consists mostly of grass, bushes and brush; sea level to 400´.

Season & Fees: Open all year; please see Appendix for reservation information, park entry fees.

Mail & Phone: Mail c/o DPR Orange Coast District Office, 18331 Enterprise Lane, Huntington Beach, CA 92648; park phone ☎(714) 494-3539.

Park Notes: The park land originally was owned by Jose Sepulveda, a "politically active" Californio who acquired it under land grants from the Mexican governor circa 1840. Sepulveda eventually sold his 48,000-acre *Rancho San Joaquin* for pennies an acre to a group of investors. The partnership in turn sold all of its 120,000 acres to one of its members, James Irvine, in 1876. That transaction led to the beginning of the Irvine Company, and of a vast agricultural and commercial empire which continues to this day. In modern times, the company's repeated refusal to subdivide the property has "antagonized land-hungry Southern Californians". Under mounting public pressure, the Irvine organization sold and gave away land for public works projects, a university, and for Crystal Cove State Park. The expanding coastal commercial zones of Newport Beach/Corona Del Mar and Laguna Beach now terminate at the north and south park boundaries, respectively.

Another nearby state park area—one that is decidedly different from Crystal Cove—is Corona Del Mar State Beach. It's operated by the City of Newport Beach near a commercial and residential district and it has the standard complement of day use and parking facilities. From California Highway 1 a mile north of Crystal Cove's northern boundary, take one of the botanical streets (Marigold, Narcissus, Orchid, Poinsettia, etc.) to Ocean Boulevard and the state beach.

Southwest Corner

California 189

DOHENY
State Beach

Location: Southern California Coast northwest of San Clemente.

Access: From Interstate 5 in Dana Point at the Beach Cities/Pacific Coast Highway/ California Highway 1 Exit (near milepost 7, 3 miles south of San Juan Capistrano, 7 miles north of San Clemente) proceed westerly on a viaduct for 1 mile and onto Pacific Coast Highway; at Del Obispo Street, turn southerly (left) onto Dana Point Harbor Drive, go 0.1 mile to Park Lantern, then swing east (left again) onto the park access road for 0.1 mile to the park entrance station; the first day use area is just beyond the entrance; the campground is 0.4 mile farther; or continue past the campground to a second day use area. (Tip: Try to hug the left lanes as soon as you exit the freeway and line up early for all of the left turns to the park.)

Day Use Facilities: Medium-large picnic areas; group picnic areas; drinking water; restrooms and freshwater rinse showers; very large parking lots; concession stand.

Overnight Facilities: 120 campsites; (hike/bike sites are also available); sites are small+, level, with minimal to nominal separation; parking pads are paved, short to short+ straight-ins plus some medium to long pull-throughs; generally enough room for small tents; fire rings; firewood is usually for sale, or b-y-o; water at several faucets; restrooms with showers; holding tank disposal station; paved driveways; complete supplies and services are available within 3 miles.

Activities & Attractions: Swimming; volleyball courts; hiking trail; fishing; interpretive center.

Natural Features: Located at the edge of the sand, with large hardwoods, palms and large shrubs that provide very light to light-medium shade/shelter in the day use and camp areas; acres of mown lawns; ocean views from many picnic and camp sites; park area is 62 acres; sea level.

Season & Fees: Open all year; please see Appendix for reservation information, park entry and campground fees.

Mail & Phone: Doheny State Beach, 25300 Dana Point Harbor Drive, Dana Point, CA 92629; ☎(714) 496-6172.

Park Notes: Getting off the Interstate might involve a minute or two of perspiration (especially if the traffic is heavy and you're hauling a big rig), but it's worth the effort. Of the trio of beach parks in the area (also see San Clemente and San Onofre), Doheny would be the one to show to your friends.

California 190 ♿

San Clemente
State Beach

Location: Southern California Coast in San Clemente.

Access: From Interstate 5 (northbound) in San Clemente, take the Cristianitos Road/Avenida del Presidente Exit to the west side of the freeway, then north for 0.9 mile on Avenida del Presidente; turn west onto Avenida Calafia and proceed 0.2 mile; turn south (left) onto the park access road for 0.2 mile to the park entrance station; the campground begins just beyond the entrance, or continue past the campground for 0.7 mile to the day use area. **Alternate Access:** From Interstate 5 (southbound) take the Avenida Calafia Exit west onto Avenida Calafia and continue as above.

Day Use Facilities: Medium-sized picnic area with ramadas (sun shelters); drinking water; restrooms; large parking lot.

Overnight Facilities: 157 campsites, including 72 with full hookups; (several hike/bike sites and a reservable group camp are also available); sites are small to small+, essentially level, with minimal to nominal separation; parking pads are paved, short to medium-length straight-ins or long pull-throughs; some sites have small ramadas for the table area; plenty of tent space; fire rings; firewood is usually for sale, or b-y-o; water at several faucets; restrooms with showers; paved driveways; complete supplies and services are available in San Clemente.

Activities & Attractions: Swimming; fishing; trail down to the beach campfire center.

Natural Features: Located on a bluff on a large, grassy flat dotted with hardwoods; picnic area is on a shelf just below the blufftop and overlooks the ocean, most campsites are some distance from the edge of the bluff; some campsites receive very light to light shade from large hardwoods; park area is 110 acres; elevation 100´.

Season & Fees: Open all year; please see Appendix for reservation information, park entry and campground fees.

Mail & Phone: Mail c/o CDPR Pendleton Coast District Office, 3030 Avenida del Presidente, San Clemente, CA 92672; park phone ☎(714) 492-3156.

Park Notes: San Clemente was the site of a former Western White House. (No, it wasn't the actor's local address; it was the home of the *other* President from California.) The facilities at the state beach are quite good. Lots of grass (albeit, worn) and a fair number of trees. Most picnic sites and only a few campsites have ocean views.

California 191

San Ononfre: Ocean Bluffs
State Beach

Location: Southern California Coast south of San Clemente.

Access: From Interstate 5 at the Basilone Road-San Onofre Exit (3 miles south of San Clemente, 17 miles north of Oceanside), turn west off the freeway, then south onto a frontage road; continue south, past the San Onofre Nuclear Generating Station (acronym is SONGS), for 2.5 miles to the main park entrance.

Day Use Facilities: Small picnic areas near the north and south ends of the park; large parking lots.

Overnight Facilities: 221 enroute campsites; (a number of hike/bike sites are also available); sites are very small, level, with minimal separation, in a long line located between the lanes of the Interstate and a bluff that parallels the beach; parking slots are paved, short straight-ins; small tent areas; water at several faucets; restrooms with freshwater rinse showers; holding tank disposal station; paved driveways; complete supplies and services are available in San Clemente.

Activities & Attractions: Swimming; fishing; several trails down to the beach; nature trail.

Natural Features: Located on a bluff; some campsites have limited ocean views; some shrubbery has been planted between sites; park area is 3000 acres; elevation 50´.

Season & Fees: Open all year; please see Appendix for reservation information, park entry and campground fees.

Mail & Phone: mail c/o CDPR Pendleton Coast District Office, 3030 Avenida del Presidente, San Clemente, CA 92672; park phone ☎(714) 492-3156 or ☎(714) 492-4872.

Park Notes: Only a chain link fence separates most of the campsites from eight-lane oblivion. The camping area is located right next to a nuclear power plant, but there are no electrical hookups. Odd. If you stop at the park, or just drive past on I-5, you might see individuals afoot scurrying across the Interstate or elusively scampering through the parklands. No, they're not on a physical-fitness exercise (not the usual kind, anyway). There's a major Border Patrol check station on the east side of the freeway across from the park.

California 192 ♿

San Onofre: San Mateo

State Beach

Location: Southern California southeast of San Clemente.

Access: From Interstate 5 at the Cristianitos Road Exit on the south edge of San Clemente at the San Diego-Orange County Line, travel northeast on Cristianitos Road for 1 mile; turn southwest (right) into the campground.

Day Use Facilities: In the Bluffs area of the state beach.

Overnight Facilities: 160 campsites, including 80 with partial hookups; sites are small to medium-sized, with minimal to nominal separation; parking pads are paved, medium-length straight-ins; a little additional leveling may be needed on many pads; large, slightly sloped areas for tents; fire rings; b-yo- firewood; water at hookup sites and at several faucets; restrooms with showers; holding tank disposal station; paved driveways; complete supplies and services are available in San Clemente.

Activities & Attractions: Ocean beach, 1.5 miles down the valley by foot trail or via the highway; amphitheater for interpretive programs; close to USMC Camp Pendleton.

Natural Features: Located in a wide, shallow valley on a southward facing slope above the north bank of San Mateo Creek; park vegetation consists of bushes, and assorted evergreens and hardwoods on a surface of sparse grass and small plants; the valley is bordered by brushy hills; (state informational literature describes the campground as having "serene coastal scrub surroundings"); elevation 100´.

Season & Fees: Open all year; please see Appendix for reservation informtion and standard California state park fees.

Mail & Phone: Mail c/o CDPR Pendleton Coast District Office, 3030 Avenida del Presidente, San Clemente, CA 92672; park office ☎(714) 361-2531.

Park Notes: San Mateo Campground is an offshoot of an agreement between California citizens and the local electrical power company. Funding for construction of the campground and the trail down to Trestles Beach were exchanged for former beach access which was obstructed by development of the San Onofre atomic juice maker, just south of here. Compare this large, modern campground to the simple national forest camps in the Santa Ana Mountains, a few miles northeast. The forest camps were built by the CCC in the 1930´s for a few thousand bucks apiece. San Mateo's facilities cost $4.7 million in 1990's dollars.

California 193

Carlsbad

State Beach

Location: Southern California Coast south of Oceanside.

Access: From San Diego County Highway S21/Carlsbad Boulevard at its intersection with Tamarack Avenue in downtown Carlsbad, walk into the park. (From Interstate 5, take the Tamarack

Avenue/Carlsbad Exit, then 0.6 mile west on Tamarack to the park.)

Day Use Facilities: Picnic tables and sitting benches; drinking water; restrooms; large parking lot at S21 & Tamarack, on the beach side of S21; (also, parking along S21 and side streets).

Overnight Facilities: None; nearest public campground is in South Carlsbad State Beach.

Activities & Attractions: Beachcombing; swimming.

Natural Features: Located on a short bluff above the beach; landscaping in the developed area consists of sections of manicured lawns and some large hardwoods, trimmed by a rail fence; park area is 23 acres; sea level.

Season & Fees: Open all year; (no fee).

Mail & Phone: c/o CDPR San Diego Coast District Office, 2680 Carlsbad Blvd., Carlsbad, CA 92008; ☎(619) 729-8947.

Park Notes: The foregoing principally describes the several acres which make up the park's very pleasantly 'developed' section; the beach itself stretches for about a mile-and-a-half approximately from the Encina Power Plant on the south edge of Carlsbad to Pine Street on the north side of town.

▲ California 194 ♿

SOUTH CARLSBAD
State Beach

Location: Southern California Coast south of Oceanside.

Access: From San Diego County Highway S21/Carlsbad Boulevard at milepost 15 +.4 (4 miles south of Carlsbad, 4 miles north of Encinitas): if southbound, turn west into the entrance; if northbound on this divided highway, watch for the signs to get you going in the right direction; you'll need to continue north on S21 past the park entrance to the Ponto Drive Exit, then swing around and double-back for 0.8 mile to the park entrance. (From Interstate 5, take the Poinsettia Lane Exit north of Encinitas, go west 0.6 mile on Poinsettia Lane to S21, then to the entrance.)

Day Use Facilities: None; nearest day use facilities are in Carlsbad State Beach.

Overnight Facilities: 226 campsites; sites are small to small+, level, with fair to fairly good separation; parking pads are sandy gravel, short to short+ straight-ins/pull-offs; generally adequate space for large tents; storage cabinets; fire rings; firewood is usually for sale, or b-y-o; water at several faucets; restrooms with showers; holding tank disposal station; paved driveways; park store; complete supplies and services are available in Carlsbad.

Activities & Attractions: Swimming; fishing; campfire center.

Natural Features: Located on a bluff just above the beach; vegetation consists mostly of large shrubs, plus a few palms; park area is 135 acres, including 3.5 miles of beach; sea level.

Season & Fees: Open all year; please see Appendix for reservation information, park entry and campground fees.

Mail & Phone: mail c/o CDPR San Diego Coast District Office, 2680 Carlsbad Boulevard, Carlsbad, CA 92008; park phone ☎(619) 438-3143.

Park Notes: South Carlsbad has twice the oceanfront property and more beachfront sites than its sister park to the south, San Elijo (see separate info). Otherwise, they are comparable. The campsites in both areas are somewhat unconventional since they really are just gravel rectangles bordered by shrubs. The sites are nearly identical in size, shape and landscaping to those in all of the campgrounds in Lake Mead National Recreation Area. Simple, practical, and cheap to construct and maintain.

▲ California 195

LEUCADIA
State Beach

Location: Southern California Coast northwest of San Diego.

Access: From San Diego County Highway S21 at its intersection with Leucadia Boulevard in the Leucadia district of Encinitas, proceed west on Leucadia Boulevard for 0.2 mile to the city parking lot at the intersection of Leucadia & Neptune Avenue (on the west side of Neptune). (From Interstate 5, take the Leucadia Boulevard Exit in Encinitas, then go west on Leucadia Boulevard for 0.6 mile to S21, then continue across S21 and west for 0.2 mile to the parking lot.)

Day Use Facilities: Small (city) parking lot.

Overnight Facilities: None; nearest public campground is in San Elijo State Beach.

Activities & Attractions: Trail down to the beach.

Natural Features: Located on a small, narrow, gravelly beach; park area is 11 acres; sea level.

Season & Fees: Open all year; (no fee).

Mail & Phone: c/o CDPR San Diego Coast District Office, 2680 Carlsbad Blvd., Carlsbad, CA 92008; ☎(619) 729-8947.

Park Notes: When you step to the edge of the parking lot, your first impulse may be to go back into town and buy some rappelling gear to get down to the beach. But it's not that bad, really. There is a steep trail (with handrails) cut into the sandstone face of the bluff that switchbacks for a hundred yards or so down to the surf.

▲ California 196 ♿

MOONLIGHT
State Beach

Location: Southern California Coast northwest of San Diego.

Access: From San Diego County Highway S21 at its intersection with Encinitas Boulevard in Encinitas, turn west onto B Street and go 2 blocks; turn south (left) onto Third Street and go another block to C Street and the main parking lot; from the lot it's a short walk down a wide, paved path to the beach. (From Interstate 5, take the Encinitas Boulevard Exit, then go west on Encinitas Boulevard for 0.4 mile to S21, then cross S21 and onto B Street to the park.)

Day Use Facilities: Several picnic tables; drinking water; restrooms with freshwater rinse showers; large parking lot above the beach, small handicapped parking area at beach level; concession stand.

Overnight Facilities: None; nearest public campground is in San Elijo State Beach.

Activities & Attractions: Swimming; fishing.

Natural Features: Located on an ocean beach and on a short bluff overlooking the ocean; park area is 14 acres; sea level.

Season & Fees: Open all year; operated by the City of Encinitas.

Mail & Phone: c/o CDPR San Diego Coast District Office, 2680 Carlsbad Blvd., Carlsbad, CA 92008; ☎(619) 729-8947.

Park Notes: Moonlight's main (upper) parking lot is in two tiers. Parking spaces in the lower tier, and those along the west edge of the upper level, are pointed seaward and have good surf views. Sitting behind the wheel in a nicely landscaped parking lot looking at the ocean may not sound like a lot of fun to many people, but on windy or rainy days it sure beats hanging around inside an inland taco stand or coffee shop.

▲ California 197 ♿

SAN ELIJO
State Beach

Location: Southern California Coast northwest of San Diego.

Access: From San Diego County Highway S21 near milepost 10 +.5 just across the railroad tracks from midtown Cardiff, turn west to the park entrance station; the campground stretches for several 10ths of a mile parallel to the highway north and south of the entrance; the day use area is at the far north end of the park, 0.5 mile from the entrance. (From Interstate 5, take the Manchester/Cardiff by the Sea or Birmingham Drive Exit south of Encinitas, then travel a mile west to Cardiff and go across the RR tracks and onto S21.)

Day Use Facilities: Medium-sized picnic area; drinking water; restrooms; large parking lot; park store.

Overnight Facilities: 171 campsites; sites are small to small+, level to somewhat sloped, with fair to fairly good separation; parking pads are gravel, short+, straight-ins/pull-offs; adequate space for a large tent (if your vehicle doesn't take up a lot of space); fire rings; firewood is usually for sale, or b-y-o; water at several faucets; restrooms with showers; holding tank disposal station; paved driveways; adequate supplies and services are available in Cardiff.

Activities & Attractions: Beach access; bikeway/jogway; swimming; campfire center.

Natural Features: Located on a short bluff or rise a few feet above the beach; vegetation includes large shrubs, hardwoods and evergreens between sites, plus tall palms; park area is 39 acres; sea level.

Season & Fees: Open all year; please see Appendix for reservation information, park entry and campground fees.

Mail & Phone: Mail c/o CDPR San Diego Coast District Office, 2680 Carlsbad Boulevard, Carlsbad, CA 92008; park phone ☎(619) 753-5091.

Park Notes: Actually, there are a lot of pretty nice, visually separated, oceanfront campsites here (although the local folks in the houses up on the bluff behind the park can probably look down and see what variety of soup you're having for lunch.) The picnic sites and many of the campsites are along the edge of the shoreside bluff overlooking the ocean. The campground is very popular with tent campers.

▲ **California 198**

CARDIFF

State Beach

Location: Southern California Coast northwest of San Diego.

Access: From San Diego County Highway S21 at a point 0.5 mile south of Cardiff-by-the-Sea, 1 mile north of the city of Solana Beach, a few yards south of the San Elijo Creek crossing, turn west into the parking lot.

Day Use Facilities: Restrooms; large parking lot.

Overnight Facilities: None; nearest public campground is in San Elijo State Beach.

Activities & Attractions: Swimming; fishing.

Natural Features: Located on a long, narrow beach; bordered by hills and bluffs north and south; park area is 25 acres; sea level.

Season & Fees: Open all year; (no fee).

Mail & Phone: c/o CDPR San Diego Coast District Office, 2680 South Carlsbad Boulevard, Carlsbad, CA 92008; ☎(619) 729-8947.

Park Notes: The beach is about a half-mile long, with a commercial district break, and some of it is along a dropoff just below the highway. It's backed-up by San Elijo Lagoon, a county ecological reserve, on the east side of the highway.

▲ **California 199** ♿

TORREY PINES

State Beach/State Reserve

Location: Southwest California northwest of San Diego.

Access: From Interstate 5 at the Carmel Valley Road/Del Mar Exit (2 miles north of the junction of Interstates 5 & 805 west of Miramar, 2 miles south of Del Mar) from the west side of the freeway, head northwest on Carmel Valley Road for 1 mile, then turn west (left) into the North Beach area; or continue northwest for another 0.4 mile, then turn south onto North Torrey Pines Road/San Diego County Highway S21 and proceed 0.8 mile to the South Beach area and the state reserve. **Alternate Access:** From Interstate 5 at the Genesee Avenue Exit on the north edge of La Jolla, go west on Genesee Avenue for 0.8 mile, then turn north onto North Torrey Pines Road and past the state reserve for 3 miles to South Beach or 4 miles to North Beach.

Day Use Facilities: Picnic tables adjacent to the North Beach parking lot; drinking water; restrooms; freshwater rinse showers; very large parking lot; restrooms and large parking lot at the South Beach area.

Overnight Facilities: None; nearest public campground is in San Elijo State Beach.

Activities & Attractions: Beachcombing; surfing; fishing; hiking and nature trails in the state reserve.

Natural Features: Located on an ocean beach (state beach) and on a forested bluff/hill above the beach (state reserve); the main parking lot is landscaped with bushes and shrubs; Los Penasquitos Marsh Natural Preserve is east of the beach; beach area is 40 acres, reserve area is 1100 acres; sea level to 400´.

Season & Fees: Open all year; (no fee).

Mail & Phone: c/o CDPR San Diego Coast District Office, 2680 Carlsbad Boulevard, Carlsbad, CA 92008; ☎(619) 729-8947.

Park Notes: What you see from the developed area is only a fraction of the more than four miles of ocean frontage here. The famous Torrey Pines Muni Golf Course (a module on the PGA circuit) is adjacent to the state reserve. The wind-swept reserve protects the small Torrey pine tree, a species which now grows naturally only here and on Santa Rosa Island in the Santa Barbara Channel.

▲ **California 200** ♿

OLD TOWN SAN DIEGO
State Historic Park

Location: Southwest California in San Diego.

Access: From Interstate 5 at the Old Town Avenue Exit, (3 miles northwest of downtown San Diego, 1 mile north of San Diego International Airport) proceed to the northeast side of the freeway then northeast on Old Town Avenue for 1 block; then northerly (left) onto San Diego Avenue and go 0.35 mile through the commercial district to a 'T' intersection; turn southwest (left) onto Twiggs Street for 1 block, then northwest (right) on Congress Street for a few yards, then swing right, into the main parking lot. (You can get your bearings from a large map posted at the corner of the parking lot; the historic district is a walk-in area).

Day Use Facilities: Picnicking/sitting area in the plaza; drinking water; restrooms; large main parking lot; additional parking is available in lots at or near the 3 other corners of the historic district as well as in several lots and parking garages in the vicinity.

Overnight Facilities: None; nearest public campground is in Silver Strand State Beach.

Activities & Attractions: Restorations or reconstructions of nearly 20 homes, commercial establishments and government buildings dating back to 1821-1872; several museums; guided tours each afternoon; self-guided tour (an excellent guide booklet is available at the park office).

Natural Features: Located principally in an area bordered by Wallace Street on the northwest and Twiggs Street on the southeast, Congress Street on the southwest and Juan Street on the northeast; the Plaza has a large mown lawn dotted with huge hardwoods; several courtyards and gardens are also landscaped appropriately; park area is 13 acres; sea level.

Season & Fees: Open all year; (no fee).

Mail & Phone: Old Town San Diego State Historic Park, 4002 Wallace Street, San Diego, CA 92110; ☎(619) 237-6770.

Park Notes: San Diego is the location of the first permanent Spanish settlement in California. Its significance has been likened to Jamestown, Virginia, site of the first English colony on the East Coast. On the hill east of the park, the Founding Father of California's missions, Junipero Serra, established Mission San Diego in July 1769. In the 1820's a small village sprung up at the base of the hill below the initial site of the mission. 'Old Town' was the original section of the city and it has been known by that name for more than a century. The park re-creates a 50-year period in the mid-nineteenth century which saw a transition from Mexican to American rule. Architecturally, it's a combination of

Mexican adobe and colonial American wood-frame. The park and the surrounding commercial district are first-rate in just about every respect. You could easily spend a day here and not see it all.

California 201 ♿

SILVER STRAND
State Beach

Location: Southwest corner of California south of San Diego.

Access: From California State Highway 75 at a point 6 miles south of the Coronado Bridge and 5 miles northwest of the Interstate 5 Exit for Highway 75/Imperial Beach/Palm Avenue, turn west then north to the park entrance station; day use facilities begin near the entrance; or continue north on the park driveway for 0.6 mile to the camping area.

Day Use Facilities: Medium-sized picnic area; drinking water; restrooms; several very large parking lots.

Overnight Facilities: 122 enroute campsites in a parking lot arrangement; sites are very small, level, with zip separation; parking slots are long straight-ins or pull-throughs; no tents allowed; vehicles must have completely self-contained facilities and must include "1 verifiable towed/towing vehicle"; complete supplies and services are available in Coronado and Imperial Beach.

Activities & Attractions: Mile-long ocean beach, plus land on San Diego Bay and bikeway on the east side of the highway.

Natural Features: Located on a long, narrow spit between the Pacific Ocean and San Diego Bay; a few palms decorate the grounds; park area is 428 acres; sea level.

Season & Fees: Open all year; please see Appendix for reservation information, park entry and campground fees.

Mail & Phone: Silver Strand State Beach, 5000 Highway 75, Coronado, CA 92118; ☎(619) 435-5184.

Park Notes: Judging from the acreage covered by the day use parking lots, it appears they would hold upwards of a thousand vehicles—and on a nice weekend they probably do.

California 202

BORDER FIELD
State Park

Location: Southwest corner of California south of San Diego.

Access: From Interstate 5 at the Dairy Mart Road Exit in San Ysidro, 1 mile north of the United States-Mexico border, travel south and west on Dairy Mart Road, which becomes Monument Road, for 3.8 miles to the park.

Day Use Facilities: Small picnic area; drinking water; vault facilities; small parking lot.

Overnight Facilities: None; nearest public campground is in Silver Strand State Beach.

Activities & Attractions: Equestrian and hiking trails; horse corral; guided nature walks scheduled periodically in Tijuana River National Estuarine Sanctuary (call for a schedule); clamming and fishing.

Natural Features: Located on a coastal plain along and near the Pacific Ocean; grassland and saltwater and freshwater marshes make up most of the vegetation; the Tijuana River estuary is within and adjacent to the park; park area is 680 acres; sea level.

Season & Fees: Open all year; please see Appendix for park entry fees.

Mail & Phone: Mail c/o CDPR Frontera District Office, 3990 Old Town Avenue, San Diego, CA 92110; phone ☎(619) 428-3034 or ☎(619) 237-6766.

Park Notes: Border Field is an especially popular place for horseback riding, as evidenced by the number of riding stables in the area. It's also an excellent place for wildlife observation. (The type of wildlife varies with the time of day; just after sundown, you may catch glimpses of shadowy figures making their way north through the marshes. Experienced observers apparently have found that their best camouflage is a plain vanilla van or other unmarked utility vehicle.)

California 203 ♿

PALOMAR MOUNTAIN
State Park

Location: Southwest California northeast of San Diego.

Access: From the junction of California State Highway 76 and San Diego County Highway S6 (3 miles east of Rincon Springs, 23 miles northwest of Santa Ysabel), turn north onto Highway S6 and climb 7 miles to the junction of SD County Highways S6 & S7; turn northwest (left) onto S7 and travel 2.9 miles to the park entrance; the Silver Crest picnic area is just beyond the entrance; or continue ahead past the picnic ground for 0.25 mile, then swing sharply north (right) and proceed 1.2 miles on a steep, narrow, paved road to Doane Pond, or an additional 0.3 mile to the Doane Valley Campground.

Alternate Access: From the junction of State Highway 76 & SD County Highway S7 (8 miles southeast of Rincon Springs, 10 miles north of Santa Ysabel) head north/northwest on S7 for 11 miles to the junction of S6 & S7, and continue on S7 to the park, as above. (Note: the first access is via steep, winding, but panoramic miles from the main highway; the second access is along a much easier route, particularly if you're pumping a 10-speed, or you're driving something larger than a van or a full-size pickup with a topper.)

Day Use Facilities: Medium-sized picnic area, drinking water, restrooms, and medium-sized parking lot at Silver Crest; several picnic sites, drinking water and restrooms are also available at Doane Pond.

Overnight Facilities: *Doane Valley Campground*: 31 sites in 2 loops (the Cedar Grove Group Camp is also available, by reservation); sites are generally small and sloped, with very little separation; parking pads are paved, short straight-ins or pull-offs; tent areas vary from small to large, and most are somewhat sloped; a few, designated, medium-sized rv and handicapped sites; storage cabinets (bear boxes); fire rings or barbecue grills; firewood is usually for sale, b-y-o is recommended; water at central faucets; restrooms with showers; paved driveways; camper supplies at the junction of Highways S6 and S7.

Activities & Attractions: A half-dozen hiking trails through several miles of forest and meadow; (a park brochure/trail map with contours is available from the park office); Doane Valley Nature Trail; fishing for stocked trout at Doane Pond; observation point; amphitheater at Doane Valley Campground; Cal Tech's world-renowned Palomar Observatory is 15 road miles northeast (visitor center/museum open daily).

Natural Features: Located on moderately sloped to steep terrain carpeted with a light to dense forest of large hardwoods and very tall conifers, intermixed with open meadows; some hillsides are thickly carpeted with ferns; elevation 4000′ to 5400′.

Season & Fees: Open all year, except during brief periods of heavy snow; please see Appendix for reservation information, park entry and campground fees.

Mail & Phone: Palomar Mountain State Park, Palomar Mountain, CA 92060; ☎(714) 742-3462.

Park Notes: The park's host-mountain was named by the early Spanish for the thousands of pigeons which made it their home. (*Palomar* means "pigeon roost" or "pigeon coop"). A number of early settlers also made this land their home, and four apple orchards in the park trace their roots to the plantings of 1880's homesteaders.

California 204 ♿

SAN PASQUAL BATTLEFIELD
State Historic Park

Location: Southwest California north of San Diego.

Access: From California State Highway 78 at milepost 25 +.5 (8 miles southeast of the junction of Highway 78 & Interstate 5 in

Escondido, 10 miles west of Ramona), turn north onto the park access road and proceed 0.2 mile up to the visitor center; or at milepost 25 (0.5 mile west of the visitor center) turn north off the highway to the monument area. (Note: From I-5 you can probably save many minutes by avoiding the traffic near midtown Escondido; take the I-5 Via Rancho Parkway Exit at the Escondido-San Diego city limits; from the east side of the freeway, go north on Bear Valley Parkway for 1 mile, then northeast on San Pasqual Road for 3.1 miles to Highway 78; from there it's 2.6 miles east to the visitor center.)

Day Use Facilities: Small picnic area, drinking water, restrooms, medium-sized parking lot at the visitor center; small-medium-sized roadside pull-off at the monument.

Overnight Facilities: None; nearest public campground is in William Heise county park off Highway 78 near Julian.

Activities & Attractions: Visitor center with interpretive exhibits about the history of the San Pasqual Valley through Indian, Mexican and American occupations, and descriptions and maps of the Battle of San Pasqual in Spanish and English; nature trail; bronze sculpture honors Lieutenant (later General) Edward Beale and scout Kit Carson (see below); living history programs, including a re-enactment of the battle each December; trail from the visitor center to the monument area; amphitheater.

Natural Features: Located on a hillside in the San Pasqual Valley; park vegetation consists of grass dotted with brush and some hardwoods; park area is 50 acres; elevation 500´.

Season & Fees: Open all year; visitor center open Thursday through Monday (subject to change).

Mail & Phone: mail c/o CDPR Frontera District Office, 3990 Old Town Avenue, San Diego, CA 92110; park phone ☎(619) 238-3380.

Park Notes: The park overlooks the site of a Mexican-American War battle and the American soldiers' campsite after the battle. The battle of San Pasqual took place December 6, 1846 between General Stephen Kearny's troops and Californios led by Major Andres Pico. The post-battle campsite is in the monument area. The American's later came under siege at a place south of here called Mule Hill and were finally rescued on December 11th by a relief party from San Diego led by Beale and Carson. The battle was only one of many in the war, but it was the bloodiest and most controversial as to its outcome. (Did the Americans win the conflict, or was it a case of "won the battle but lost the war" for the Californios?)

▲ California 205 ♿

CUYAMACA RANCHO: PASO PICACHO
State Park

Location: Southwest California northeast of San Diego.

Access: From California State Highway 79 at milepost 9 +.3 (12 miles north of Interstate 8 Julian/Japatul Road Exit, 11 miles south of Julian), turn west into the Paso Picacho entrance station; just inside the entrance, turn right to the picnic area, or bear left and continue for 0.1 mile to the campground. **Additional Access** (for the Stonewall Mine area): From State Highway 79 at milepost 10 +.3 (10 miles south of Julian, 1 mile north of the Paso Picacho area) turn northeast onto a paved access road and proceed 0.8 mile to the mine site.

Day Use Facilities: Medium-sized picnic area; drinking water; restrooms; medium-sized parking area.

Overnight Facilities: 85 campsites in a complex network of loops; (2 group camps and a number of environmental campsites are also available in this area, 2 horse camps are available near the Stonewall Mine area); sites are small+, with nominal to fair separation; parking pads are short to medium-length straight-ins, most of which will probably require additional leveling; large, but sloped, tent areas; fire rings; firewood is usually for sale, or b-y-o; water at central faucets; restrooms with showers; narrow, paved driveways; holding tank disposal station; gas and groceries in Julian;

nearest source of complete supplies and services is El Cajon, 35 miles southwest.

Activities & Attractions: Over a hundred miles of hiking and horse trails, including a 3.5 mile trail from here to the summit of 6512´ Cuyamaca Peak; Paso Nature Trail; small interpretive center; campfire center; Stonewall Mine site dates back to the 1860's.

Natural Features: Located on forested slopes in the Peninsular Range; park vegetation consists of a light to medium-dense mixture of hardwoods and conifers and some open grassy areas; Cuyamaca Lake is 2 miles north; total park area is 25,000 acres; park elevation ranges from 4000´ to 6500´; elevation at Paso Picacho is 4900´.

Season & Fees: Open all year, depending upon winter weather conditions; please see Appendix for reservation information, park entry and campground fees.

Mail & Phone: Cuyamaca Rancho State Park, 12551 Highway 79, Descanso, CA 92016; ☎(619) 765-0755.

Park Notes: From Paso Picacho, a moderately difficult trail winds to the summit of Cuyamaca Peak. At the top you look out to the Pacific Ocean, Mexico, Anza-Borrego Desert and the Salton Sea. The Stonewall Mine is said to have been the most productive of the gold mines in Southern California. It took its name from nearby Stonewall Peak which had been named for Confederate General Thomas "Stonewall" Jackson, Robert E. Lee's principal field commander during the early years of the War Between the States.

▲ **California 206** ♿

CUYAMACA RANCHO:
GREEN VALLEY
State Park

Location: Southwest corner of California northeast of San Diego.

Access: From California State Highway 79 at milepost 4 +.2 (7 miles north of Interstate 8 Julian/Japatul Road Exit, 16 miles south of Julian), turn west into the Green Valley entrance station; turn right and proceed 0.3 mile to a fork; take the right fork for campsites 1-22; take the left fork and go another 0.1 mile, then turn right into the Arroyo Seco day use area; or continue ahead for 0.1 mile to the main camp loops; or continue past the main camp loops for an additional 0.3 mile to the Falls/River day use area parking lots. **Additional Access** (for the museum): From Highway 79 at milepost 6 +.25 (2 miles north of the Green Valley area) turn east onto a paved access road and proceed 0.35 mile to the museum parking lot.

Day Use Facilities: Medium-sized picnic area at Arroyo Seco, large picnic area at Falls/River; drinking water and restrooms in both areas; 3 medium-sized parking lots; small picnic spot, small parking lot and restrooms at the museum.

Overnight Facilities: 81 campsites in 2 loops, plus an extension; (hike/bike campsites and a primitive camp, accessible by trail, are available nearby); sites are small+, quite sloped, with nominal to fair separation; parking pads are mostly paved, short to medium-length straight-ins; additional leveling would be needed in virtually all sites; medium to large tent areas; fire rings; b-y-o firewood; water at most sites; restrooms with showers; paved driveways; gas and groceries in Julian; nearest source of complete supplies is El Cajon, 30 miles southwest.

Activities & Attractions: Trails, trails, trails—the park has more than a hundred miles of equestrian and foot trails, several of which lead off from this area; short trail from the day use area to the falls (but don't get your expectations up too high about the drop of these tumbling waters); interpretive displays; campfire center; museum houses exhibits and artifacts about the local Kumeya-ay Indians and the early Spanish explorers.

Natural Features: Located on rolling slopes near the edge of a ravine in a densely forested river valley; the Sweetwater River flows past the day use areas and campground loops; some of the state's largest canyon live oaks are within the park; surrounding mountainous areas have moderately dense forestation interspersed with meadows; elevation at Green Valley 4000´.

Season & Fees: Open all year, subject to winter weather conditions; please see Appendix for reservation information, park entry and campground fees.

Mail & Phone: Cuyamaca Rancho State Park, 12551 Highway 79, Descanso, CA 92016; ☎(619) 765-0755.

Park Notes: Green Valley's campground apparently is popular mostly with pickup, van and tent campers. The nearby park museum is in an old, attractive two-story building with walls made of local stone which was the home of the previous owner of Cuyamaca Rancho. (The state bought this sizeable spread in 1933 at reportedly half its appraised value.) The handiwork of the Civilian Conservation Corps can still be identified in certain places around the park—the CCC built the park's first trails and campgrounds during the Great Depression. (Incidentally, *Cuyamca* is pronounced like *Coo-yah-mah´-kah*.)

California

South Central Inland

California 207

San Luis Reservoir: Basalt-Main Reservoir

State Recreation Area

Location: West-central California south of Modesto.

Access: From California State Highway 152 at milepost 10 +.95 (5 miles west of the Los Banos/Highway 152 Exit on Interstate 5, 36 miles east of Gilroy), turn south onto a paved access road; proceed 2.1 miles to the entrance station, then 0.3 mile to the Basalt Campground. (If you're southbound on Interstate 5, you can save 3 miles by taking the Santa Nella/Gilroy Exit, then go south for 3 miles on State Highway 33 to Highway 152, then west on 152 for 3 miles to the park turnoff.)

Day Use Facilities: Vault facilities and parking lot at the boat launch.

Overnight Facilities: *Basalt Campground*: 79 campsites in 2 loops; sites are medium+ in size, with nominal separation; parking pads are paved, medium to long, wide, straight-ins; pads are basically level, but those in the south loop may require a little additional leveling; excellent tent areas; fireplaces; b-y-o firewood; water at several faucets; restrooms with showers; holding tank disposal station; nearly complete supplies and services are available in Los Banos, 11 miles east.

Activities & Attractions: Fishing for black bass, shad, striped bass, channel catfish; boating; boat launch (2 miles west of the campground, launch fee); visitor center with audio-visual programs (at Highway 152 milepost 8, west of the Basalt Turnoff); interpretive programs on weekends.

Natural Features: Located in the eastern foothills of the Coast Range, near the south shore of San Luis Reservoir, on the west edge of the San Joaquin Valley; a variety of large, full hardwoods provide a fairly generous amount of shelter/shade within the campground; ringed by grassy hills sparingly dotted with brush and small trees; higher, more forested hills lie in the near distance; hot and often windy in summer, mild in winter; scant annual rainfall, mostly in winter; total park area is 26,000 acres; elevation 400´.

Season & Fees: Open all year; please see Appendix for reservation information, park entry and campground fees.

Mail & Phone: San Luis Reservoir State Recreation Area, 31426 West Highway 152, Santa Nella, CA 93635; ☎(209) 826-1196 or ☎(209) 826-1197.

Park Notes: Basalt is one of two established campgrounds within the recreation area. The other is a 22-unit primitive campground with ramadas, water and vault facilities, which can also be used by picnickers. It's located at Los Banos Creek Reservoir, 10 miles southeast of San Luis Reservoir. Los Banos Creek is accessible via a roundabout route from State Highway 152 just west of the city of Los Banos, then south on Volta Road, east on Pioneer Road and south on Canyon Road (crossing over to the southwest side of I-5) for a total of eight paved miles to the park. The area also has a primitive horse camp.

California 208

SAN LUIS RESERVOIR:
SAN LUIS CREEK-O'NEIL FOREBAY

State Recreation Area

Location: West-central California south of Modesto.

Access: From California State Highway 152 at milepost 9 +.8 (6 miles west of the Los Banos/Highway 152 Exit on Interstate 5, 35 miles east of Gilroy), turn northeast onto a paved access road and proceed 1.4 miles to the park. **Additional Access:** From State Highway 33 at a point 0.4 mile north of its junction with Highway 152, 2.5 miles south of Santa Nella, proceed west on a park access road for 1 mile to the Madeiros picnic/camp area. (If you're southbound on I-5, see the short cut info in the Access section under the Main Reservoir.)

Day Use Facilities: Large-picnic area with ramadas (sun shelters), drinking water, restrooms and several medium-sized parking lots at San Luis Creek; picnic/camp area at Madeiros.

Overnight Facilities: Large, open camp/picnic area, with drinking water and vault facilities and large parking area at Madeiros; nearly complete supplies and services are available in Los Banos, 11 miles east.

Activities & Attractions: Swimming beach; boating; boat launch and docks; fishing for striped bass, black bass, channel cat, crappie, bluegill; visitor center, 2 miles west.

Natural Features: Located on grassy slopes dotted with trees above the west shore (San Luis Creek) and on the south shore (Madeiros) of O'Neil Forebay, a 2000-acre secondary impoundment associated with San Luis Reservoir; picnic sites receive light to light-medium natural shade from large hardwoods; bordered by grassy, tree-dotted hills and low mountains; elevation 300´.

Season & Fees: Open all year; please see Appendix for park entry and campground fees.

Mail & Phone: San Luis Reservoir State Recreation Area, 31426 West Highway 152, Santa Nella, CA 93635; ☎(209) 826-1196 or ☎(209) 826-1197.

Park Notes: O'Neil Forebay acts as an "hydraulic junction" (a liquid buffer zone) between the main reservoir, a local canal, and the California Aqueduct, in what is a more complex water system than first meets the eye. (The complete story unfolds at the visitor center.) San Luis Reservoir SRA provides the only major picnicking and camping facilities in the San Joaquin Valley, other than the freeway rest areas, within a few easy miles of Interstate 5.

California 209 ♿

MILLERTON LAKE

State Recreation Area

Location: Central California north of Fresno.

Access: From the junction of California State Highways 41 & 145 (19 miles north of Fresno, 15 miles east of Madera, 27 miles south of Oakhurst), travel east on County Road 145 (an extension of State Highway 145) for 3.3 miles to a 'Y'; bear slightly north (left) continuing on Road 145 for 1.2 miles; turn east (right, remaining on Road 145) and proceed 2.6 miles to the park entrance station (at the southwest corner of the lake); the main picnic areas are just east of the entrance on the south shore; camp areas are located over the next 2.5 miles on the north shore along the main park road.

Day Use Facilities: 2 medium-sized picnic areas near the park entrance, plus numerous picnic sites scattered around the lake shore; large group picnic area with ramada; drinking water near some areas; vault facilities; small parking areas.

Overnight Facilities: 160 campsites in a half-dozen areas; (2 group camps, a boat-in camp and a trail camp are also available); sites in the sections closest to the entrance (Rocky Point, Mono, Fort Miller, etc.) are medium-sized, and generally well separated; parking pads are gravel, somewhat sloped, short to medium-length straight-ins; sites in the area farthest from the entrance (the "Meadow" area), are more level and have longer pads, but less separation; some sites have storage cabinets; fire rings; b-y-o firewood; water at several faucets in the first sections; water at faucets throughout the Meadow area; restrooms with showers, supplemented by vault facilities; holding tank disposal station; paved driveways; groceries 3 miles west, on Road 145.

Activities & Attractions: Designated swimming area; fishing for the standard warm water species; boating; boat launches; marina; hiking and horse trails; relocated, original Millerton courthouse (one-time Fresno County Courthouse, moved from what is now a submerged location.)

Natural Features: Located along the shore of Millerton Lake, an impoundment on the San Joaquin River in the western foothills of the Sierra Nevada; picnic sites are lightly shaded by hardwoods; campsites in the sections closest to the entrance are on a series of tree-dotted hills and slopes; Meadow area above the north/east shore is primarily on a large hilltop, somewhat shaded by hardwoods; park area is 6550 acres; elevation 600´.

Season & Fees: Open all year; please see Appendix for reservation information, park entry and campground fees.

Mail & Phone: Millerton Lake State Recreation Area, P.O. Box 205, 5290 Millerton Rd, Friant, CA 93626; ☎(209) 822-2332.

Park Notes: There are some really nice picnic and camp sites here, so a look around might be worthwhile. Summer weekends are busy, (reportedly, more than 30,000 people and over 1000 boats have used the park on certain holiday weekends), but early in the week the place is often nearly deserted.

▲ **California 210** ♿

COLONEL ALLENSWORTH
State Historic Park

Location: South-central California north of Bakersfield.

Access: From California State Highway 43 at milepost 5 +.5 in the small community of Allensworth (19 miles north of Wasco, 18 miles south of Corcoran) turn west onto Palmer Avenue and into the park; turn north (right) and follow the road around the north side of the townsite; the day use area and visitor center are at the mid-west edge of the park, the campground is in the far northwest corner.

Day Use Facilities: Medium-sized picnic area with ramadas (sun shelters); drinking water; restrooms; medium-sized parking lots near the picnic area and visitor center; other small parking areas throughout the park.

Overnight Facilities: 15 campsites; sites are small+ to medium-sized, level, with nominal separation; parking pads are gravel, medium to long straight-ins; large tent areas; medium-sized, central ramadas (sun shelters); fire rings; b-y-o firewood; water at central faucets; restrooms; holding tank disposal station; gravel driveway; limited to adequate supplies in Earlimart, 9 miles east, and Delano, 13 miles southeast.

Activities & Attractions: Original townsite of a pioneer community of the early 1900's and restorations or reconstructions of some of the original buildings; (about half of the two-dozen historic sites and buildings which have been identified to date have been completed or are planned for development, including the schoolhouse, library, hotel, general store, drug store, the homes of several families, and the Allensworth residence); small visitor center with orientation film and interpretive displays.

Natural Features: Located on a vast, semi-arid plain near the south end of the San Joaquin Valley; park vegetation consists of sections of watered lawns, natural grass, low brush and scattered hardwoods; park area is 240 acres; elevation 200´.

Season & Fees: Open all year; please see Appendix for reservation information, park entry and campground fees.

Mail & Phone: Colonel Allensworth State Historic Park, Star Route Box 148, Earlimart, CA 93219; ☎(661) 849-3433.

Park Notes: Allen Allensworth was born a slave in Louisville, Kentucky in 1842, fought for the Union during the Civil War, earned an education, and went back into the army as a chaplain in 1886. Twenty years later he retired as a lieutenant colonel—and as the highest ranking African-American in the armed forces. The small rural community here was founded by Allensworth in 1908 as a means of giving Black pioneers an opportunity to live and work free of what might euphemistically be termed the "social and economic pressures" of the era.

The town flourished for a while and, according to historical accounts, life here was exemplary of pioneer life elsewhere on the American frontier. (Indeed, the lonesome location and the style of architecture bear more than just a passing resemblance to those small, classic communities on the Great Plains of Western Kansas.) But the water supply slowly decreased and the importance of the town's railroad-side location diminished as trucks became more commonly used to transport supplies and farm products. The town of Allensworth quite literally "dried up", and most of the population of what had been hundreds moved on. It is noteworthy that two of the first of the original buildings selected for restoration were the elementary school and the library. (If you drive away from your visit to this outlying place in empathy of *who* these people were rather than just with knowledge of *what* they were, perhaps the park will have served its most important purpose.)

California 211 ♿

TULE ELK
State Reserve

Location: Southern California west of Bakersfield.

Access: From Interstate 5 at the Stockdale Road Exit (32 miles northwest of the junction of I-5 & California State Highway 99 near Wheeler Ridge, 4.5 miles southeast of the junction of I-5 & State Highway 58 near Buttonwillow), travel west on Stockdale Road for 1.2 miles; turn south (left) onto Morris Road for 1.5 miles, then go west on Station Road for 0.2 mile to the day use area and the park office.

Day Use Facilities: Small picnic area; parking lot.

Overnight Facilities: None; nearest public campground is in Kern River county park, off Highway 178 east of Bakersfield.

Activities & Attractions: Herd of Tule elk; interpretive exhibits; interpretive talks for groups, by appointment.

Natural Features: Located on a grassy plain garnished with stands of large hardwoods near the south end of the San Joaquin Valley; the Elk Hills lie to the west; park area is 946 acres; elevation 300′.

Season & Fees: Open all year; (no fee).

Mail & Phone: Tule Elk State Reserve, Route 1 Box 42, Buttonwillow, CA 93206; ☎(805) 765-5004.

Park Notes: Tule elk once ruled the valley, but their numbers were decimated in the 1800's by agriculturization and unrestrained hunting. The reserve now protects a herd of these monarchs of the plains. In case the elk aren't cooperating by being viewably close to the picnic area and office, you can gain additional observation points by continuing west on Station Road for another 0.7 mile, then traveling southeast on Tupman Road, which parallels the west side of the reserve property.

California 212 ♿

FORT TEJON
State Historic Park

Location: Southern California south of Bakersfield.

Access: From Interstate 5 (northbound) at the Fort Tejon Exit (6 miles north of Tejon Pass, 36 miles south of Bakersfield), at the end of the freeway ramp continue north on a frontage road for 0.3 mile, then the road swings around to the west over the Interstate then south for 0.2 mile to the park. **Alternate Access:** From Interstate 5 (southbound) at the Fort Tejon Exit, at the end of the short exit way, turn north (a hairpin right) and proceed 0.1 mile to the park.

Day Use Facilities: Small picnic area; drinking water and restrooms at the visitor center; medium-sized parking lot.

Overnight Facilities: None; nearest public campground is Oak Flat (Angeles National Forest) 26 miles south at the I-5 Templin Highway Exit.

Activities & Attractions: Restoration and reconstruction of an 1854-1864 U.S. Army post; small visitor center.

Natural Features: Located in Grapevine Canyon on the north slope of the Tehachapi Mountains; park vegetation consists of large grassy areas dotted with mostly hardwoods; park area is 205 acres; elevation 3300´.

Season & Fees: Open all year; please see Appendix for park entry fees.

Mail & Phone: Fort Tejon State Historic Park, P.O. Box 895, Lebec, CA 93243; ☎(805) 248-6692.

Park Notes: At its peak of activity, Fort Tejon was the military, political and social hub of the land between Los Angeles and the upper San Joaquin Valley. The fort was the western terminus of the 'Jefferson Davis Highway' from San Antonio, Texas. As U.S. Secretary of War in the 1850's, Davis sponsored an experiment in the use of camels to haul supplies over the Southwest's rugged terrain to the West Coast. (Davis, who later became President of the Confederate States of America, is credited with being the "Father of National Highways".) The U.S. Army 'Camel Corps', under the command of Lt. Edward Beale (also see San Pasqual Battlefield SHP), made its first appearance here in November 1857 at the end of a trial run from Fort Defiance, New Mexico. The first and only U.S. Army Camel Brigade was then organized and is said to have performed admirably on the route from San Antonio to Fort Tejon from 1857-1861. The camel experiment ended with the beginning of the War Between the States and the coming of the railroad.

California 213

CASTAIC LAKE

State Recreation Area

Location: Southern California north of Los Angeles.

Access: From Interstate 5 at the Castaic Exit near milepost 59 +.5, from the east side of the freeway, proceed east on lake Hughes Road for 0.4 mile to a 4-way intersection; turn north (left) onto Ridge Route Road and go 0.4 mile, then turn right, to the visitor center/office, day use and boat launch areas; or continue east from the intersection for 0.2 mile to the launch and parking area on the lagoon's south shore.

Day Use Facilities: Very large picnic area; ramadas (sun shelters) for some sites; drinking water; restrooms; large parking lots; concessions.

Overnight Facilities: Camping for tents and rv's is being developed (please contact the park office for current information); a reservable group camp is available.

Activities & Attractions: Swimming at 4 beaches on the lagoon; limited boating (manual, sail, or electric power) on the lagoon; boating with some restrictions on the main lake; boat launches; fishing for stocked trout, also bass, catfish and crappie; playground.

Natural Features: Located principally on a 180-acre lagoon or afterbay below Castaic Dam, and on the main body of twin-armed, 2000-acre Castaic Lake; developed areas around the lagoon are landscaped with expansive, groomed lawns well-dotted with hardwoods and some conifers; total park area is 8000 acres; elevation 1100´-1500´.

Season & Fees: Open all year (days vary seasonally); park entry fee $4.00 per vehicle, $6.00 for an rv, plus $4.00 for boat launching (subject to change); operated by Los Angeles County.

Mail & Phone: Castaic Lake State Recreation Area, 32132 Ridge Route Road, Castaic, CA 91384; ☎(805) 257-4050.

Park Notes: Castaic Lake SRA is locally called Warren M. Dorn Recreation Complex. About 18 miles up the Interstate from Castaic's first-class facility is, technically, Pyramid Lake State Recreation Area. The state unit is administered by the USDA Forest Service, which, in turn, leases the operation to a concessionaire. Any similarity between Pyramid Lake and other state park areas is purely coincidental. (Q: When is a bear not a bear? A: When it's a turkey. Ed.)

California 214 ♿

ANTELOPE VALLEY CALIFORNIA POPPY
State Reserve

Location: Southern California north of Los Angeles.

Access: From Interstate 5 at the Lancaster/Palmdale Exit (3 miles south of Gorman, 19 miles north of Castaic) travel east on California State Highway 138 for 15 miles; turn south (right) onto Lancaster Road and proceed south and then east for 12 miles; turn north (left) onto a gravel park access road and proceed 0.5 mile to the visitor center parking lot. **Alternate Access:** From California State Highway 14 1 mile north of Lancaster, take the Avenue I Exit and head west on Avenue I for 15 miles to the park access road and continue as above.

Day Use Facilities: Small picnic area with ramadas (sun/partial wind shelters); drinking water; vault facilities; restrooms inside the visitor center; medium-sized parking lot.

Overnight Facilities: None; nearest public campground is in Saddleback Butte State Park.

Activities & Attractions: Spectacular spring blooms of the California poppy (roughly March through May); hiking trails (paved and unpaved); visitor center has interpretive displays and programs about the poppy, local environment, solar energy.

Natural Features: Located on grassy, treeless hills on the west side of Antelope Valley; nearly encircled by high mountains; park area is 1745 acres; elevation 2800´.

Season & Fees: Available all year for day use; visitor center open principally in spring; no dogs allowed; please see Appendix for park entry fees (charged seasonally).

Mail & Phone: c/o CDPR High Desert District Office, 4555 West Avenue G, Lancaster, CA 93536; ☎(661) 942-0662; visitor center phone (seasonally) ☎(661) 724-1180.

Park Notes: The California poppy may grace these windswept slopes with its golden presence (or *presents*) only in spring, but the park is quite enjoyable for a picnic or a hike just about anytime. During much of the 'off-season' at Antelope Valley California Poppy State Reserve you might have the place and its excellent viewpoints all to yourself.

California 215 ♿

SADDLEBACK BUTTE
State Park

Location: Southern California north of Los Angeles.

Access: From California State Highway 14 in Lancaster, take the Avenue J Exit and travel east on Avenue J/LA County Road N5 for 20.5 miles to the intersection of N5 & 170th Street; continue east for another 0.1 mile, then turn south (right) onto a gravel access road into the day use area; or turn south onto 170th Street and proceed 1 mile, then turn east (left) onto a gravel access road for 0.15 mile, then turn left into the campground. (Note: the picnic and camp grounds are connected by a 1-mile gravel road through the park, but this route will keep you on the pavement as long as possible.)

Day Use Facilities: Medium-sized picnic area; many sites have ramadas (sun/partial wind shelters); drinking water; vault facilities; parking at sites.

Overnight Facilities: 50 campsites; (a reservable group camp is also available);

sites are small+ to medium-sized, reasonably level, with fair to fairly good separation; parking pads are gravel, short to long straight-ins; adequate space for medium to large tents; ramadas (sun/partial wind shelters) for most sites; barbecue grills and fire rings; b-y-o firewood; water at central faucets; restrooms; holding tank disposal station; gravel driveways; gas and groceries+ in the community of Lake Los Angeles, 4 miles south.

Activities & Attractions: Saddleback Butte Trail (1.6 miles); Joshua Nature Trail (a guide pamphlet is available); (an unusual "Birdwatcher's Guide to the Antelope Valley" may also be available—check around in the campground).

Natural Features: Located in Antelope Valley in the Mojave Desert near the west slope of 3651´ Saddleback Butte; park vegetation consists of Joshua Trees and desert brush; park area is 2900 acres; elevation 2600´-3651´.

Season & Fees: Open all year; please see Appendix for reservation information, park entry and campground fees.

Mail & Phone: Saddleback Butte State Park, 17102 Avenue J East, Lancaster, CA 93534; no park phone; CDPR High Desert District Office phone ☎(661) 942-0662.

Park Notes: From the picnic area especially, there are really neat views of the entire valley, of Saddleback Butte itself, and of the 10,000´ San Gabriel Mountains to the south. A principal feature here are the Joshua trees which grow throughout most of the park. Oddly enough, the plant is botanically classified as a distant relative of the lily and not as a tree at all. The Joshua tree supposedly was named by the early Mormons to whom its outstretched arms fancifully resembled the biblical character Joshua pointing toward the Promised Land. If you're looking for something to do in addition to admiring the fine surroundings at Saddleback Butte, the Antelope Valley Indian Museum, another unit operated under the park system, is a few minutes' drive from any picnic or camp site. Just head south on 170th Street to Avenue M, then west on 'M' for 2 miles to the museum. The museum holds a collection of Indian artifacts and crafts from California and the Desert Southwest. It regularly features 'hands on' demos. (Phone 805-942-0662.) But why is an Indian museum located in a Swiss chalet snuggled up against a boulder-cloaked hillside in the middle of the California desert? The answer can be found inside.

California 216 ♿

RED ROCK CANYON
State Park

Location: South-east California east of Bakersfield.

Access: From California State Highway 14 near milepost 40 +.5 (17 miles south of the junction of California State Highways 14 and 178 at Freeman Junction near Inyokern, 25 miles north of Mojave) turn west, then immediately north onto Abbott Drive (paved); continue for 0.75 mile, then turn southwest (left) onto a gravel access road to the park entrance station and the visitor center; the picnic area is just west of the v.c.; the campground is 0.5 mile farther west; or near milepost 40 (0.5 mile south of the v.c. turnoff) turn east into the Red Cliffs area.

Day Use Facilities: Small picnic area with ramada, drinking water, vault facilities and small parking area at the visitor center; vault facilities and large parking lot at Red Cliffs.

Overnight Facilities: *Ricardo Campground*: 50 campsites; sites are generally small to medium in size, with nominal to fairly good separation; parking pads are gravel, medium to long, level straight-ins; tent areas are large, somewhat level; fire rings; definitely b-y-o firewood; water at central faucets; vault facilities; gravel driveway; gas and camper supplies, 6 miles south; limited supplies in Inyokern; adequate supplies and services are available in Mojave.

Activities & Attractions: Red Cliffs Natural Preserve (open only to hiking); several miles of hiking trails; (vehicle travel permitted only on designated roads);

campfire center near the visitor center/ranger station.

Natural Features: Located on a Mojave Desert plain; campground is partly encircled by eroded, low, white cliffs (locally called "White House Cliffs") campground vegetation consists of small Joshua trees and short, desert brush; Red Cliffs area has high, red and white cliffs shaped into columns; the Sierra Nevada rises a few miles to the west; park area is 4000 acres; elevation 2600´.

Season & Fees: Open all year; please see Appendix for reservation information, park entry and campground fees.

Mail & Phone: Red Rock Canyon State Park, RRC Box 26, Cantil, CA 93519; no park phone; High Desert District Office phone ☎(760) 942-0662.

Park Notes: Red Rock Canyon itself flanks about a four-mile stretch of highway within the park, so you can enjoy the area to a limited extent just by taking a few extra minutes to stop at one or more of the several roadside pull-outs. Probably the most spectacular of the easily accessible viewpoints is at the large Red Cliffs parking lot. Although some visitors do take advantage of the desert tranquility here in summer, it makes a much better fall through spring park. Skywatching can be highly gratifying in these clear desert skies.

Mojave Desert & San Bernardino Mountains

California 217

PROVIDENCE MOUNTAINS
State Recreation Area

Location: South-east California west of Needles.

Access: From Interstate 40 at the Essex Road Exit at milepost 100 (44 miles west of Needles, 100 miles east of Barstow), at the north side of the Interstate head northwest on a paved local road for 14 miles to the park boundary; here the road begins a long, moderately steep climb for the final 2 miles to the visitor center, picnic area and campground.

Day Use Facilities: Small picnic area; drinking water; vault facilities; small parking lot.

Overnight Facilities: 6 campsites; sites are very small, with minimal to nominal separation; parking surfaces are gravel, reasonably level, short straight-ins or pull-offs; enough space for small tents; fire rings and barbecue grills; firewood is usually for sale, b-y-o to be sure; water at several faucets; (b-y-o water and shade is suggested because of a limited supply of both in the park); vault facilities; gas and camper supplies in Essex, 6 miles southeast of the Interstate exit.

Activities & Attractions: Guided tours of Mitchell Caverns (1.5 miles round trip, 1 hour); Mary Beal Nature Trail (a nice guide booklet is available); short hiking trails; East Mohave National Scenic Area (BLM-administered) borders the park.

Natural Features: Located on a mountainside (and within the mountain) on the east slope of the 7200´ Providence Mountains; picnic sites are minimally shaded, campsites are unshaded; the vast reaches of the Mojave Desert plains lie several thousand feet below the park's vantage point; park area is 5900 acres; visitor center elevation 4300´.

Season & Fees: Open all year; cavern tours are given in the early afternoon on weekdays and several times daily on weekends and holidays from September to June, weekends and holidays in the early afternoon from June to September; tour fees about $4.00 for adults, $2.00 for children 6-17; (it is suggested that you contact the park or the district office for a current time and fee schedule); please see Appendix for reservation information, park entry and campground fees.

Mail & Phone: Providence Mountains State Recreation Area, P.O. Box 1, Essex, CA 92332; no park phone; Mojave River District Office phone ☎(760) 389-2281.

Park Notes: Most visitors are drawn here by the prospect of going deep inside the mountain to pursue stalactites and stalagmites (but no bats, at last report.) A huge, fallen stalactite is on display in the visitor center, so even if you shun dark, close-in places, you can still get a feel for what lies inside the caverns. Outside in the daylight, the desert views are first-rate.

▲ **California 218** ♿

SILVERWOOD LAKE

State Recreation Area

Location: Southern California north of San Bernardino.

Access: From California State Highway 138 at milepost 26 +.4 (10 miles north of Crestline, 11 miles east of the Palmdale/Silverwood Lake Exit on Interstate 15), turn east onto the park access road and proceed 0.6 mile to the entrance station; just beyond the entrance, turn north (left) to the Cleghorn day use area, swimming beach and campsites 96-136; or continue easterly for 0.2 mile to the lower-numbered campsites, or another 1 mile to the Sawpit Canyon day use area, swimming beach and main boat launch. (Note that there is a 'mini interchange' on Highway 138 that serves the park access road; additional, automatic (self-pay) gates are located on Highway 138 at the far east end of the park, 3 miles east of the main entrance, and also on Highway 173 on the north shore of the lake near the dam, 3 miles east of the junction of Highways 138 & 173.)

Day Use Facilities: 2 major picnic areas, plus a third smaller area; 3 group picnic areas; 3 boat-in picnic areas; drinking water; restrooms; 6 medium-sized parking lots; concession stands.

Overnight Facilities: *Mesa Campground*: 136 campsites; (hike-bike sites and 3 group camps are also available); sites are small+ to medium-sized, with fair to good separation; at least half of the sites are basically level, remainder are slightly sloped; parking pads are paved, mostly short+ to medium+ straight-ins, and many are extra wide; also some medium+ pull-off pads; large tent areas in most sites; fire rings and barbecue grills; firewood is usually for sale, or b-y-o; water at several faucets; restrooms with showers; coin-op laundry; holding tank disposal station; paved driveways; adequate supplies and services are available in Crestline.

Activities & Attractions: Designated swimming areas; boating; boat launches; fishing for largemouth bass, striped bass, catfish, bluegill, crappie, rainbow trout; ('fish attractors' have been left at several locations around the lake); 13 miles of paved hiking and bicycling trails; campfire circle; small visitor center.

Natural Features: Located principally on the south and southwest shores of 976-acre Silverwood Lake; the lake lies behind a dam across the West Fork of the Mojave River in a small valley in the San Bernardino Mountains; medium-high oaks and pines and shrubs provide ample shade/shelter for most campsites; wooded hills and low mountains encircle the 200´-deep lake; park area is 2200 acres; elevation 3400´.

Season & Fees: Open all year; please see Appendix for reservation information, park entry and campground fees; automatic gates require payment in crisp greenbacks.

Mail & Phone: Silverwood Lake State Recreation Area, Star Route Box 7A, Hesperia, CA 92345; ☎(909) 389-2303.

Park Notes: There are good views of the surrounding mountains from most picnic sites and many campsites, particularly from the bike camps. Although the lake lies over the West Fork of the Mojave River and a tributary, most of the water doesn't come from local runoff, as might be expected. (But the area does get nearly 40 inches of precip annually). Silverwood's contents originate (theoretically) nearly 700 miles from here, in the upper Feather River in northeast California. A complex system of reservoirs, rivers, aqueducts and pumping stations brings the water to Silverwood Lake. From here, gravity takes the water through a four-mile tunnel and finally into Lake Perris, spinning a set of electric generating turbines on the way for good measure. Also along the entire route, of course, much of the water is divvied-up to assorted users.

California 219

Chino Hills
State Park

Location: Southern California west of Riverside.

Access: From California State Highway 71 (northwestbound) at a point 5.5 miles northwest of the junction of State Highways 71 & 91 west of Corona, 9 miles southeast of Pomona, jog left, then right onto Pomona-Rincon Road and travel northwest (parallel to Highway 71) for 0.9 mile; turn southwest (left) onto Soquel Canyon Parkway and proceed 1 mile, then turn left onto Elinvar Drive, go 0.2 mile, turn left onto Sapphire Drive for another 0.2 mile, then turn southwest (right) onto the park access road (gravel/dirt) and continue southwest then southeast for 3.5 miles to the park headquarters. **Alternate Access:** From State Highway 71 (southeastbound) at a point 8 miles southeast of Pomona, turn southwest (right) onto Los Serranos Avenue (Los Serranos is a continuation of Central Avenue from Chino), go 50 yards, then swing southeast (left) onto Pomona-Rincon Road, travel 0.2 mile, then turn southwest onto Soquel Canyon Road and continue as above. (Note: the park access road may be closed during and just after rainy periods.)

Day Use Facilities: Small picnic area; drinking water; vault facilities; parking area.

Overnight Facilities: A small, primitive camping area and trail camps are available; nearest standard public campgrounds are in Prado Regional Park, 8 miles east, off State Highway 83, and Featherly Regional Park, 10 miles south.

Activities & Attractions: Over 30 miles of hiking, horse, and bike trails (some restrictions apply); horse-handling facilities.

Natural Features: Located on the grass-coated, nearly treeless Chino Hills; short to medium-high grass comprises most of the vegetation, but some draws and pockets contain stands of hardwoods; park area is 11,000 acres; elevation 1000′ to 1800′.

Season & Fees: Open all year, subject to weather conditions.

Mail & Phone: c/o CDPR Chino Hills District Office, 1879 Jackson Street, Riverside, CA 92504; ☎(714) 780-6222.

Park Notes: From a moderate distance, these smooth-to-moderately contoured hills seem to have a surface that's painted on: Kelly green in late winter and spring, cycling to tawny yellow in summer and fall. Actually, these "hills" could qualify as "mountains" in just about anybody's lexicon. This great "open space" will undoubtedly be a welcome isle of solitude to the present and future residents of the many subdivisions sprouting up around the lower slopes of Chino Hills.

California 220 ♿

Lake Perris
State Recreation Area

Location: Southern California southeast of Riverside.

Access: From California State Highway 60 near milepost 19 (11 miles west of the junction of Highway 60 & Interstate 10 near Beaumont, 6 miles east of the junction of Highway 60 & Interstate 215 east of Riverside) take the Moreno Beach Drive Exit and travel south on Moreno Beach Drive for 3.2 miles, then southwest (right) on Via Del Lago for 1.2 miles to the Moreno (north) park entrance station; just beyond the entrance, turn southwest (right) and follow the well-marked route for 1.4 miles to the main campground entrance station; or continue ahead (south) past the park entrance for 0.1 mile, then swing southwest (right) to the day use areas.

Alternate Access: From California State Highway 215 (Escondido Freeway) in Val Verde (4 miles northwest of the city of Perris, 4 miles southeast of the junction of Highway 215 & California State Highway 60 east of Riverside), head east on Pomona Expressway for 2.3 miles; turn north (left) onto Lake Perris Drive and proceed 1.2 miles to the Perris (southwest) entrance station; continue northeast for 0.7 mile to the day use areas or for another 1.2 miles to the campground. (There are at least a dozen other possible routes to the park, but the above accesses should serve the majority of visitors.)

Day Use Facilities: Large picnic areas with ramadas (sun shelters); group picnic areas with ramadas (reservable by groups, contact the park office); drinking water; restrooms; more than a dozen medium to large parking lots; concession stand.

Overnight Facilities: 431 campsites, including 264 with partial hookups; (several group camp areas and a primitive equestrian camp are also available); sites are small- to small+, with minimal to nominal separation; hookup sites are clustered in small 'parking lot' arrangements; most parking pads are paved, short straight-ins; about half of the pads will require a little additional leveling; enough space for medium to large tents in most sites; fireplaces and/or fire rings; b-y-o firewood; storage cabinets (bear boxes); water at several faucets; restrooms with showers; waste water receptacles; holding tank disposal station; paved driveways; complete supplies and services are available within 5 miles west/northwest.

Activities & Attractions: Boating; several boat launches; marina; designated sailing area; fishing for bass, also stocked trout, catfish, bluegill, sunfish; fishing piers; designated swimming beaches; water slide; playground; 9-mile-long (mostly paved) hiking/biking trail around the lake; hiking trails to overlook points; equestrian trail around the lake and into natural lands on the east/northeast corner of the park; designated rock-climbing area on the south side of the lake; designated upland game hunting areas; Regional Indian Museum has interpretive displays related to the history and culture of Mojave Desert Indians; campfire circle and interpretive center; nature walks, evening campfire programs, fishing clinics and other outdoor-related activities, scheduled seasonally.

Natural Features: Located on rolling, sloping terrain around the shore of Lake Perris; picnic and camp sites are on the north shore and are very lightly to lightly shaded by scattered hardwoods and conifers on a surface of sparse grass; sandy beach; bordered by dry, boulder-strewn rolling hills and low mountains; total park area is 8800 acres; elevation 1600´.

Season & Fees: Open all year; Moreno entrance open 24 hours, Perris entrance open daytime hours (subject to change); campsite reservations are "definitely recommended" for weekends, spring through fall; please see Appendix for reservation information, park entry and campground fees.

Mail & Phone: Lake Perris State Recreation Area, 17801 Lake Perris Drive, Perris, CA 92370; ☎(909) 657-0676.

Park Notes: All picnic sites and just about all camp spots have good lake and mountain views. Alessandro Island, a massive, solitary mound, rises from the lake just offshore of the campground and one of the two day use areas. Tent campers have much better sites than rv-ers here. Lake Perris has the largest developed campground in the California state park system. Another lake park with a large campground in the general vicinity is Lake Elsinore State Recreation Area, located at the northwest end of Lake Elsinore, near the city of the same name, a dozen miles southwest of Lake Perris. Recreational facilities on the state land are operated by a concessionaire. Lake Elsinore SRA is located on State Highway 74, two miles southwest of 74's junction with Interstate 5.

California 221

Mount San Jacinto: Idyllwild-Headquarters

State Wilderness & State Park

Location: South-central California southeast of Riverside.

Access: From California State Highway 243 at milepost 5 (on the north edge of the community of Idyllwild, 24 miles southeast of Banning), turn west, go past the ranger station, and into the campground. **Additional Access** (San Jacinto Peak and interior area): From State Highway 111 (Palm Canyon Drive) on the northwest corner of Palm Springs, turn southwest onto Tramway Road (paved) and proceed 4 miles to Valley Station; from there, take the aerial tram to Mountain Station; a short walk will take you to the trailhead and ranger station at Long Valley.

Day Use Facilities: 2 small picnic areas, drinking water; restrooms, small parking areas at Headquarters; small picnic area at Long Valley.

Overnight Facilities: *Headquarters Campground*: 33 campsites; (4 trail camps in the State Wilderness are also available, by reservation only); sites are small+ to medium-sized, with some separation provided by vegetation; parking pads are sand/dirt, mostly short straight-ins, many are extra wide; additional leveling will probably be required in most sites; medium to large tent areas, about half are fairly level; fire rings; some firewood may be available for gathering on nearby national forest lands, or b-y-o; water at several faucets; restrooms with showers; limited supplies within walking distance in Idyllwild; nearest source of complete supplies and services is Banning.

Activities & Attractions: Campfire center for evening programs in summer; trails into the San Jacinto Wilderness; cross-country skiing.

Natural Features: Located near the heart of the high, rugged, San Jacinto Mountains; vegetation consists of tall conifers, large oaks, and some low-level, bushy hardwoods; 10,800′ San Jacinto Peak rises a half-dozen miles north of here; total park area is 13,500 acres; park elevation 5400′ to 10,800′; Idyllwild elevation 5400′; Long Valley elevation 8500′.

Season & Fees: Open all year; please see Appendix for reservation information, park entry and campground fees.

Mail & Phone: Mount San Jacinto State Park, 25905 Highway 243, P.O. Box 308, Idyllwild, CA 92349; ☎(909) 659-2607.

Park Notes: This park has somewhat of a dual personality: in summer, it's popular with Southern Californians who find it's a convenient place to come to escape the sizzle in the lowlands; and snow-campers and x-c skiers find it's a convenient place to escape the mid-winter blahs. Certainly the best way to see the park is to take a backpacking trip through the wilderness. There are three main routes over the top. The shortest trip starts at the Humber Park Trailhead, two miles northeast of Idyllwild. From there it's eight miles—first over a portion of the national San Jacinto Wilderness, then continuing through the state wilderness—to the tram ride at Mountain Station. From there it's 6000 feet down the mountain to the desert floor. Of course, the reverse trip can be taken; the pros and cons of either direction just about balance out.

California 222

Mount San Jacinto: Stone Creek

State Wilderness & State Park

Location: South-central California southwest of Palm Springs.

Access: From California State Highway 243 at milepost 9 +.85, (200 yards south of the Forest Service Alandale Fire Station, 19 miles southeast of Banning, 5 miles northwest of Idyllwild), turn northeast onto a paved access road, and proceed 0.2 mile to the campground.

Day Use Facilities: None; nearest picnic ground is in the park's Headquarters area.

Overnight Facilities: 50 campsites; sites are small+ to medium-sized, with fair to good separation; parking pads are short, gravel/dirt straight-ins, including several extra-wides; good-sized, but somewhat sloped, tent spots; fire rings; some firewood may be available for gathering on adjacent national forest lands, or b-y-o; water at several faucets; vault facilities; hard-surfaced driveway; gas and groceries at Pine Cove, 2 miles southeast; limited supplies in Idyllwild; nearest source of complete supplies is Banning.

Activities & Attractions: Quite respectable mountain views to the east and north from the campground area.

Natural Features: Located in a lightly forested area of tall conifers, brushy hardwoods, and lower level mountain shrubbery; elevation at Stone Creek 6100′.

Season & Fees: Principal season is April to November; may be available at other times, subject to weather conditions; please see Appendix for reservation information, park entry and campground fees.

Mail & Phone: Mount San Jacinto State Park, 25905 Highway 243, P.O. Box 308, Idyllwild, CA 92349; ☎(909) 659-2607.

Park Notes: There are some really good to excellent campsites here. This is one of the comparatively few state park campgrounds that normally (emphasis on *normally*) isn't booked solid every weekend. The price is comparable to that of the local national forest campgrounds, and the sites are, overall, a little nicer.

▲ **California 223** ♿

ANZA-BORREGO DESERT: BORREGO PALM CANYON

State Park

Location: Southwest California northeast of San Diego.

Access: From San Diego County Highway S22 at milepost 17 +.5, at the intersection of Palm Canyon Drive and Montezuma Valley Road, (1.4 miles west of the town circle—called "Christmas Circle"—in the city of Borrego Springs) proceed 0.2 mile west on the park access road; turn north onto the campground access road and continue for 1 mile to the campground entrance station; or continue west past the turnoff onto the campground access road for another 0.2 mile to the visitor center. (Note: From the west boundary of the park for 11 miles down to Borrego Palm Canyon, County Highway S22 is steep and twisty, so if you're driving something—or someone—which doesn't take well to curves and grades, a better route might be via County Highway S3 over Yaqui Pass; but the vast views from the highwayside pull-outs along S22 are incredible.)

Additional Access (for the Desert Gardens/Coyote Canyon area): From County Highway S22/Palm Canyon Drive at a point 0.5 mile east of Christmas Circle, turn north onto DiGiorgio Road and proceed 4.7 miles to the end of the pavement; continue ahead on a narrow, dirt/sand road for another 1.5 miles to the gardens, on the northeast side of the road. (Note: it is suggested that you size-up the road conditions to determine if your vehicle can handle this sand track; beyond Desert Gardens the road up Coyote Canyon becomes very narrow and very rocky, but the scenery gets better, too.)

Day Use Facilities: Medium-sized picnic area near the west end of the campground, with ramadas (sun shelters) for all sites; drinking water; restrooms; parking at each site; good-sized parking lot at the visitor center; small picnic area at Desert Gardens.

Overnight Facilities: 117 campsites, including 52 with full hookups, in 3 sections; (an equestrian camp and a number of group camps are also available, by reservation); sites are generally medium-sized, with fair to fairly good separation; hookup sites tend to be larger; parking pads are paved, level, long pull-throughs in the hookup section; parking pads in the tent section are gravel/earth and tend to be slightly sloped; adequate space for large tents; ramadas (sun shelters) in many of the tent sites; fire rings; b-y-o firewood; water in the hookup units and at central faucets; restrooms with showers; paved driveways; limited+ to adequate supplies and services are available in Borrego Springs.

Activities & Attractions: Visitor center with a large botanical garden and interpretive exhibits and slide programs about desert vegetation, wildlife and geology; Borrego Palm Canyon Nature Trail (an excellent guide pamphlet is available); hiking trails; campfire center; botanical displays at Desert Gardens.

Natural Features: Located at the east edge of the San Ysidro Mountains overlooking the vast Borrego Valley to the east; visitor center area has an extensive and varied collection of desert trees and plants; picnic/campground vegetation includes large, desert bushes and a few palms; the park is highly regarded for its spectacular early spring wildflower bloom; elevation within the park varies from 15′ to 6200′; elevation at Borrego Palm Canyon is about 1200′.

Season & Fees: Open all year; please see Appendix for reservation information, day use and campground fees.

Mail & Phone: Anza-Borrego Desert State Park, P.O. Box 299, Borrego Springs, CA 92004; ☎(760) 767-4684 or ☎(760) 767-5311. (For information about the best spring wildflower viewing periods: sometime during the winter enclose a self-addressed, stamped post card in an envelope, and mail the envelope to "Wildflowers" c/o the park address above; the card will be returned to you about 2 weeks before the expected peak bloom.)

Park Notes: Try to plan your itinerary so the visitor center is one of your first stops when you come to Anza-Borrego. The visitor center is an underground operation. (Well it really *is*—the earth berming helps to keep the place cool.) The excellent exhibits and information inside, and the botanical displays outside, will strengthen your appreciation of the park's unique environment. Borrego Palm Canyon is the largest and most highly developed area in the park. There are some tremendous daytime and nighttime vistas of the valley from here. Some of the palms look like characters from Sesame Street.

▲ California 224

ANZA-BORREGO DESERT: TAMARISK GROVE

State Park

Location: Southwest California northeast of San Diego.

Access: From San Diego County Highway S3 at a point 0.3 mile northeast of the junction of Highway S3 with California State Highway 78, 18 miles northeast of Julian and 12 miles south of Borrego Springs, turn south into the picnic area and campground.

Day Use Facilities: Small picnic area; drinking water; restrooms nearby; small parking area.

Overnight Facilities: 27 campsites; (small, primitive camp areas are available nearby at Yaqui Well, 0.3 mile southwest, and just north of the summit of Yaqui Pass, 2 miles northeast) sites are level, about average in size, with fair to fairly good separation; parking pads are paved, short, but extra wide; adequate space for a medium to large tent in most sites; all sites have ramadas (sun shelters); fire rings; b-y-o firewood; water at central faucets; restrooms with showers; paved driveway; limited+ to adequate supplies and services are available in Borrego Springs.

Activities & Attractions: Cactus Loop Trail; campfire center; interpretive garden; small visitor center/ranger station.

Natural Features: Located in a desert canyon flanked by Pinyon Ridge to the west and Yaqui Ridge to the east; most picnic and camp sites are fairly well shaded/sheltered by huge Tamarisk trees; other local vegetation consists of a good cross-section of typical desert plants; Yaqui Pass, 2 miles northeast; elevation 1400'.

Season & Fees: Open all year; reservations available October to May, and advised for holidays and weekends.

Mail & Phone: Anza-Borrego Desert State Park, P.O. Box 299, Borrego Springs, CA 92004; ☎(760) 767-4684 or ☎(760) 767-5311.

Park Notes: Anza-Borrego's 600,000 acres make it the largest state park in the contiguous United States. Weekend traffic during 'perfect' weather in spring and fall can make it seem a little smaller than that, but it's pretty quiet on weekdays during most of the year. Although a lot of people don't think so, it can even be thoroughly enjoyed in summer, provided you bring your sense of adventure (and, of course, your standard complement of hot-weather supplies as well). While summer picnicking and camping in the desert isn't for everyone, you might consider doing it at least once. (There won't be any crowds.)

▲ California 225

ANZA-BORREGO DESERT: BOW WILLOW

State Park

Location: South-central California northeast of San Diego.

Access: From San Diego County Highway S2 at milepost 48.3 (14 miles northwest of the Ocotillo Exit on Interstate 8, 31 miles southeast of the junction of Highway S2 & California State Highway 78) turn south onto a gravel access road and proceed 1.5 miles to the campground.

Day Use Facilities: None.

Overnight Facilities: 15 campsites; sites are medium-sized, somewhat sloped, with minimal separation; parking pads are medium-length, sloped, with a sandy gravel surface; tent areas are fairly large, with a sandy base, best for free-standing tents, or tents with sand anchors; ramadas (sun shelters) for most sites; no fires allowed; limited water at a central faucet, for drinking and cooking only; vault facilities; sandy gravel driveway; gas and groceries during the winter at a small store 10 miles northwest on S2 near Aqua Caliente Park; limited supplies in Ocotillo.

Activities & Attractions: A half-dozen foot trails lead off from the campground into the hills and mountains for several miles; desert flora and fauna exhibit; Carrizo Badlands Overlook on Highway S2, 3 miles southeast.

Natural Features: Located on a sandy slope at the base of a rocky hillside near the southern boundary of the state park; local vegetation consists of an extensive variety of typical desert plants; barren mountains in most directions, particularly northeast across the badlands; elevation 1000′.

Season & Fees: Principal season is October to May, available for limited use remainder of the year; please see Appendix for campground fees.

Mail & Phone: Anza-Borrego Desert State Park, P.O. Box 299, Borrego Springs, CA 92004; ☎(760) 767-4684 or ☎(760) 767-5311.

Park Notes: This camp has a nice, simple, natural ambience about it. Another state park primitive camping area (dry camp), Mountain Palm Springs, is located 1.2 miles northwest of here, and a half mile west of the highway on a sandy track. Mountain Palm Springs has several small clusters of native California fan palms which are naturally watered by springs in a small canyon. The palm area can be reached via a short trail from the camp area. The three sections of Anza-Borrego described in this volume (Borrego Palm Canyon, Tamarisk Grove and Bow Willow), plus their nearby areas constitute the principal developed facilities in the park. Detailed information and maps covering the park's 600,000 square miles of wilderness and near-wilderness can be readily obtained at the park visitor center.

▲ **California 226** ♿

SALTON SEA: HEADQUARTERS

State Recreation Area

Location: Southeast California between Indio and El Centro.

Access: From California State Highway 111 at milepost 7 +.6 (21 miles southeast of Indio, 67 miles northwest of El Centro) turn west, go 0.1 mile to the park entrance station, then south (left) 0.4 mile to the campground.

Day Use Facilities: 2 small picnic areas with ramadas; drinking water; restrooms; small and large parking areas.

Overnight Facilities: 40 campsites, including 15 with full hookups, in 2 areas; hookup sites are medium-sized, parallel pull-throughs in a paved, semi-parking lot arrangement; standard sites are in a separate section, with short, straight-in parking pads and large, sandy tent spots; standard sites have ramadas (sun shelters); all sites are level; fire rings; b-y-o firewood; water at hookup sites and at central faucets; restrooms with showers; holding tank disposal station; limited supplies and services are available in Mecca, 11 miles north.

Activities & Attractions: Boating; boat launch, dock, and boat wash; fishing for sargo, tilapia, gulf croaker, and orangemouth corvina; self-guided nature trail; visitor center.

Natural Features: Located on the northeast shore of the Salton Sea; a few palm trees and hardwoods are planted in the separators between the hookup sites; a fair amount of shade/shelter is provided by planted hardwoods in the standard campsite section; the west shore of the sea is lined by high and dry desert mountains; annual rainfall is 2.5 inches; total park area is 18,000 acres; 220´ below sea level.

Season & Fees: Open all year; please see Appendix for reservation information, park entry and campground fees.

Mail & Phone: Salton Sea State Recreation Area, P.O. Box 3166, North Shore, CA 92254; ☎(760) 393-3052 or (760) 393-3059.

Park Notes: Locals often refer to the Salton Sea as the "ocean", since it still is an inland ocean, of sorts. Millenia ago, the basin in which it lies was part of the Gulf of California. The modern "sea" is the result of recent human error. During the spring floods of 1905, a levee on a Colorado River canal burst. Just like an electrical current, the river water took the path of least resistance and flooded the Salton Sink. It took two years of frantic work to bring the rampaging waters under control. During that time a new 700-square mile inland sea was formed.

Evaporation has brought the surface area of the Salton Sea down to about 360 square miles, but the sea is shallow: soundings to about 50 feet have been recorded, but the average depth is more like 20 feet. For years, that size was naturally maintained by runoff water. In recent years, however, the surface area has receded, probably as a result of greater use of the fresh runoff water for domestic and agricultural uses. The surface of the sea is at about 225 feet below sea level. Like several other inland oceans, including the Great Salt Lake, the Salton Sea has no outlet. The salt content of the water is similar to that of the Pacific Ocean, but it still falls far short of the Salt Lake's salinity of two to five times that of seawater. Because of runoff and evaporation factors, however, the salt content of the water continues to increase and eventually it may exceed the level which most aquatic life can tolerate.

▲ California 227

SALTON SEA:
MECCA BEACH
State Recreation Area

Location: Southeast California between Indio and El Centro.

Access: From California State Highway 111 at milepost 6 +.2 (23 miles southeast of Indio, 65 miles northwest of El Centro), turn west, go 0.1 mile to the entrance station, then 0.2 mile farther to the campground.

Day Use Facilities: None; picnic sites are available at the headquarters area.

Overnight Facilities: 108 campsites; sites are small, level, with virtually no separation, in what is basically a large parking lot; parking slots are short, paved, straight-ins; small, gravel, table and tent area behind each site; fire rings; b-y-o firewood; water at central faucets; restrooms with showers; holding tank disposal station; limited supplies in Mecca, 12 miles north; adequate supplies and services are available in Indio.

Activities & Attractions: Boating; boat launch, dock, and boat wash accessible from 1.5 miles north, near park headquarters; fishing for sargo, tilapia, gulf croaker, and the ever-elusive orangemouth corvina; visitor center near park headquarters.

Natural Features: Located on the northeast shore of the Salton Sea; the table/tent areas in the campground are somewhat shaded by small hardwoods and a few palm trees; the west shore of the sea is bordered by the Santa Rosa Mountains; the Chocolate Mountains serve as the backdrop for the east shore; some peaks reach to 10,000´; 220´ below sea level.

Season & Fees: Open all year; please see Appendix for reservation information, park entry and campground fees.

Mail & Phone: Salton Sea State Recreation Area, P.O. Box 3166, North Shore, CA 92254;☎(760) 393-3052 or (760) 393-3059.

Park Notes: Great fishing is what brings most people to the Salton Sea, and the creel (or cooler) limits are generous. A wealth of fishing info is readily available locally. Depending upon which of the seagoing transplants you're going after, you'll need jigs, spoons, spinners, live bait or canned corn. (Whole kernel corn, not the creamed variety; and if the fish aren't cooperating, you can always dine on the corn.) Mecca Beach, and Headquarters next door, are the only two developed campgrounds in the park. Three other areas south of Mecca can provide undeveloped ("beach") camping for several hundred campers for several bucks a night. One more item: depending upon the season, the specific location, and your own sense of smell, you may faintly detect (or be clobbered by) the briny fragrance of this region.

▲ California 228 ♿

Picacho

State Recreation Area

Location: Southeast California north of Yuma, Arizona.

Access: From Interstate 8 at the Winterhaven/4th Avenue Exit on the *east* edge of Winterhaven, (the easternmost exit in California, 1 mile west of Yuma), drive northwest on a local road for 0.3 mile; swing east (a sharp right) onto Picacho Road/Imperial County Road S24 (paved) and proceed east for 0.3 mile, pass under the railroad tracks, and head north out of town; after 3.5 miles, S24 takes off to the east, but continue north on Picacho Road for another 0.6 mile, then the pavement ends and the trip begins; press on in a generally northerly direction along a gravel/dirt/sand/dust road (soon you'll zigzag across a canal, pass the city dump, drive under some high-voltage power lines, then bear slightly right at a fork, and that's the last evidence of civilization you'll probably encounter) toward and then past a prominent group of peaks for another 19.5 miles to the park.

Day Use Facilities: Small picnic area; drinking water; vault facilities; small parking lot.

Overnight Facilities: 50 campsites; (2 group camps, 1 of them for boat-in use, plus 2 individual boat-in camps, are also available; group camps are reservable); sites are small, with nominal separation; parking pads are gravel straight-ins; adequate space for tents; fire rings; b-y-o firewood; water at faucets; vault facilities; showers; gravel driveways; gas and groceries+ in Winterhaven; complete supplies and services are available in Yuma.

Activities & Attractions: Boating (more than 50 miles of open river are accessible from here); boat launch; fishing; Picacho Mills Historic Trail.

Natural Features: Located in the Mojave Desert along the west bank of the Colorado River; the Chocolate Mountains and Picacho Peak, a 1947-foot volcanic 'plug', dominate the landscape; several backwater lakes lie on both sides of the river; some riverside and lakeshore areas are lined with canes, reeds and stands of Tamarisk; the desert is dotted with beavertail cactus and ocotillo, but it's wild with flowers in spring; (mosquitos can be quite bothersome here in spring and early summer); park area is 7000 acres; elevation 200´.

Season & Fees: Open all year; please see Appendix for reservation information, park entry and campground fees.

Mail & Phone: Picacho State Recreation Area, P.O. Box 848, Winterhaven, CA 92283; no park phone; Picacho District Office phone ☎(760) 339-5110.

Park Notes: This isn't just a trip—it's a genuine adventure. Note that some maps depict other roads and jeep trails in the region. However, this is really the *only* way to get into this place without a boat or a 'copter—unless you can get the *Enterprise* to beam you in.

Special Section

Ramblin' Rec's

State Vehicular Recreation Areas

Unique to California is a system of State Vehicular Recreation Areas (SVRA's). These sites have been set aside for off highway vehicles (ohv's), off road vehicles (orv's), all terrain vehicles (atv's), dune buggies (db's), four wheel drives (4wd's) and motorcycles (dirt bikes). Because of the specialized nature of the svra's, only brief information about them is listed here. Each area has its own detailed brochure/map which can be obtained from the local svra office or from state park HQ in Sacramento. Most areas have provisions for picnicking and primitive camping and most require a use fee. Days and hours of operation vary seasonally. The areas are listed north to south.

California 229

Clay Pit
SVRA

Located 3 miles west of Oroville on East Oroville Dam Boulevard; 220 acres; c/o Lake Oroville State Recreation Area, 400 Glen Dr., Oroville, CA 95965; ☎(530) 534-2409.

California 230

Prairie City
SVRA

Located at 13300 White Rock Road in Rancho Cordova; 900 acres; mail c/o OHMVR Division, P.O. Box 942896, Sacramento, CA 94296; (no phone).

California 231

Carnegie
SVRA

Located at 18600 Corral Hollow Road off Interstate 580 southwest of Tracy; 1500 acres; park office P.O. Box 1105, Tracy , CA 95376; ☎(415) 447-9027.

California 232

Hollister Hills
SVRA

Located at 7800 Cienega Road southwest of Hollister; 5200 acres; park office 7800 Cienega Road, Hollister, CA 95023; ☎(408) 637-3874.

California 233

Pismo Dunes
SVRA

Located west and south of Pismo State Beach; 2500 acres; c/o CDPR 576 Camino Mercado, Arroyo Grande, CA 93420; ☎(805) 549-3433.

California 234

Hungry Valley
SVRA

Located on Peace Valley Road just off Interstate 5 near Gorman; 19,000 acres; park office Box 1360, Lebec, CA 93243; ☎(805) 248-6447.

California 235

Ocotillo Wells
SVRA

Located on State Highway 78 just east of Anza-Borrego Desert State Park; 14,000 acres; park office 5172 Highway 78, Borrego Springs, CA 92004; ☎(760) 767-5391.

Notes & Sketches

Nevada State Parks

Lake Tahoe Nevada State Park

 Nevada 

West

Nevada 1

LAKE TAHOE NEVADA: SAND HARBOR
State Park

Location: Western Nevada west of Carson City.

Access: From Nevada State Highway 28 at milepost 2 +.5, (5.5 miles south of the junction of Highway 28 & State Highway 431 in Incline Village, 2.5 miles north of the Washoe County-Carson City line) turn west into the Sand Harbor unit; proceed 0.2 mile to the day use areas and the beach. **Additional Access:** From Highway 28 at milepost 2 +.7 (0.2 mile north of Sand Harbor), turn west into the boat launch/parking area; or at milepost 3 +.3, turn west into the viewpoint parking lot.

Day Use Facilities: Large picnic area; group picnic area with ramada (reservations recommended); drinking water; restrooms; 2 large parking lots (rv parking in the south lot); medium-large parking lot for the boat launch; medium-sized lot for the viewpoint.

Overnight Facilities: Primitive camping in 2 backcountry campgrounds, 1 at the north end of the park, one approximately in the center of the park; (a backcountry pamphlet/map with contour lines is available).

Activities & Attractions: Swimming beach; Sandy Point Nature Trail (guide pamphlet available); designated scuba cove; visitor station/office; hiking, horseback riding and mountain biking on more than 20 miles of old logging roads; hiking on the Tahoe Rim Trail; Lake Tahoe Shakespeare Festival, July and August; cross-country skiing.

Natural Features: Located along and above the east shore of Lake Tahoe in the Sierra Nevada; light conifers and tall bushes are the predominant forms of vegetation; total park area is 13,100 acres; park elevation 6200′ to 9000′, Sand Harbor elevation 6200′.

Season & Fees: Open all year, with limited services October to April; please see Appendix for park entry fees.

Mail & Phone: Lake Tahoe Nevada State Park, 2005 Highway 28, P.O. Box 3283, Incline Village, NV 89450; ☎(775) 831-0494.

Park Notes: Sand Harbor's parking lots are usually filled from 11:00 am to 3:00 pm on summer weekends, (even though as many as 500 vehicles are packed in) and a lot of people get turned away. Walk-ins are OK, but you'll probably have to have someone drop you off because very limited roadside parking is available along the highway. When you see the park, it'll be clear why: the long, curved, sandy beach is a real crowd-pleaser. You can't beat the scenery, near or far, either. In his classic *Roughing It*, Mark Twain said of Lake Tahoe: "I thought it must surely be the fairest picture the whole earth affords". Right on.

Nevada 2

LAKE TAHOE NEVADA:
SPOONER LAKE
State Park

Location: Western Nevada west of Carson City.

Access: From Nevada State Highway 28 at a point 0.6 mile north of the junction of Highway 28 & U.S. Highway 50 west of Carson City and 13 miles south of the junction of Highway 28 & State Highway 431 in Incline Village, turn east onto a paved access road and proceed 0.15 mile to the park.

Day Use Facilities: Medium-sized picnic area; group picnic area (reservable); drinking water; restrooms; medium-sized parking lot.

Overnight Facilities: Primitive camping at 2 designated backcountry campgrounds, at the north end of the park, and also roughly in the center of the park; (a backcountry pamphlet/map with contour lines is available).

Activities & Attractions: Fishing for stocked trout (catch-and-release, artificial flies and lures only); limited boating (small, motorless craft); Tahoe Rim Trail extends 4 miles north of the lake to 3.5 miles south; hiking, horseback riding and mountain biking on more than 20 miles of former logging roads; 55 km of groomed x-c ski tracks, (trail pass required from the park office).

Natural Features: Located on a hillside above Spooner Lake in the Sierra Nevada, 2.5 miles east of the east shore of Lake Tahoe; vegetation consists of light to medium-dense, tall conifers and some undergrowth; Spooner Lake elevation 7000´.

Season & Fees: Open all year, with limited services October to April; please see Appendix for park entry fees.

Mail & Phone: Lake Tahoe Nevada State Park, 2005 Highway 28, P.O. Box 3283, Incline Village, NV 89450; ☎(775) 831-0494.

Park Notes: The park holds much, much more land than even the sizeable chunk which most visitors see as they drive Highway 28. The backcountry is what could be called "reclaimed near-wilderness". Most of it was logged off during the mining boom of the 1800's, but much of it has regrown to a freshly forested state. Another small unit of Lake Tahoe Nevada State Park near here is Cave Rock. It's located on State Highway 28, 5.5 miles south of the junction of Highway 28 & U.S 50. Cave Rock has a boat launch, parking lot and restrooms on the shore of Lake Tahoe. It's one of the few spots on the east shore where you can park at the water's edge.

If you come to Tahoe and would prefer not to 'pick up the pace' with everyone else, you might consider bypassing the California parks and coming over to the Nevada side. To be sure, Lake Tahoe Nevada won't be totally unpopulated, but you probably will stand a better chance of finding a parking spot on a midsummer weekend. A good way to take in the Tahoe circuit might be to tour the Nevada segment early in the day, beginning at the north end of the lake. Then gradually work your way around to the south and west shores, getting to the California parks late in the afternoon as other visitors begin to leave. That way the sunlight will also be in your favor most of the day, optimizing your viewing and picture-taking opportunities.

Nevada 3

WASHOE LAKE
State Recreation Area

Location: Western Nevada north of Carson City.

Access: From U.S. Highway 395 (northbound) at Exit 42 (4 miles north of Carson City, 26 miles south of Reno), turn northeast onto East Lake Boulevard and travel 3.25 miles; turn west (left) into the park entrance; turn south (left) and go 0.4 mile to the day use area; or turn north (right) and proceed 0.2 mile, then turn west (left) into the campground. **Alternate Access:** From U.S. 395 (southbound) at milepost 10 +.25 (16 miles south of Reno, 14 miles north of Carson City), turn southeast onto East Lake Boulevard; proceed 7 miles south; turn west (right) into the park entrance and continue as above.

Day Use Facilities: Medium-sized picnic area; vault facilities; large parking lot.

Overnight Facilities: 49 campsites in 2 loops; (a group camp and an equestrian area are also available); sites are generally large, with nominal separation; parking pads are paved, level, long pull-throughs or straight-ins; tent spots are large and level; some pads for tent/table areas; several sites have ramadas (sun shelters); fire rings; b-y-o firewood; water at several faucets; restrooms with showers; holding tank disposal station; paved driveways; gas and groceries in New Washoe City, 4 miles north; complete supplies and services are available in Carson City.

Activities & Attractions: Boating; sailing; windsurfing; boat launch; fishing for perch and catfish; sandy beach in the day use area; short hiking and equestrian trails.

Natural Features: Located on a sage plain in Washoe Valley on the southeast shore Washoe Lake; the lake is 6 miles long, 5000-acres in area, and 6 to 15 feet deep; the lake is ringed by low dry hills to the north, high dry mountains to the east, higher barren peaks to the south, and forested mountains to the west; picnic sites are shaded by large hardwoods on watered lawns; vegetation in the campground consists of large sagebrush, sparse grass and a some trees; typically breezy; elevation 5000´.

Season & Fees: Open all year, with limited services November to April; please see Appendix for park entry and campground fees.

Mail & Phone: Washoe Lake State Recreation Area, 4855 East Lake Boulevard, Carson City, NV 89701; ☎(775) 687-4319.

Park Notes: This is a good, high desert park. The day use area, especially, is quite nice. The sagebrush around here is so huge that it provides more shade than most of the trees. Very good to excellent views in all directions. There's a lot of recreational potential here.

▲ **Nevada 4**

MORMON STATION
State Historic Park

Location: Western Nevada south of Carson City.

Access: From U.S. Highway 395 at milepost 25 +.9 (13 miles south of Carson City, 4 miles north of Minden), turn west onto Nevada State Highway 206 (Genoa Lane) and travel 3.6 miles to a 'T' junction in the community of Genoa; the park is on the northeast corner of the 'T'. (Note: southbound from Carson City, you can shave off a couple of miles by taking Jacks Valley Road from milepost 33 +.1, 1.4 miles south of the junction of U.S. 395 & U.S. 50, then southwesterly for 8 miles into Genoa.)

Day Use Facilities: Medium-sized picnic area inside the compound; medium-sized ramada, drinking water and restrooms adjacent to (north of) the compound.

Overnight Facilities: None; nearest public campground is in Washoe Lake State Park.

Activities & Attractions: Reconstruction of the first white settlement in what is now Nevada; small museum in the park; also, local museum across the street in the restored courthouse.

Natural Features: Located on the west edge of a valley at the foot of the Carson Range; park area is lightly shaded by large hardwoods; park area is 5 acres; elevation 4800´.

Season & Fees: May to October; please see Appendix for park entry fees.

Mail & Phone: Mormon Station State Historic Park, Genoa, NV 89411; ☎(775) 782-2590.

Park Notes: In 1851, a band of 18 men crossed the desert from the Great Salt Lake Valley and built the first trading post in Nevada on this spot, calling it "Mormon Station". Later came more Mormons who settled and established the town of Genoa, which became the county seat of Carson County, Utah. (It was some years later that Nevada and Utah were split into two states.) The Mormons have always had a reputation for their sharp business transactions, and Mormon Station undoubtedly was the scene of many bargaining bouts. (A Nevada grass roots historian who, like his father and grandfather before him, spent the better part of a lifetime in the mining towns of Nevada and California, relates: "When the pioneers who came overland got to where they were headed, they said they were never sure which was the greater of the two major perils they faced along the way—fighting the Indians or trading with the Mormons".)

▲ **Nevada 5**

DAYTON
State Park

Location: Western Nevada northeast of Carson City.

Access: From U.S. Highway 50 at milepost 6 +.5 (1.4 miles east of Dayton, 22 miles west of Silver Springs), turn south into the south unit of the park; proceed 0.1 mile to the entrance station; picnic sites are just southwest of the entrance, or turn west (right) into the campground; or from milepost 6 +.4, turn north into the park's north (mill site) unit.

Day Use Facilities: Small picnic area; group picnic area with ramada (available by reservation only); drinking water; restrooms; small and medium-sized parking areas.

Overnight Facilities: 10 campsites; sites are smallish, level, with nominal to fair separation; parking pads are gravel, medium-length straight-ins or pull-offs; sandy/gravel, framed tent/table pads are adequate for large tents; fire rings; b-y-o firewood; water at several faucets; restrooms; holding tank disposal station; gravel driveways; limited supplies in Dayton; complete supplies and services are available in Carson City.

Activities & Attractions: Hiking along the Carson River Trail; fishing; horseback riding; historical exhibits, including the site of the Rocky Point Mill, in operation from 1861 to 1920.

Natural Features: Located on a desert plain bordered by low hills dotted with a few trees; the Carson River flows past the southern edge of the park; large hardwoods provide very light shade for several picnic and camp sites; the Sierra Nevada rises a few miles west; park area is 160 acres; elevation 4400´.

Season & Fees: Open all year, with limited services November to April; please see Appendix for reservation information, park entry and campground fees.

Mail & Phone: Dayton State Park, P.O. Box 412, Dayton, NV 89403; ☎(775) 885-5678.

Park Notes: Dayton has quite a bit of Nevada history behind it. The area was once a traditional Washoe Indian winter camp. It was also an important Pony Express station. Dayton is the first known site where gold was discovered in Nevada, and it became an early gold mining tent city. With the discovery of the Comstock Lode and the advent of the Silver Rush, the first ore-crushing stamp mill was constructed here and the town served as an important silver ore processing site. Like so many others in the Far West, the boom was short-lived.

▲ **Nevada 6**

FORT CHURCHILL
State Historic Park

Location: Western Nevada east of Carson City.

Access: From U.S. Highway 95A at milepost 36 +.1 (8 miles south of Silver Springs, 24 miles north of Yerington), turn west onto Fort Churchill Road (paved);

proceed westerly for 0.9 mile; angle southwest into the park entrance; at a 3-way intersection just inside the entrance, turn south (left) to the museum and the day use area; or continue southwest past the museum turnoff for another 0.7 mile to a fork; take the right fork onto a gravel road for 0.2 mile to the campground.

Day Use Facilities: Small picnic area; group picnic/camp area (available by reservation only); drinking water; restrooms at the museum; small parking lot.

Overnight Facilities: 20 campsites; (a group camp/picnic are is also available); sites are generally quite spacious, fairly level and well-separated; parking pads are gravel, medium to very long, straight-ins or pull-throughs; ample space for large tents; fire rings and fireplaces; firewood is usually for sale, or b-y-o; water at several faucets; vault facilities; holding tank disposal station; gravel driveways; gas and groceries in Silver Springs.

Activities & Attractions: Ruins of Fort Churchill, a U.S. Army post established in 1860 and left to the desert 10 years later; museum/visitor center has historical exhibits; trail from the campground to the ruins.

Natural Features: Located along or near the north bank of the Carson River; very tall cottonwoods provide a substantial amount of shade for picnic and camp sites; a small stream trickles past the campground; surrounding desert plains and hills are rocky and sage-covered; distinctive purple mountains are visible on the horizon; park area is 210 acres; elevation 4300´.

Season & Fees: Open all year, with limited services November to April; please see Appendix for park entry and campground fees.

Mail & Phone: Fort Churchill State Historic Park, Silver Springs, NV 89406; ☎(775) 577-2345.

Park Notes: Fort Churchill is located along the pioneer trail, the Carson Route of the California Trail. The fort served as a desert outpost to protect the Pony Express and other travelers during the years of the Indian Wars. All that remains of the fort are the adobe walls of some of its buildings. The park's tall cottonwoods are part of a long, continuous line of trees which stretch along the river for many miles through the otherwise harsh desert terrain.

Nevada 7

LAHONTAN: SILVER SPRINGS BEACH

State Recreation Area

Location: Western Nevada east of Carson City.

Access: From U.S. Highway 95A at milepost 41 +.4 (2.8 miles south of Silver Springs, 29 miles north of Yerington), turn east onto Fir Avenue and travel 1.6 miles to a 3-way intersection; turn north (left) and proceed 0.35 mile to the park entrance station; at a point 0.2 mile beyond the entrance, turn east (right) and go 0.7 mile to the day use area, swimming beach and boat launch; or continue past the day use turnoff for 1.6 miles, then turn east (right) into the campground. (Note: the above directions will take you to Silver Springs Beaches 3, 5, 7, and 9; by continuing east on Fir Avenue at the 3-way intersection, then south on a dirt road, you can reach the primitive areas on Beaches 4, 6, 8, and 10.)

Day Use Facilities: Medium-sized picnic area; drinking water; restrooms; medium-sized parking lot.

Overnight Facilities: *Beach 7 Campground*: 27 campsites; sites are small to medium-sized, with nominal to fair separation; parking pads are paved, level, medium to very long straight-ins; tent spots are grassy or sandy, mostly level, and adequate for large tents; barbecue grills and fire rings; b-y-o firewood is recommended; water at several faucets; restrooms with showers (nearby); holding tank disposal station; paved driveways; (primitive, 'dispersed' camping is also permitted along most of the shore of the reservoir); gas and groceries+ in Silver Springs; nearest source of complete supplies and services is Carson City, 45 miles west.

Activities & Attractions: Boating; sailing; boat launch; designated swimming beach;

fishing for channel catfish, white bass, crappie; (a detailed boating and fishing guide is available); swimming; hiking; campfire circle at Beach 7 for scheduled summer evening programs.

Natural Features: Located on the west shore of Lahontan Reservoir, an impoundment on the Carson River; predominant vegetation is sparse grass, tall cottonwoods and a few small bushes; desert hills and mountains surround the lake; the reservoir is 16 miles long and has upwards of 60 miles of shoreline; dozens of small bays and coves provide shelter and add interest to the shoreline; total park area is in excess of 12,000 acres; elevation 4200´.

Season & Fees: Open all year, with limited services November to April; please see Appendix for park entry and campground fees.

Mail & Phone: Lahontan State Recreation Area, 16799 Lahontan Dam, Fallon, NV 89406; ☎(775) 577-2226 (Silver Springs ranger station).

Park Notes: Silver Springs Beach is a desert park but, since it is situated in groves of trees on the shore of this large reservoir, it offers good choices of sun or shade. The recreation area is available year 'round, but if you venture here in winter, keep in mind that this is a *high* desert park—it consistently drops below freezing at night and there's occasional snow, too.

▲ Nevada 8

LAHONTAN: RIVERSIDE & CHURCHILL BEACH

State Recreation Area

Location: Western Nevada east of Carson City.

Access: From U.S. Highway 50 near milepost 5 (0.5 mile northwest of the dam, 10.5 miles northeast of Silver Springs, 15 miles southwest of Fallon), turn south onto a park access road and proceed 0.6 mile top the Riverside camp area or continue for an additional 0.2 mile to the day use area (just south of the dam.)

Day Use Facilities: Medium-sized picnic area; drinking water; restrooms; site-side parking.

Overnight Facilities: Primitive (open) camping along the river (also on beaches, unless otherwise designated); gas and groceries+ in Silver Springs; nearest source of adequate supplies and services is Fallon, 16 miles northeast.

Activities & Attractions: Boating, sailing; boat launch, 1 mile southwest in the Cove area, just off U.S. 50; designated swimming beach; fishing for catfish, white bass, crappie, plus some walleye; swimming.

Natural Features: Located along the east shore of Lahontan Reservoir (day use areas/beaches), and along the Carson River just downstream of Lahontan Dam (camping); predominant vegetation is desert brush, plus some hardwoods along the lake shore; bordered by a desert plain, with desert hills and mountains in most directions; elevation 4200´.

Season & Fees: Open all year, with limited services November to April; please see Appendix for park entry and campground fees.

Mail & Phone: Lahontan State Recreation Area, 16799 Lahontan Dam, Fallon, NV 89406; park hq office ☎(775) 867-3500.

Park Notes: Lahontan is named for the Ice-Age Lake Lahontan which once covered nearly 9000 square miles of the Great Basin to a depth of hundreds of feet. If you look closely, you may be able to distinguish a portion of the ancient lake's former shoreline around the nearby mountainsides. The new Lahontan is a bit smaller. When the reservoir is full it has about 10,000 surface acres of water, but the average area is probably closer to half of that figure. It's still a good-sized body of water, considering the present-day desert climate.

▲ Nevada 9

WALKER LAKE

State Recreation Area

Location: Western Nevada northwest of Hawthorne.

Access: From U.S. Highway 95 at milepost 62 +.5 (13 miles northwest of Hawthorne, 60 miles south of Fallon), turn east and proceed 0.2 mile to the park.

Day Use Facilities: Medium-sized picnic area with ramadas (sun shelters); vault facilities; medium-sized parking area.

Overnight Facilities: None; nearest public campground is Sportsman's Beach (BLM), 3 miles north.

Activities & Attractions: Boating; boat launch; fishing; designated swimming beach.

Natural Features: Located on a rocky flat along the west shore of 25-mile-long Walker Lake, a natural freshwater (more or less) lake; park vegetation consists primarily of sparse desert brush; the mostly barren Wassuck Range rises directly west of the lake; elevation 4100´.

Season & Fees: Open all year; please see Appendix for park entry fees.

Mail & Phone: c/o Nevada State Parks District Office, 16799 Lahontan Dam, Fallon, NV 89406; ☎(775) 867-3001.

Park Notes: Jedediah Smith, one of the boldest of all the West's early explorers, and who was the first American to set foot in Nevada, passed by here during his extraordinary trek across the state in 1828. A year later, Peter Skene Ogden, who journeyed throughout the Great Basin and the Pacific Northwest, and was the first American to see Mount Shasta, came this way as well. John C. Fremont commanded an expedition through here on his trip to California in 1845 and named the lake after his tour guide, Joseph Walker. (Fremont's task, assigned to him by President Polk, was to stir up sentiment against Mexican rule among California settlers in order to win the territory for the United States.)

You can imagine what these early adventurers thought as they stood on the lake's treeless, rocky shore. Even today, finding such an enormous body of water in this incredibly desolate terrain is an undeniably curious encounter. The countryside near the lake's south shore is planted with scores of concrete storage bunkers used by the Army ammunition plant in Hawthorne. The large-caliber ammo dump, although it might look a bit bizarre in other surroundings, fits right in with this asteroidal landscape.

Nevada 10

RYE PATCH

State Recreation Area

Location: Northwest Nevada northeast of Reno.

Access: From Interstate 80 Exit 129 (120 miles northeast of Reno, 22 miles northeast of Lovelock, 45 miles southwest of Winnemucca), turn west (I-80 runs north/south in this section) onto Nevada State Highway 401/Ryepatch Road (paved); proceed for 1.1 miles to the park entrance station; just beyond the entrance turn south (left) and proceed 0.2 mile down to the River picnic area; continue 0.3 mile west (across the dam); turn south (left) and proceed 0.1 mile down a paved driveway to the River camping area; or continue west then north beyond the River camp area turnoff for another 0.8 mile to the Westside picnicking and camping area.

Day Use Facilities: Small picnic area, drinking water, vault facilities and small parking area in the River section; small picnic area, vaults and parking lot near the Westside swim beach; group picnic area with ramada (sun shelter) near Westside.

Overnight Facilities: 43 campsites; River area sites are medium to large, level, with nominal to fair separation; parking pads are paved, mostly medium to long straight-ins; tent spots are grassy, and roomy enough for large tents; Westside area sites are around the edge of a paved parking lot with small tent spots and short straight-in parking pads; small ramadas (sun shelters) for a few sites in Westside; fire rings and barbecue grills; b-y-o firewood; water at several faucets; restrooms with showers, plus auxiliary vaults; holding tank disposal station; paved driveways; gas and groceries at the Interstate; adequate supplies and services are available in Lovelock and Winnemucca.

Activities & Attractions: Boating; boat launch at Westside; fishing for channel cat, crappie, white bass, black bass; designated swimming beach.

Natural Features: Located on the southwest shore of Rye Patch Reservoir (Westside area) and on the banks of the Humboldt River (River area); Westside sites are near the lake shore and have a few small trees between them; River area sites are on a grassy shelf slightly above the river; some River sites are located alongside a grove of hardwoods; 10,000-acre (when full) Rye Patch Reservoir stretches for several miles, and is bordered by chalk-colored, sage-dotted bluffs and hills and distant mountains; maximum depth of the reservoir is about 50 feet; elevation 4100´.

Season & Fees: Open all year, with limited services November to April; please see Appendix for park entry and campground fees.

Mail & Phone: Rye Patch State Recreation Area, Star Route #1, Box 215, Lovelock, NV 89419; ☎(775) 538-7321.

Park Notes: This is a welcome stop along an otherwise barren 500-mile stretch of high desert 'tween Reno and Salt Lake City. (There are also a couple of good freewayside rest areas in Nevada; but for all practical purposes, the only other greenery along I-80 is in the Nevada casinos, or inside the cash registers at the fuel stops in Utah.)

▲ Nevada 11

BERLIN-ICHTHYOSAUR
State Park

Location: Central Nevada southwest of Austin.

Access: From Nevada State Highway 361 at a point 1 mile north of the community of Gabbs (34 miles north of the junction of Highway 361 & U.S. 95 east of Hawthorne, 28 miles south of the junction of Highway 361 & U.S. 50 between Austin and Fallon), head east on a paved local road for 22 miles to Berlin; or continue southeasterly past Berlin for 2 miles to the Ichthyosaur area.

Day Use Facilities: Small picnic area, drinking water, vault facilities, medium-sized parking lot in the ichthyosaur area.

Overnight Facilities: 14 campsites; sites are small to medium sized, with fair to good separation; parking pads are gravel, short to short+ straight-ins; adequate space for medium to large tents; ramadas (sun shelters); fireplaces; b-y-o firewood; water at central faucets; vault facilities; holding tank disposal station; limited to adequate supplies and services are available in Hawthorne, Fallon, Austin, and Tonopah.

Activities & Attractions: Mining ghost town of Berlin; exhibits of the fossils of ancient fish-lizards; ranger-naturalist talks scheduled in summer.

Natural Features: Located on the west slope of the Shoshone Mountains on the east edge of the high desert plain of Ione Valley (Berlin), and in Union Canyon (Ichthyosaur); park area is 900 acres; elevation 6500´.

Season & Fees: Open all year, subject to winter weather conditions; tours $2.00; please see Appendix for campground fees.

Mail & Phone: Berlin-Ichthyosaur State Park, Route 1 Box 32, Austin, NV 89310; ☎(775) 867-3001.

Park Notes: Smaller and less famous than California's Bodie State Park (see separate information), Berlin too is described as being in a state of "arrested decay" in a high desert environment. Berlin is also a bit harder to reach from civilization. (For that matter, just about *any* place in Nevada is hard to reach from civilization—and perhaps that's the whole point in coming here.) The little mining town's history is short, spanning only the calendar space between 1897 and 1910; and it was small (300 souls) by western mining boom town standards. Poking around the residential/commercial district and the mill can still consume a couple of hours, though.

The ichthyosaur exhibit contains the fossilized remains of a trio of large sea serpents caught on the beach when the tide went out on a primordial sea about 100 million years ago. The threesome were members of the largest species of animals of their time—the biggest of the critters were 70 feet long and weighed-in (on the fish scale) at up to 60 tons. Another small historic spot is in this neighborhood, relatively speaking. Belmont Courthouse State Historic Site is a partially restored building in the ghost town of Belmont, 45 miles northeast of Tonopah. If you're into the history of Nye County, Nevada, it would be a worthwhile stop.

Nevada

East

Nevada 12

WILD HORSE
State Recreation Area

Location: Northeast Nevada north of Elko.

Access: From Nevada State Highway 225 at milepost 92 +.1 (19 miles south of Mountain City, 35 miles south of the Nevada-Idaho Border, 65 miles north of Elko), turn west onto a paved park access road and proceed 0.2 mile to the entrance station and another 0.3 mile to the campground or another 0.3 mile to the day use area.

Day Use Facilities: Small picnic area; vault facilities; 2 small parking lots.

Overnight Facilities: 33 campsites in 2 loops; sites are small+ to medium-sized with minimal separation; parking pads are gravel, medium to long straight-ins or pull-throughs and most are level; some sites have good, level tent spots; a few sites are extra-large, with very long parking pads; fire rings; b-y-o firewood; water at central faucets; restrooms, plus auxiliary vault facilities; showers; holding tank disposal station; gravel driveways; gas and groceries in Mountain City; adequate supplies and services are available in Elko.

Activities & Attractions: Fishing for rainbow trout, plus some kokanee salmon, brown trout and largemouth bass; boating; boat launch; weekend interpretive programs in summer; special programs for groups of 10 or more, available by reservation.

Natural Features: Located on windswept hills overlooking Wild Horse Reservoir; park vegetation consists mostly of tall grass and sage; the park is above the northeast shore of the 3000-acre reservoir, in a broad, high desert valley ringed by nearly treeless hills and mountains; park area is 80 acres; elevation 6200′.

Season & Fees: Open all year, subject to winter weather conditions, with limited services November to May; please see Appendix for park entry and campground fees.

Mail & Phone: Wild Horse State Recreation Area, Elko, NV 89801; ☎(775) 758-6493.

Park Notes: Most picnic and camp sites have an almost totally unrestricted, 360 degree panoramic view of this high desert region. Tent campers do stay here, but the campground is probably much better suited to pickup, van and rv camping because of the total lack of shelter (unless you seek out shade under a big sage bush or in the shower). The reservoir was built to provide irrigation water for hay meadows on the Duck Valley Indian Reservation. Water levels are variable.

Nevada 13

SOUTH FORK
State Recreation Area

Location: Northeast Nevada southwest of Elko.

Access: From Interstate 80 (westbound) Exit 303 at the east edge of Elko, travel into midtown Elko to the intersection of Idaho Street (the main drag) and 12th Street; turn south (left) onto 12th Street and go 0.8 mile; turn southeast (left) onto Nevada State Highway 227 (Lamoille Road) and travel 5.3 miles; turn south (right) onto Nevada State Highway 228 (Jiggs Highway) and proceed 5.5 miles to milepost 12 +.4; turn west (right) onto a local road and proceed west and south for 3.8 miles; turn west (right) onto the park access road and proceed 0.5 mile into the park.

Alternate Access: From Interstate 80 (eastbound) Exit 301 at the west edge of

Elko, travel into midtown Elko to the intersection of Idaho & 5th Streets; turn south (right) onto 5th Street and go 0.8 mile; the road will then curve easterly (left) and become State Highway 227; continue for 6 miles to the junction of Highways 227 & 228 and continue as above. (The above routings should help you to minimize the time spent in Elko's traffic jams.)

Day Use Facilities: Vault facilities; gravel/dirt parking areas; (see Park Notes section).

Overnight Facilities: Open camping along the shore of the lake; vault facilities; (see Park Notes section).

Activities & Attractions: Fishing (including ice fishing); boating; boat launch; the Hastings Cut-Off of the California Trail passed through this area; impressive Northeast Nevada Museum in Elko.

Natural Features: Located along the shore of a reservoir on the South Fork of the Humboldt River; vegetation consists mostly of sparse grass and brush; bordered by low hills, plus the lofty Ruby Mountains to the east; elevation 5200´.

Season & Fees: Open all year, subject to winter weather conditions; please see Appendix for park entry and campground fees.

Mail & Phone: South Fork State Recreation Area, Lower South Fork, Elko, NV 89801; ☎(775) 744-4346.

Park Notes: This is one of Nevada's newer state parks. Improvements in facilities are said to be "in the works", so by the time you arrive, there could be more in the way of creature comforts here. Some of the scenic views are so-so, but others, especially toward the 11,300´ mountains to the east, are excellent.

▲ **Nevada 14**

CAVE LAKE
State Recreation Area

Location: Eastern Nevada east of Ely.

Access: From U.S. Highways 6/50/93 at a point 6 miles southeast of Ely, turn east onto Steptoe Creek Road (also called Success Summit Road, gravel) and travel 5.5 miles east and northeast; turn east (right) into the park.

Day Use Facilities: Medium-sized picnic area; drinking water; vault facilities; several small parking areas.

Overnight Facilities: 20 camp/picnic sites; sites are small, with nominal separation; parking surfaces are gravel, medium-length straight-ins or pull-offs; adequate space for tents; fire rings; b-y-o firewood; water at central faucets; vault facilities; gravel driveways; limited+ supplies and services are available in Ely.

Activities & Attractions: Fishing for stocked rainbow and brown trout; limited boating; boat launch; ice fishing, snowmobiling, x-c skiing (if you have a vehicle that'll make it up the road to the park).

Natural Features: Located on the north shore of Cave Lake, a 32-acre reservoir on Cave Creek, in the Schell Creek Range; closely bordered by rocky, evergreen-dotted hills and mountains; elevation 7300´.

Season & Fees: Open all year, subject to weather conditions; principal season is May to October; please see Appendix for campground fees.

Mail & Phone: Cave Lake State Recreation Area, P.O. Box 761, Ely, Nevada 89301; ☎(775) 728-4467.

Park Notes: Cave Lake has the reputation of being one of the better trout fishing spots in the state. Besides that, its a really pretty spot. An historic site near Cave Lake might be worth a short side trip. Ward Charcoal Ovens State Historic Site preserves six charcoal kilns south of the hamlet of Ward. The stone, beehive-shaped ovens converted the local pine forests into charcoal for the mining camp of Ward. The turnoff from U.S. Highways 6/50/93 is 4.9 miles southeast of midtown Ely. From there it's 9 miles south down the valley on a gravel/dirt road. U.S. 50 between Ely and Fernley has gained some renown as "The Loneliest Road in America". If you journey to Ely from the west, you'll learn precisely how it earned that title.

Nevada 15

Spring Valley
State Park

Location: Southeast Nevada northeast of Las Vegas near the Nevada-Utah border.

Access: From U.S. Highway 93 at milepost 119 at the east edge of the community of Pioche, turn east onto Nevada State Highway 322 and proceed east, then northeast, for 19 miles to the park. (Note: many maps are somewhat ambiguous in their numbering of the state highways around Pioche; best thing to remember is to head for, then past, Ursine, to Eagle Valley Dam and reservoir.)

Day Use Facilities: Small picnic area; drinking water; restrooms; medium-sized parking lot.

Overnight Facilities: 37 campsites in 2 loops; (a group camp area is also available); site size is slightly larger than average, with fairly good separation; parking pads are gravel, and most are medium to long straight-ins which may require a little additional leveling; medium to large, fairly level, tent areas; ramadas (sun shelters) over table areas; fireplaces or barbecue grills; firewood is usually for sale, or b-y-o; water at several faucets; restrooms with showers; holding tank disposal station; gravel driveways; limited+ to adequate supplies and services are available in Pioche.

Activities & Attractions: Fishing for trout and bass in the reservoir; stream fishing for trout below the dam; limited boating; boat launch and dock; fish cleaning station; small amphitheater.

Natural Features: Located in a small canyon on the west shore of 65-acre Eagle Valley Reservoir; campground is in a small side canyon; vegetation consists of some junipers and pinon pines, plus sparse grass and sage, in a semi-arid, high desert environment; surrounded by low hills dotted with evergreens and brush; total park area is 1630 acres; elevation 5800´.

Season & Fees: Open all year, with limited services November to April; please see Appendix for park entry and campground fees.

Mail & Phone: Spring Valley State Park, Star Route # 89063, Pioche, NV 89043; ☎(775) 962-5102.

Park Notes: All in all, this is a nice place to spend some time. The surroundings, while not spectacular, are interesting. In the mid-1860's, a group of pioneers named the area Spring Valley after they had counted more than 150 springs in a single day. Remains of settlers' ranches can be seen in the park area.

Nevada 16

Echo Canyon
State Recreation Area

Location: Southeast Nevada northeast of Las Vegas near the Nevada-Utah border.

Access: From U.S. Highway 93 at milepost 119 at the east edge of the community of Pioche, turn east onto Nevada State Highway 322 and drive east for 4 miles to milepost 4 +.76; turn south onto a paved local road signed (hopefully, still) for "Echo Dam"; proceed 7.6 miles to the park boundary and continue straight ahead for another 0.4 mile to the campground, on the north (left) side of the road. (Note: road signs around here tend to be a little vague; best thing to remember might be that, if you find yourself in Utah, you missed it.)

Day Use Facilities: Small picnic area; group picnic area with ramadas; drinking water; restrooms; small parking areas.

Overnight Facilities: 34 campsites; (a group camp area is also available); sites are small+ to medium-sized, with nominal to fair separation; parking pads are gravel, medium to long straight-ins, which may require a slight amount of additional leveling; small to medium-sized, gravel pads for tents; ramadas (sun shelters) over table areas; fire rings and barbecue grills; b-y-o firewood; water at faucets throughout; restrooms; holding tank disposal station; gravel driveways; limited+ to adequate supplies and services are available in Pioche.

Activities & Attractions: Fishing for trout and panfish; boating; boat launch; Ash Canyon Nature Trail (2.5 miles, trail guide available).

Natural Features: Located on sage slopes around and above the shore of 65-acre Echo Canyon Reservoir; some hardwoods and evergreens provide a small amount of natural shade; surrounded by dry, low hills; some views of distant mountains; park area is 920 acres; elevation 5500´.

Season & Fees: Open all year, with limited services November to April; please see Appendix for park entry and campground fees.

Mail & Phone: Echo Canyon State Recreation Area, Star Route Box 295, Pioche, NV 89043; ☎(775) 962-5103.

Park Notes: The reservoir is subject to drastic decreases in water level by midsummer, so fishing, boating and the lake view might not be in their prime then. But, really, it's worth staying here regardless of the water level. You might very well have this park nearly all to yourself.

▲ **Nevada 17**

CATHEDRAL GORGE
State Park

Location: Southeast Nevada northeast of Las Vegas.

Access: From U.S. Highway 93 at milepost 108 +.9 (9 miles south of Pioche, 15 miles north of Caliente), turn west onto a paved access road and proceed west and north for 0.8 mile; turn west (left) and proceed west and north again for another 0.7 mile to the picnic area and the campground, on the west (left) side of the park road; or continue north for another 2 miles to the scenic overlook.

Day Use Facilities: Small picnic area with ramada.

Overnight Facilities: 22 campsites; sites are small to medium in size, level, with nominal separation; parking pads are gravel, extra wide straight-ins; good, large tent areas; some sites have small ramadas (sun shelters); waste water disposal basins; fireplaces or barbecue grills; b-y-o firewood; water at several faucets; restrooms with showers; holding tank disposal station; limited+ to adequate supplies and services are available in Pioche and Caliente.

Activities & Attractions: Unusual, pastel rock formations; nature trail; small amphitheater; scenic overlook.

Natural Features: Located in a shallow canyon bordered by rocky bluffs and spire-shaped rock formations; medium to large hardwoods provide very light to light-medium shade/shelter in most picnic and camp sites; canyon floor has tall grass and brush; high mountains in the near distance; park area is 1600 acres; elevation 4500´.

Season & Fees: Open all year, with limited services November to April; please see Appendix for park fees.

Mail & Phone: c/o Nevada State Parks District Office, P.O. Box 176, Panaca, NV 89042; ☎(775) 728-4467.

Park Notes: Cathedral Gorge is closest to the main highway (U.S. 93) of the five state parks/recreation areas which offer virtually all of the public picnicking and camping opportunities in this sparsely populated region. Overall, it may be the most scenically interesting of the quintet as well. Unlike the others, which have water features, this park is in a bone-dry, high desert environment.

▲ **Nevada 18**

BEAVER DAM
State Park

Location: Southeast Nevada southeast of Caliente.

Access: From U.S. Highway 93 at milepost 100 (18 miles south of Pioche, 6.5 miles north of Caliente), head east-southeast on a local gravel road for 29 miles to the park. (Note: The road is graded a couple times a year, but nonetheless can become pretty slick and rutty in wet weather.)

Day Use Facilities: Small picnic area; other facilities are shared with campers.

Overnight Facilities: 45 campsites; (a group camp is also available); sites are small to medium-sized, with nominal to fair separation; parking pads are gravel, mostly short to medium-length straight-ins; medium to large tent areas; some sites have small ramadas (sun shelters); fire rings; b-y-o firewood; water at central faucets; vault facilities; nearest sources of supplies and services (limited+ to adequate) are in Pioche and Caliente.

Activities & Attractions: Hiking and interpretive trails; lake fishing for trout (accessible via foot trail).

Natural Features: Located among small canyons along a stream and near the west shore of a small reservoir; picnic and camp sites are lightly sheltered by piñon pines and junipers; bordered by lightly to moderately forested hills and canyon walls; elevation 5100´.

Season & Fees: Open all year, with limited services and reduced fees November to April; 14 day limit; please see Appendix for standard state park fees.

Mail & Phone: c/o Nevada State Parks District Office, P.O. Box 176, Panaca, NV 89042; ☎(775) 728-4467.

Park Notes: This park is available and accessible—at a price. In addition to the nominal park entry and camping fees, the 'cost of admission' is a somewhat grueling drive across high desert hills and plains almost to the Nevada-Utah border. Worth it? Probably at least once.

▲ Nevada 19

Kershaw-Ryan
State Recreation Area

Location: Southeast Nevada south of Caliente.

Access: From Nevada State Highway 317 at milepost 56 +.9 (2 miles south of the junction of Highway 317 & U.S. Highway 93 on the west edge of Caliente, 19 miles north of Elgin), turn east onto a paved park access road and proceed 2 miles to the park.

Day Use Facilities: Small picnic area; other facilities are shared with campers.

Overnight Facilities: 12 campsites; sites are small, level, with nominal separation; parking pads are gravel, mostly short to medium-length straight-ins; adequate space for tents; fire rings; b-y-o firewood; water at central faucets; restrooms; limited+ to adequate supplies and services are available in Caliente.

Activities & Attractions: Hiking trails.

Natural Features: Located along a stream in rugged but colorful Rainbow Canyon; camp and picnic area vegetation consists of grass and scattered hardwoods which provide some shade for picnic and camp sites; canyon walls are dotted with brush and small evergreens; developed park area is 6 acres, total park area is 240 acres; elevation 5000'.

Season & Fees: Open all year, with limited services November to April; 14 day limit; please see Appendix for standard state park fees.

Mail & Phone: c/o Nevada State Parks District Office, P.O. Box 176, Panaca, NV 89042; ☎(775) 728-4467.

Park Notes: Early settlers in this canyon planted grape vines, trees and lawns around a spring-fed pond which stood in sharp contrast to the rocky walls of the gorge. This park was badly damaged by a flood in the mid-1980's and has been re-opened on a limited basis. It is suggested that you contact the state parks district office in Panaca for current information about its availability.

▲ Nevada 20

Valley of Fire
State Park

Location: Southeast Nevada northeast of Las Vegas.

Access: From Interstate 15 Exit 75 for Valley of Fire (34 miles northeast of Las Vegas, 46 miles southwest of Mesquite) travel east on Nevada State Highway 169 for 14 miles to the west park boundary; proceed easterly for another 2 miles, then turn northwest (left) onto the campground access road for 0.3 mile to the first camp loop, or go another 0.7 mile (around the large 'island' of rock) to the second camp loop; or continue for another 1.9 miles past the campground turnoff to the visitor center; or go past the visitor center for an additional 3.3 miles to the east park boundary. **Alternate Access:** From the Lake Mead North Shore Road at milepost 46 +.1 (9 miles south of Overton, 46 miles northeast of Henderson), turn west on Nevada State Highway 169 and travel 2 miles to the east park boundary and proceed in reverse of the above directions.

Day Use Facilities: Several small picnic areas with vault facilities and parking lots are along or just off the main road; picnicking is also available in the campground.

Overnight Facilities: 59 campsites, including 12 walk-ins, in 2 loops; (a group area is also available); sites are small+ to large, reasonably level, with nominal to good separation; parking pads are gravel, short to medium-length straight-ins; a number of sites have framed gravel tent/table pads and ramadas (sun shelters) over the tables; adequate space for medium to large tents; barbecue grills; b-y-o firewood; water at several faucets; restrooms with showers, plus auxiliary vault facilities; holding tank disposal station; gravel driveways; gas and groceries+ in Overton.

Activities & Attractions: Hiking and equestrian trails; nature trail; Atlatl Rock with Indian Petroglyphs; petrified wood exhibits; visitor center; Lake Mead National Recreation Area (Overton Beach area), 7 miles east.

Natural Features: Located on 46,000-acres of desert, with red sandstone rock formations and darker hills and mountains visible in every direction; a few creosote bushes and yucca plants dot the sandy desert floor; a number of campsites are separated by huge, colorful boulders; park area is 46,000 acres; elevation 1500´.

Season & Fees: Open all year; please see Appendix for park entry and campground fees.

Mail & Phone: Valley of Fire State Park, P.O. Box 515, Overton, NV 89040; ☎(702) 397-2088.

Park Notes: Valley of Fire resembles places like Canyonlands, Monument Valley or Arches, only on a smaller, less-overwhelming scale. In midsummer, it quite regularly reaches 120° around here; but in spring and fall the temps are nearly ideal (depending upon your individual preferences). If you hit the Lake Mead region on a busy weekend, this park should provide a little more tranquility than the large rec areas south of here along Lake Mead's shore, (which the locals call the "war zone"). There's plenty of water at Valley of Fire (although it all comes from spigots, unless a flash flood occurs), and the facilities are on par with (or better than) those in the national recreation area.

▲ **Nevada 21** ♿

FLOYD LAMB
State Park

Location: Southeast corner of Nevada northwest of Las Vegas.

Access: From U.S. Highway 95 near milepost 89 (13 miles northwest of the junction of U.S. 95 & Interstate 15 in downtown Las Vegas) turn northwest onto North Durango Drive (paved) and proceed 1.3 miles to a fork; bear right at the fork and continue for another 0.6 miles to the park entrance station; the park extends for 0.8 mile beyond the entrance.

Day Use Facilities: Very large picnic area; medium-sized ramadas (sun shelters) all over the place; a half-dozen group picnic areas (reservable); drinking water; restrooms; several medium-sized parking lots along the main park road.

Overnight Facilities: None; nearest public campgrounds are in the Charleston Peak area of Toiyabe National Forest, 18 miles west of this park.

Activities & Attractions: Paved walk, jog, and bike path winds through the park; kids' fishing; historic area.

Natural Features: Located on a desert plain; park landscaping consists of acres and acres of mown lawns dotted with large hardwoods, some evergreens, a few palms, plus a chain of several large ponds; peacocks roam the lawns, ducks paddle the ponds and geese waddle along the walkways; bordered by high desert mountains to the north and the Spring Mountains, topped by 11,900´ Charleston Peak to the southwest; elevation 2100´.

Season & Fees: Open all year, daylight hours; please see Appendix for reservation information and park entry fees.

Mail & Phone: Floyd Lamb State Park, 9200 Tule Springs Road, Las Vegas, NV 89131;☎(702) 486-5413.

Park Notes: Was this a former golf course? It almost could pass for one. No, it started out in the 1950's as Tule Springs Ranch, a guest ranch where a lot of people waited out their six-week residence requirement prior to getting that traditional Las Vegas *bon voyage* present, the quickie divorce. If you want to catch some rays, some shade, a few afternoon zzzzz's, or just want to watch the antics of birdlife, try this place. (If a denomination of ducks is a "flock", and a gathering of geese is a "gaggle", what would you call a population of peacocks? A 'passel of peacocks' maybe?) The park proves that all of the 'naturals' in 'Vegas aren't at the craps tables and all of the showplaces aren't on the Strip.

▲ Nevada 22 ♿

SPRING MOUNTAIN RANCH
State Park

Location: Southeast corner of Nevada west of Las Vegas.

Access: From Interstate 15 (northbound) Exit 33 for Blue Diamond/Pahrump near the south edge of Metro Las Vegas, head west on Nevada State Highway 160 (Pahrump Valley Road) for 10.5 miles to the junction of State Highways 160 & 159; bear north (right) onto State Highway 159 and travel north (through the burg of Blue Diamond) for another 5.5 miles; turn west (left) onto the paved park access road and proceed 1 mile to the parking lot. **Alternate Access:** From I-15 (southbound) in midtown Las Vegas, take Exit 41 for Charleston Boulevard/Nevada State Highway 159 and travel west then south for 20.5 miles to the park turnoff and continue as above.

Day Use Facilities: Medium-sized picnic area; group picnic area; drinking water; restrooms; medium-large parking lot.

Overnight Facilities: None; nearest useable public campgrounds are in the Mount Charleston area of Toiyabe National Forest off U.S. 95 northwest of the park, and in Lake Mead National Recreation Area.

Activities & Attractions: Well-preserved/renovated buildings of a ranch dating back to the mid-19th Century; self-guided and guided tours of the buildings and grounds; visitor center with historical information.

Natural Features: Located on the edge of a desert plain at the eastern foot of the Wilson Range; the Wilson Cliffs rise sharply from the plain to 7,000´ just west of the park; park vegetation consists of large hardwoods and lawn areas around the ranch grounds, Joshua trees and desert brush in the surrounding area; wild burros freely roam the adjacent public lands; elevation 2300´.

Season & Fees: Open all year; visitor center is open and guided tours are generally available on weekends and holidays; (it is suggested that you contact the park for a current schedule); please see Appendix for park entry fees.

Mail & Phone: Spring Mountain Ranch State Park, P.O. Box 124, Blue Diamond, NV 89004; ☎(702) 875-4141.

Park Notes: Because of abundant spring water in the nearby mountains, this area was for centuries a residence of the Paiute Indians, then a campsite on the Old Spanish Trail. The ranch was originally established as the Bill Williams Ranch (named for the region's greatest frontiersman) in the mid-1860's. The list of the ranch's previous owners includes the names of several Hollywood and show biz people (none of whom you'll likely recognize). Don't come here expecting to find a bucolic, single-pit cow camp—this is Rancho Deluxe.

Another state park in the Las Vegas area that's currently being developed is called Mormon Fort State Park. It's the archaeological site of an adobe fortress built during the mid-1850's on what is now the Las Vegas Strip. The site was discovered while a lot was being excavated for a new commercial developmnent Although it's now mostly just a 'dig', plans call for eventually ading a visitor/interpretive center and exhibits.

Notes & Sketches

Special Section

Creative Traveling

In its most elementary form, traveling requires very little in the way of extensive planning or highly specialized and sophisticated equipment. A stout knife, some matches, a few blankets, a free road map, a water jug, and a sack of p.b.& j. sandwiches, all tossed onto the seat of an old beater pickup, will get you started on the way to a lifetime of outdoor adventures.

Idyllic and nostalgic as that scenario may seem, most of the individuals reading this *Double Eagle*™ Guide (as well as those *writing* it) probably desire (and deserve) at least a few granules of comfort sprinkled over their car or mini van, and around their tent or rv.

There are enough books already on the market or in libraries which will provide you with plenty of advice on *how* to travel.In this series we've concentrated your hard-earned *dinero* into finding out *where* to travel. However, there are still a few items that aren't widely known, or which bear repeating, so we've included them in the following paragraphs.

Resourcefulness. When putting together your equipment, it's both challenging and a lot of fun to make the ordinary stuff you have around the house, especially in the kitchen, do double duty. Offer an 'early retirement' to serviceable utensils, pans, plastic cups, etc. to a 'gear box'.

Resource-fullness. Empty plastic peanut butter jars, pancake syrup and milk jugs, ketchup bottles, also aluminum pie plates and styrofoam trays, can be washed, re-labeled and used again. (The syrup jugs, with their handles and pop-up spouts, make terrific 'canteens' for kids.) The lightweight, break-resistant plastic stuff is more practical on a camping trip than glass containers, anyway. *El Cheapo* plastic shopping bags, which have become *de rigueur* in supermarkets, can be saved and re-used to hold travel litter and picnic or camping trash. When they're full, tie them tightly closed using the 'handles'.

Redundancy. Whether you're traveling in a car, pickup, van, boat, motorhome or trailer, it pays to think and plan like a backpacker. Can you make-do with fewer changes of clothes for a short weekend trip? How about getting-by with half as much diet cola, and drink more cool, park spring water instead? Do you really *need* that third curling iron? Real backpackers (like the guy who trimmed the margins off his maps) are relentless in their quest for the light load.

Water. No matter where you travel, *always* carry a couple of gallons of drinking water. Backwoods water sources may be out of order (e.g., someone broke the handle off the hydrant or the well went dry). Because of the possibility of encountering the widespread 'beaver fever' (*Giardia lamblia*) parasite and other diseases in lakes and streams, if treated or tested H_2O isn't available, boil the surface water for a full five minutes.

Juice. If you're a tent or small vehicle camper who normally doesn't need electrical hookups, carry a hotplate, coffee pot, or hair dryer when traveling in regions where hookup campsites are available. The trend in public campground management is toward charging the full rate for a hookup site whether or not you have an rv, even though there are no standard sites available for you to occupy. In many popular state parks, hookup sites far outnumber standard sites. At least you'll have some use for the juice.

Fire. A really handy, clean option to using wood or charcoal is to carry a couple of synthetic 'fire logs'. The sawdust-and-paraffin logs are made from byproducts of the lumber and petroleum industries and burn about three hours in the outdoors. The fire logs can also be used to start and maintain a regular picnic or camp fire if the locally gathered firewood is wet.

Styrofoam. This flimsy synthetic may not be environmentally acceptable, but it's a fact of modern life. After you stop for a fuel-up and a rest break along the highway, save the foam cups which contained your coffee, cocoa or soft drinks; then rinse them out at the next stop or when you arrive at your picnic or camp site. The cups can be used again for drinks, collecting specimens for nature study, or to hold nightcrawlers gathered from under a log for fishing bait.

Styrofoam or paper cups weighted with a few stones occasionally can be seen holding a small collection of wildflowers and left on the picnic table as a centerpiece for the next visitors.

Rattlers. Anywhere you go in the West, expect to find rattlesnakes or other poisonous reptiles, so place your hands and feet and other vital parts accordingly. (While preparing the *Double Eagle*™ series, one of the publishers inadvertently poked her zoom lens to within a yard of a coiled rattler's snout. The photographer's anxieties were vocally, albeit shakily, expressed; the level of stress which the incident induced on the snake is unknown.)

Mosquitoes. The winged demons aren't usually mentioned in the text because you just have to *expect* them almost anywhere except perhaps in the driest desert areas. Soggy times, like late spring and early summer, are the worst times. If you're one of us who's always the first to be strafed by the local mosquito squadron, keep plenty of anti-aircraft ammo on hand. The most versatile skin stuff is the spray-on variety. Spray it all over your clothes to keep the varmints from poking their proboscis through the seat of your jeans. A room spray comes in handy for blasting any bugs which might have infiltrated your car, tent or rv. Fortunately, in most areas the peak of the mosquito season lasts only a couple of weeks, and you can enjoy yourself the rest of the time. Autumn traveling is great!

Plants. Poison ivy, oak and sumac can be found in many wooded regions throughout the West. Avoid off-trail brush-busting or side-swiping trailside vegetation with bare skin. Oleander, those beautifully flowering bushes planted in parks all over the Western Sunbelt are toxic, so keep your pets and your kids from nibbling on them. Likewise, in the desert regions, steer plenty clear of cholla cactus. The Indians call it the "jumping cactus" with good reason.

Creepy-crawlers. In arid Desert Southwest regions, watch for scorpions and other ground-based critters. In the Southwest Plains, tarantulas make their appearances in spring and fall, but the fuzzy arachnids will leave you alone if you reciprocate.

Horsepower. Your vehicle will lose about four percent of its power for each 1000′ gain in altitude above sea level. Keep that in mind in relation to the "pack like a backpacker" item mentioned previously. You might also keep it in mind when you embark on a foot trip. The factory-original human machine loses about the same amount of efficiency at higher elevations.

Air. To estimate the temperature at a park in the mountains while you're still down in the valley or on the plains, subtract about three degrees Fahrenheit for each 1000′ difference in elevation between the valley and the park. Use the same method to estimate nighttime lows in the mountains by using weather forecasts for valley cities.

Reptile repellent. Here's a sensitive subject. With the rise in crimes perpetrated against travelers in the nation's parks and forests and on its highways and byways, it's become increasingly common for legitimate travelers to pack a 'heater'—the type that's measured by caliber or gauge, not in volts and amps. To quote a respected Wyoming peace officer: "Half the pickups and campers in Wyoming and Montana have a .45 automatic under the seat or a 12-gauge pump beneath the bunk". If personal safety is a concern to you, check the laws, get competent instruction, practice a lot, and join the NRA.

Vaporhavens. Be skeptical when you scan highway and forest maps and see hundreds of little symbols which indicate the locations of alleged parks and campsites; or when you glance through listings published by government agencies or promotional interests. A high percentage of those 'recreation areas' are as vaporous as the mist rising from a warm lake into chilled autumn air. Many, many of the listed spots are actually simple picnic areas, fishing access sites, and even highway rest stops; dozens of camps are ill-maintained remnants of their former greatness, located at the end of rocky jeep trails; many others no longer exist; still others *never* existed, but are merely a mapmaker's or recreational planner's notion of where a recreation area *might* or *should* be. Make certain that a park exists and what it offers before you embark on 20 miles of washboard gravel travel in the never-ending quest for your own personal Eden.

We hope the foregoing items, and information throughout this series, help you conserve your own valuable time, money, fuel and other irreplaceable resources. ***Good Traveling!***

Appendix A

$ Far West Standard State Park Fees

California State Parks

Daily park entry fee/parking (per vehicle, most parks)	$4.00-$14.00
Daily entry/parking fee, primitive parks	$3.00
Primitive/semi-developed campsite	$9.00-$15.00
Standard/developed/enroute campsite	$11.00-$25.00
Hookup campsite	$9.00 add'l
Backcountry or hike/bike campsite (per person)	$3.00
Enroute/Overflowing camping	$11.00-$25.00
Group campsite (depends on occupancy)	$53.00-$450.00
Showers	$0.25-$0.50
Walk-in fee (per person)	$2.00-$5.00
Overnight camping, premium sites	$10.00 add'l
Peak season, per campsite	$3.00-$5.00 add'l
Boating, motorized vessels	$5.00-$8.00

(The basic campsite fee varies with the level of amenities, niceties, and creature comforts provided in each campground. A substantial majority of campsites throughout the state park system are priced near the top end of the range. Off-season rates are available in most parks. Limits of stay vary from 7 to 30 days.)

Nevada State Parks

Daily park entry fee (per vehicle)	$3.00-$5.00
Primitive/semi-developed campsite	$6.00
Standard/developed campsite	$8.00
Group campsite	$15.00 + $8.00/vehicle

Both California and Nevada offer annual permits and discount permits for handicapped individuals, disabled veterans, and seniors. Annual park entry permits offer substantial savings for frequent park users.

The above list covers fee information needed by most park visitors.

It is recommended that you call your selected park a few days prior to arrival to determine the exact campsite fees you'll be charged.

In both states, fees for the use of group facilities and for special activities like boat launch and moorage, vary considerably. As an example, expect to pay a minimum of $10.00 for a small group picnic to $100.00 or more for a large gathering, plus a substantial (but refundable) cleaning deposit.

Please remember that fees are subject to change without notice.

Far West State Park Reservations

Reservations for individual and group campsites in most California state parks, as well as for guided tours of Hearst San Simeon State Historical Monument, may be obtained from 10 to 56 days in advance by calling the independent reservationms agent, ReserveAmerica:

☎(800) 444-PARK (800-444-7275) or ☎TDD (800)-274-7275

Telephone reservations require a VISA/MC. A non-refundable service fee of $7.00 is charged for a campsite reservation; a service fee of $6.00 is charged for a cancellation.

In summer, it is recommended that you make reservations for most California state parks well in advance. For southern coastal parks, reservations are recommended for weekends year 'round. If you're running on a loose schedule, or you prefer not to plunk down your hard-earned greenbacks for a reservation fee, your best bet might be to plan to arrive at a park between 10:00 a.m and 2:00 p.m., as the previous night's campers are checking out.

When making a reservation by telephone, having a touch-tone phone in your slightly sweaty palms will help speed your way through the 'decision tree' of verbal 'menus' along the info-rez primrose path.

Reservable campsites are usually assigned, but you can request an rv or a tent site; rv sites are generally a little larger and most will accommodate tents. When making a reservation, be prepared to tell the reservation agent about the major camping equipment you plan to use: size and number of tents, type and length of rv, additional vehicles, boat trailers, etc. Be generous in your estimate. In many cases, a park's *best sites* are also those which are *reservable*. Most of the park campgrounds *usually* can accommodate a *limited* number of drop-ins on a first-come, first-served basis.

Reservations for other areas must be obtained directly from the selected California or Nevada state park. Specific information and procedures will be provided upon initial contact.

For additional information about picnic or camp site reservations, availability, current conditions, or regulations about the use of state parks, we suggest that you contact your selected park directly, using the *Mail & Phone* information in the text. (Detailed lists of fees, as well as reservation forms, are available at any state park office or entrance station.)

These offices might also be helpful:

California

California Department of Parks and Recreation
P.O. Box 942896
Sacramento, CA 94296
☎(916) 445-6477

Nevada

Nevada Division of State Parks
123 West Nye Lane, Room 207
Capitol Complex
Carson City, NV 89710
☎(702) 687-4384

Please remember that all reservation information is subject to change without notice.

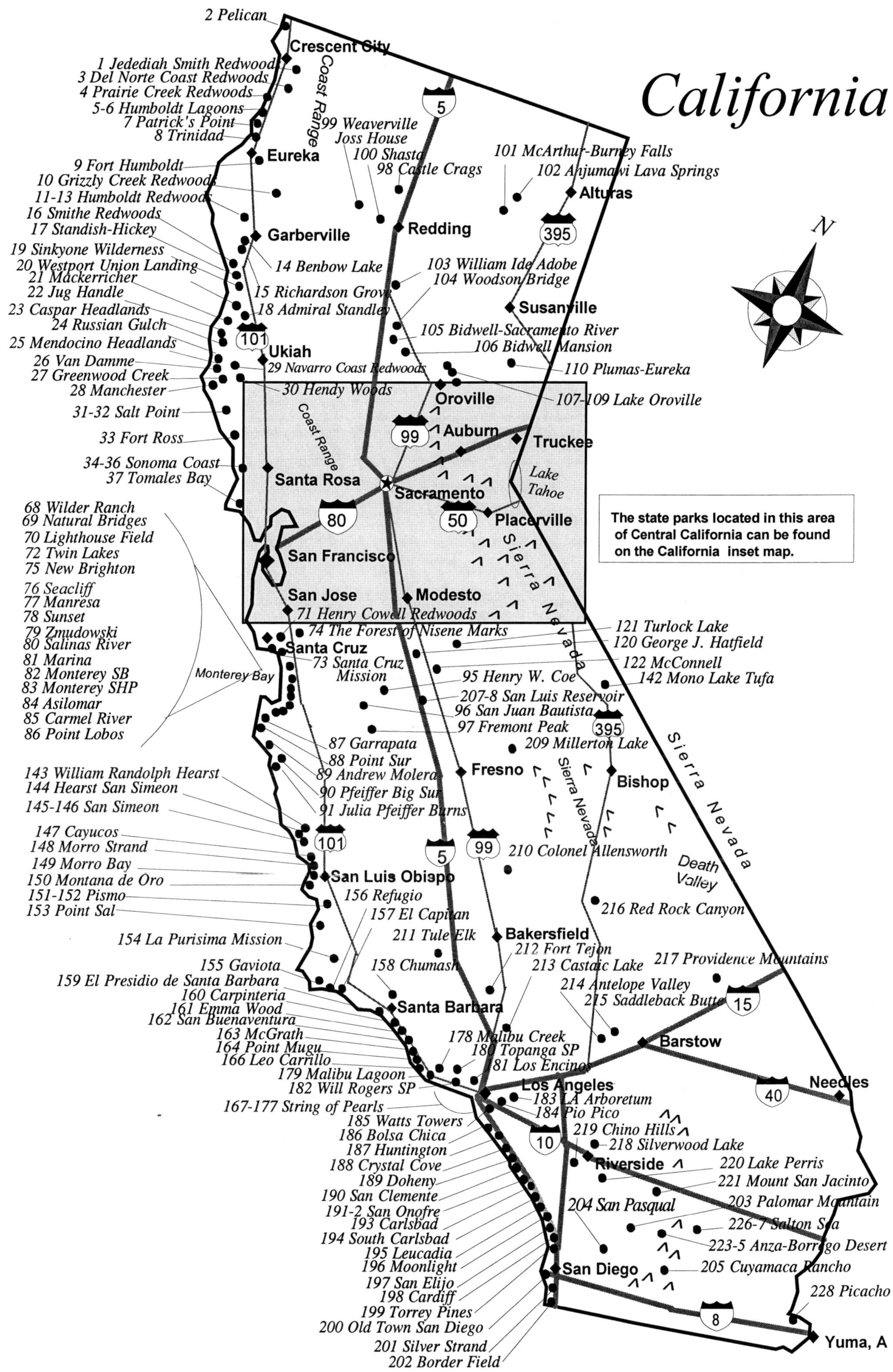

California
N
The state parks located in this area of Central California can be found on the California inset map.
2 Pelican
Crescent City
Coast Range
1 Jedediah Smith Redwoods
3 Del Norte Coast Redwoods
4 Prairie Creek Redwoods
5-6 Humboldt Lagoons
7 Patrick's Point
8 Trinidad
Eureka
9 Fort Humboldt
10 Grizzly Creek Redwoods
11-13 Humboldt Redwoods
16 Smithe Redwoods
17 Standish-Hickey
Garberville
19 Sinkyone Wilderness
20 Westport Union Landing
21 Mackerricher
22 Jug Handle
23 Caspar Headlands
24 Russian Gulch
25 Mendocino Headlands
26 Van Damme
27 Greenwood Creek
28 Manchester
31-32 Salt Point
33 Fort Ross
34-36 Sonoma Coast
37 Tomales Bay
14 Benbow Lake
15 Richardson Grove
18 Admiral Standley
101
Ukiah
29 Navarro Coast Redwoods
30 Hendy Woods
99 Weaverville Joss House
100 Shasta
98 Castle Crags
5
Redding
101 McArthur-Burney Falls
102 Ahjumawi Lava Springs
Alturas
395
103 William Ide Adobe
104 Woodson Bridge
Susanville
105 Bidwell-Sacramento River
106 Bidwell Mansion
110 Plumas-Eureka
107-109 Lake Oroville
Oroville
99
Auburn
Truckee
Lake Tahoe
Coast Range
Santa Rosa
Sacramento
80
50
Placerville
Sierra Nevada
San Francisco
San Jose
Modesto
71 Henry Cowell Redwoods
74 The Forest of Nisene Marks
Santa Cruz
73 Santa Cruz Mission
Monterey Bay
68 Wilder Ranch
69 Natural Bridges
70 Lighthouse Field
72 Twin Lakes
75 New Brighton
76 Seacliff
77 Manresa
78 Sunset
79 Zmudowski
80 Salinas River
81 Marina
82 Monterey SB
83 Monterey SHP
84 Asilomar
85 Carmel River
86 Point Lobos
121 Turlock Lake
120 George J. Hatfield
122 McConnell
142 Mono Lake Tufa
95 Henry W. Coe
207-8 San Luis Reservoir
96 San Juan Bautista
97 Fremont Peak
395
209 Millerton Lake
87 Garrapata
88 Point Sur
89 Andrew Molera
90 Pfeiffer Big Sur
91 Julia Pfeiffer Burns
Fresno
Bishop
Sierra Nevada
Sierra Nevada
143 William Randolph Hearst
144 Hearst San Simeon
145-146 San Simeon
101
5
99
147 Cayucos
148 Morro Strand
149 Morro Bay
150 Montana de Oro
151-152 Pismo
153 Point Sal
210 Colonel Allensworth
Death Valley
San Luis Obispo
156 Refugio
157 El Capitan
216 Red Rock Canyon
154 La Purisima Mission
211 Tule Elk
Bakersfield
212 Fort Tejon
213 Castaic Lake
217 Providence Mountains
155 Gaviota
159 El Presidio de Santa Barbara
160 Carpinteria
161 Emma Wood
162 San Buenaventura
163 McGrath
164 Point Mugu
166 Leo Carrillo
179 Malibu Lagoon
182 Will Rogers SP
167-177 String of Pearls
158 Chumash
Santa Barbara
214 Antelope Valley
215 Saddleback Butte
15
178 Malibu Creek
180 Topanga SP
181 Los Encinos
Barstow
Los Angeles
183 LA Arboretum
184 Pio Pico
Needles
40
185 Watts Towers
186 Bolsa Chica
187 Huntington
188 Crystal Cove
189 Doheny
190 San Clemente
191-2 San Onofre
193 Carlsbad
194 South Carlsbad
195 Leucadia
196 Moonlight
197 San Elijo
198 Cardiff
199 Torrey Pines
200 Old Town San Diego
201 Silver Strand
202 Border Field
10
219 Chino Hills
218 Silverwood Lake
Riverside
220 Lake Perris
221 Mount San Jacinto
204 San Pasqual
203 Palomar Mountain
226-7 Salton Sea
223-5 Anza-Borrego Desert
San Diego
205 Cuyamaca Rancho
228 Picacho
8
Yuma, A

Central California Area Map Inset

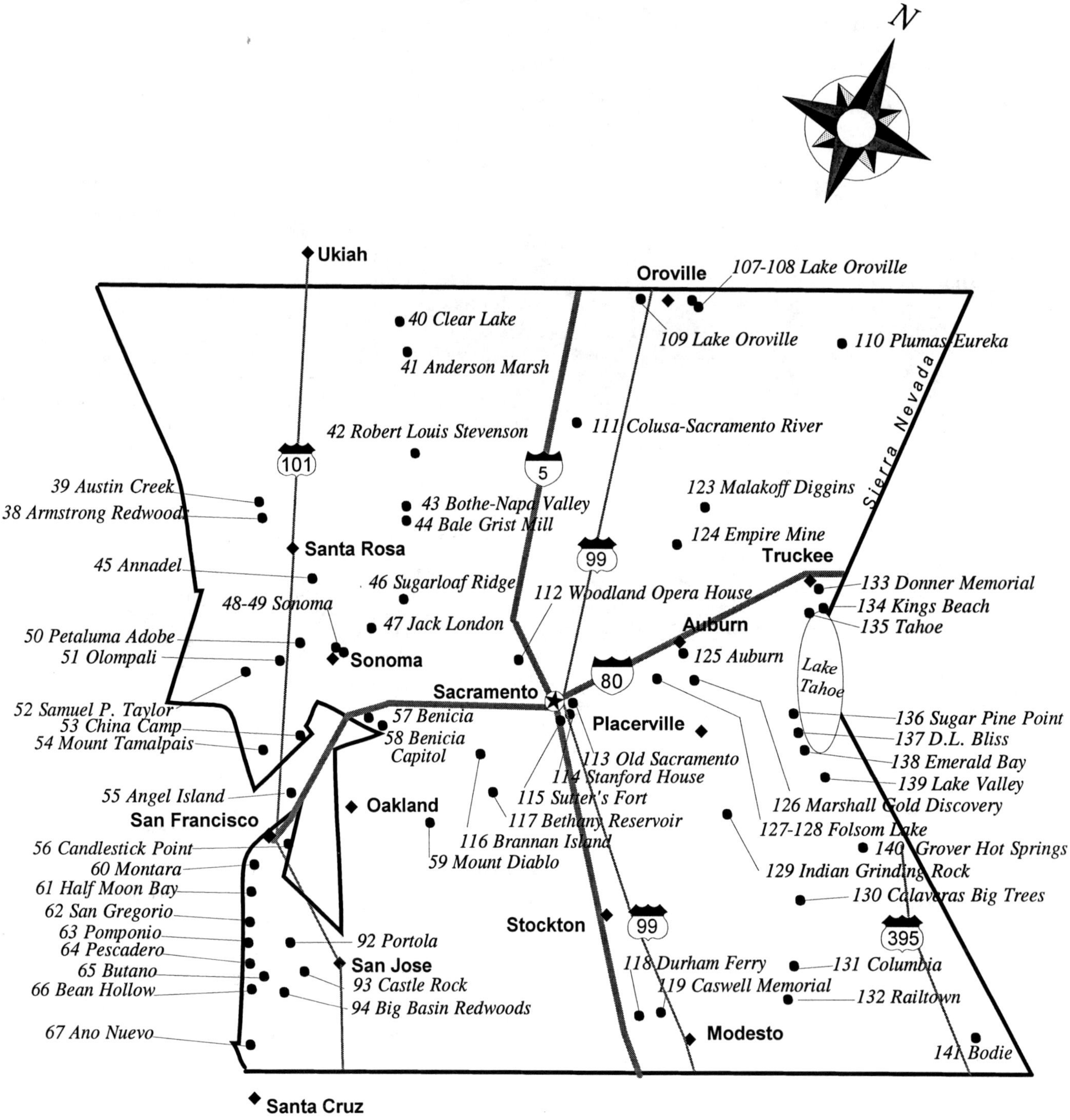

Ukiah
Oroville
107-108 Lake Oroville
40 Clear Lake
109 Lake Oroville
110 Plumas Eureka
41 Anderson Marsh
Sierra Nevada
42 Robert Louis Stevenson
111 Colusa-Sacramento River
101
5
39 Austin Creek
38 Armstrong Redwoods
43 Bothe-Napa Valley
44 Bale Grist Mill
123 Malakoff Diggins
124 Empire Mine
Santa Rosa
99
Truckee
45 Annadel
46 Sugarloaf Ridge
112 Woodland Opera House
133 Donner Memorial
48-49 Sonoma
134 Kings Beach
135 Tahoe
47 Jack London
Auburn
50 Petaluma Adobe
51 Olompali
Sonoma
125 Auburn
Lake Tahoe
80
Sacramento
52 Samuel P. Taylor
53 China Camp
54 Mount Tamalpais
57 Benicia
58 Benicia Capitol
Placerville
136 Sugar Pine Point
137 D.L. Bliss
113 Old Sacramento
138 Emerald Bay
114 Stanford House
139 Lake Valley
55 Angel Island
115 Sutter's Fort
San Francisco
Oakland
117 Bethany Reservoir
126 Marshall Gold Discovery
127-128 Folsom Lake
56 Candlestick Point
116 Brannan Island
140 Grover Hot Springs
60 Montara
59 Mount Diablo
129 Indian Grinding Rock
61 Half Moon Bay
130 Calaveras Big Trees
62 San Gregorio
Stockton
99
395
63 Pomponio
92 Portola
64 Pescadero
San Jose
118 Durham Ferry
131 Columbia
65 Butano
93 Castle Rock
119 Caswell Memorial
66 Bean Hollow
94 Big Basin Redwoods
132 Railtown
67 Ano Nuevo
Modesto
141 Bodie
Santa Cruz

Nevada

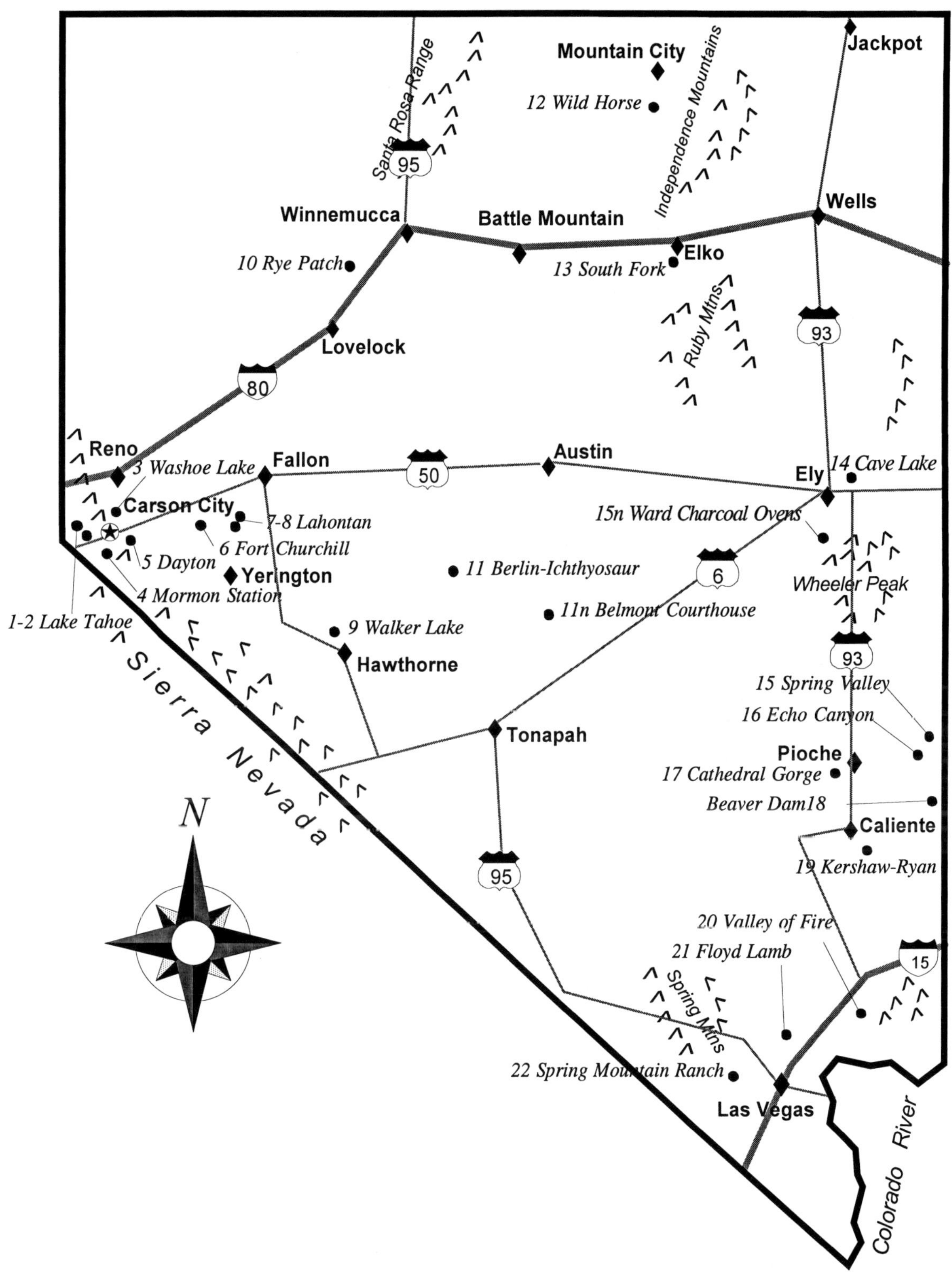

Mountain City
12 Wild Horse
Santa Rosa Range
Independence Mountains
Jackpot
95
Winnemucca
Battle Mountain
Wells
10 Rye Patch
Elko
13 South Fork
Ruby Mtns
93
Lovelock
80
Reno
3 Washoe Lake
Fallon
50
Austin
Ely
14 Cave Lake
Carson City
7-8 Lahontan
15n Ward Charcoal Ovens
6 Fort Churchill
5 Dayton
Yerington
11 Berlin-Ichthyosaur
6
Wheeler Peak
4 Mormon Station
1-2 Lake Tahoe
11n Belmont Courthouse
9 Walker Lake
Hawthorne
93
15 Spring Valley
16 Echo Canyon
Sierra Nevada
Tonapah
Pioche
17 Cathedral Gorge
Beaver Dam18
N
Caliente
95
19 Kershaw-Ryan
20 Valley of Fire
21 Floyd Lamb
15
Spring Mtns
22 Spring Mountain Ranch
Las Vegas
Colorado River

Notes & Sketches

INDEX

Important Note:

* A thumbnail description of a state park marked with an asterisk is found in the *Park Notes* section of the principal numbered state park.

California

F

G

H

I

J

K

L

M

Nevada

Notes & Sketches

The Double Eagle Guide to

CAMPING *in* WESTERN PARKS *and* FORESTS

__*Volume 1*	*Pacific Northwest* Washington∗Oregon∗Vancouver Island	ISBN 0-929760-17-4 Hardcover	 $21.95*
__*Volume 2*	*Far West* Northern California∗Southern California ∗ Lake Tahoe	ISBN 0-929760-28-X Hardcover	 $21.95*
__*Volume 3*	*Desert Southwest* Nevada∗Utah∗Arizona	ISBN 0-929760-30-1 Hardcover	 $21.95*
__*Volume 4*	*Northern Rocky Mountains* Montana∗Idaho∗Wyoming	ISBN 0-929760-40-9 Hardcover	 $21.95*
__*Volume 5*	*Southern Rocky Mountains* Colorado∗New Mexico	ISBN 0-929760-56-5 Hardcover	 $21.95*
__*Volume 6*	*Northern Great Plains* North Dakota∗South Dakota∗Nebraska∗Kansas	ISBN 0-929760-67-0 Hardcover	 $21.95*
__*Volume 7*	*Southern Great Plains* Texas∗Oklahoma	ISBN 0-929760-70-0 Hardcover	 $21.95*

∗ **Save $3.00** Softcover, spiral-bound editions are also available. Recommended for light-duty, personal use only. Subtract $3.00 from the standard hardcover price and ✓here: ☐

Please add $4.00 for shipping the first volume, and $2.00 for each additional volume.

Please include your check/money order, and complete the shipping information in the indicated space below.

Total amount enclosed $________________

Name____

Address____

City________________________________ State______ Zip____________________

Please mail your completed order to:

Discovery Publishing P.O. Box 50545 Billings, MT 59105 (Phone 1-406-245-8292)

Thank You Very Much For Your Order!

Prices, shipping charges, and specifications are subject to change.
(A photocopy or other reproduction may be substituted for this original form.)

The Double Eagle Guide to

WESTERN STATE PARKS

__Volume 1	Pacific Northwest		ISBN 0-929760-10-7
	Washington*Oregon*Idaho Hardcover 8½x11		$21.95^
__Volume 2	Rocky Mountains		ISBN 0-929760-19-0
	Colorado*Montana*Wyoming Hardcover 8½x11		$21.95^
__Volume 3	Far West		ISBN 0-929760-37-9
	California*Nevada Hardcover 8½x11		$21.95^
__Volume 4	Desert Southwest		ISBN 0-929760-38-7
	Arizona*New Mexico*Utah Hardcover 8½x11		$21.95^
__Volume 5	Northern Great Plains		ISBN 0-929760-39-5
	The Dakotas*Nebraska*Kansas Hardcover 8½x11		$21.95^
__Volume 6	Southern Great Plains		ISBN 0-929760-59-X
	Texas*Oklahoma Hardcover 8½x11)		$21.95^

^ **Save $3.00** Softcover, spiral-bound editions are also available. Recommended for light-duty, personal use only. Subtract $3.00 from standard hardcover price and ✓ here: ❑

Please add $4.00 for shipping the first volume, and $2.00 for each additional volume.

Please include your check/money order, and complete the shipping information in the indicated space below.

Total amount enclosed $________________

Name____

Address____

City________________________________ State______ Zip____________________

Please mail your completed order to:

Discovery Publishing P.O. Box 50545 Billings, MT 59105 (Phone 1-406-245-8292)

Thank You Very Much For Your Order!

Prices, shipping charges, and specifications are subject to change.

(A photocopy or other reproduction may be substituted for this original form.)